# DEPENDENCY AND MARXISM

# Latin American Perspectives Series

*Dependency and Marxism:*
*Toward a Resolution of the Debate*
edited by Ronald H. Chilcote

Continuing the debate on dependency, this collection critically assesses the relationship of dependency to a theory of Marxism, as well as its significance for an analysis of class and class struggle, and concludes that dependency has not led to developmental solutions for Latin America and the rest of the Third World.

The book includes an introductory synthesis identifying theoretical issues central to dependency and Marxism, three in-depth critiques of current dependency theory, and seven position papers offering a range of perspectives. A concluding essay reviews the recent literature on dependency and Marxism. The articles, first published in a special issue of the journal *Latin American Perspectives* and supplemented here by a new preface by the editor, are intended especially for use in the classroom.

Ronald H. Chilcote is professor of political science at the University of California, Riverside. He is founder and managing editor of *Latin American Perspectives* and author and editor of numerous books and articles, including *Latin America: The Struggle with Dependency and Beyond* and *Theories of Comparative Politics: The Search for a Paradigm* (Westview, 1981).

# DEPENDENCY AND MARXISM
## Toward a Resolution of the Debate
### edited by Ronald H. Chilcote

Westview Press / Boulder, Colorado

*Latin American Perspectives Series, Number 1*

Published in 1982 in the United States of America by
  Westview Press, Inc.
  5500 Central Avenue
  Boulder, Colorado 80301
  Frederick A. Praeger, President and Publisher


Library of Congress Cataloging in Publication Data
Main entry under title:
Dependency and Marxism.
  1. Dependency—Addresses, essays, lectures.  2. Communism—Addresses, essays, lectures.
I. Chilcote, Ronald H.  II. Series.
HB199.D44    1982              335.4'01              82-11056
ISBN 0-86531-457-8
ISBN 0-86531-458-6 (pbk.)


Printed and bound in the United States of America

# Contents

# Preface

In the exploited and backward areas of what has been loosely characterized as the Third World there have been many attempts to define development and underdevelopment. A plethora of theories and ideas about these concepts emerged in the period after the Second World War, and today we continue to sort them out and to seek a theoretical basis for analysis and understanding.

Many who favored capitalism as a solution to the problems of deformation and decay that characterized much of Africa, Asia, Latin America, and the Middle East have emphasized the diffusionist character of capitalism. Political writers from James Bryce to Seymour Martin Lipset and Lucian Pye stressed values and practices of Western democracy, in particular constitutional legitimacy, electoral participation, multiparty systems, and competitive politics. These features of Western democracy were associated with political development in capitalist economies. Political scientists like Karl Deutsch related nationalism and the emergence of national states in the world to development in capitalist countries. The economic historian Walt W. Rostow outlined stages of economic growth in a linear direction toward modernization, while Samuel P. Huntington argued that authority, control, and regulation might be employed to avoid the political instability that typically accompanies rapid social and economic change. The ideas of these writers remain important in contemporary social science conceptions of capitalist development.

The writers of the Third World sought answers as to why capitalist development did not reproduce itself as it had done in Western Europe and the United States. The economists of the United Nations Economic Commission for Latin America argued that capitalist development could be promoted by limiting imports, establishing an infrastructure for industrialization, and encouraging autonomous national development. Although their approaches differed as to detail, the Argentine economist Raúl Prebisch, the Brazilian economist Celso Furtado, and the Chilean economist Osvaldo Sunkel all offered analyses within this reformist, nationalist, and capitalist framework. Their structural distinction between the advanced capitalist center and the backward periphery was inherent in the scheme of internal colonialism suggested by the Mexican sociologist Pablo González Casanova. These and many other writers began to associate their structuralism with the idea of dependency so that the metropolitan center was seen as dominant over dependent peripheral areas. The break with the center and with imperialism could be accompanied by the development of an autonomous national capitalism.

These distinctions between center and periphery and metropolis and satellite also were incorporated into approaches that advocated revolution and socialism. As early as 1947, the Argentine Trotskyist Silvio Frondizi provided a basis for the understanding of dependency, identified the weakness of the national bourgeoisie in the face of imperialism and its dependence on world capitalism, and called for revolution and the establishment of socialism. The Argentine historian Sergio Bagú had developed some of these ideas in the middle 1940s and argued that capitalism had affected Latin America as early as the sixteenth century: the subjugation of the colonial economies to the world market left them in a condition of stagnation and deformation. The Brazilian economic historian Caio Prado Júnior concurred with this position and argued that feudalism had never existed in Brazil. Thus, Brazil and other dependent nations must break with imperialism and the international system of capitalism. Capitalism, not feudalism, was the issue, and a progressive bourgeoisie could never lead the revolution in Brazil. All three of these thinkers advocated socialism as a solution to the underdevelopment and dependency that had shaped the periphery since colonial times.

This revolutionary tradition was embraced by André Gunder Frank in his writings on the capitalist development of underdevelopment. Frank believed that capitalist contradictions had generated underdevelopment in the peripheral satellites, whose economic surplus was expropriated for the economic development of the metropolitan centers. Frank had been influenced by Paul Baran's writings on surplus and backwardness. Walter Rodney offered a similar conception of how Europe underdeveloped Africa. Brazilian sociologist Theotonio dos Santos and his notion of new dependency, Brazilian economist Ruy Mauro Marini and his emphasis on subimperialism, and Peruvian sociologist Aníbal Quijano also followed in this revolutionary tradition, while another Brazilian, Fernando Henrique Cardoso, emphasized the compatibility of dependency and capitalist development in the periphery and later dismissed altogether the theory of dependency.

I have been involved over the past decade in identifying and synthesizing approaches, models, and lines of thinking about development and underdevelopment. The present volume represents another contribution to the continuing debate over questions of underdevelopment and dependency. However, this collection of essays focuses explicitly on the relationship of dependency to a theory of Marxism. Interpretations and descriptions of dependency and underdevelopment are found in the writing of Marx, Lenin, and Trotsky and have influenced many of the thinkers identified above. The assessment that follows addresses such questions as the significance of dependency for analysis of class and class struggle and concludes that dependency has not led to developmental solutions for Latin America and the rest of the Third World.

These essays were originally published in the quarterly journal *Latin American Perspectives*, whose pages have been filled with the debate over dependency since the appearance of its first issue in 1974. The journal attempts to organize some of its material around topics that are especially useful in the classroom. Because the issue on dependency has generated great interest in the academic community, among instructors and students alike, the editors of the journal sought to publish it in book form. Thus, this volume, the first of a series to be published by Westview Press. Readers who would like more information about the journal itself, manuscript submissions, subscriptions, and so on should address the Managing Editor, Latin American Perspectives, P.O. Box 5703, Riverside, California 92517-5703.

Acknowledgments are due to the contributors, who struggled with the challenge of reassessing their past work and that of others on dependency, underdevelopment, and

Marxism. The coordinating editors of *Latin American Perspectives* carefully reviewed the various essays and offered valuable suggestions for revision. Frances Chilcote copy edited the manuscripts for printing. Finally, appreciation must be expressed to Lynne Rienner of Westview Press, who encouraged the idea for this volume and series.

*Ronald H. Chilcote*

# DEPENDENCY AND MARXISM

# 1

## ISSUES OF THEORY IN DEPENDENCY AND MARXISM

*by*
*Ronald H. Chilcote*\*

Students of dependency have struggled over the past decade to integrate their ideas with a theory of Marxism. Their work has opened up new questions and areas of investigation and stimulated interest in many issues that run through the thought of Marx, Engels, Lenin, and Trotsky. Criticism has evolved in the contemporary study of dependency with the acknowledgement of theoretical weaknesses: confusion over terminology, undue emphasis on market in the domestic and international economy, and so on. Controversy has arisen around various explanations of dependency which are rooted in the Latin American experience. Fernando Henrique Cardoso (1980), Theotônio dos Santos (1978), Ruy Mauro Marini (1974), and André Gunder Frank (1967) have offered ideas and theories about Latin America, while Samir Amin (1976), Walter Rodney (1972), and Clive Thomas (1974) have incorporated a conception of dependency in their writings about other areas. Considerable debate has ensued.

The debate over dependency theory, unlike some scholarly controversies, has been rich in content and relevant in application. Theorists of dependency have been concerned with nothing less than unraveling the essence of past historical processes, and they have presented contending interpretations of historical reality. These theorists have contributed to some remarkable historical breakthroughs as well as to detours and setbacks in theory and revolutionary practice. The critics of dependency have shown no less complexity in their contributions.

An introductory review of the debate in general and this journal issue in particular should be convincing of the proposition that scholars have indeed struggled over a praxis of some consequence. Since the world does not present us with unequivocal and verifiable responses to the questions that ensue from the debate, the polemics over dependency continue. The present purpose is to draw upon the implications of these polemics, especially in this journal.

---

\*The author is managing editor of *Latin American Perspectives* and teaches in the Department of Political Science at the University of California, Riverside.

3

This introductory essay begins with a review of the debate in the pages of *Latin American Perspectives* since the journal's founding 'eight years ago, then examines the substance of the debate in the current issue. An evaluation of responses to four central questions folows. Finally, a conclusion offers a summary of the principal criticisms of dependency as well as of new directions for theory and inquiry suggested by various writers.

The present issue represents this journal's third serious effort to assess the relevancy of dependency to a theory of Marxism. The first was contained in the initial issue of this journal and involved my own synthesis of the literature from its beginnings until early 1974. My discussion offered prevailing definitions of the concept, illustrated the impact of dependency on experiences in my university classes, and explained how questions over the relevancy and irrevelancy of dependency to Marxist theory had accompanied the founding of this journal. Two of my observations pertain today to an assessment of dependency. One was that dependency offers no unified thoery, and to support this position, I identified four formulations in the literature: development of underdevelopment, a thesis set forth by André Gunder Frank (1966); the new dependency suggested by Dos Santos (1970) who observed the technological and industrial dominance established by multinational corporations after the Second World War; dependent capitalist development, a view applied by Fernando Henrique Cardoso (1972) to the Brazilian situation; and dependency as a reformulation of classical theories of imperialism, found in the work of Aníbal Quijano (1971). I also identified many weaknesses in the dependency formulations: the failure to relate explicitly to a class analysis, the tendency to emphasize relations of exchange, the exaggerated emphasis on questions of nationalism and development, and the possibility of obscuring analysis of imperialism.

Many of these ideas on dependency pervaded Latin America. At the time, criticism by Marxist scholars, for example, Laclau (1971) and Warren (1973), had tended to focus on the work of Frank, in particular on his view that Latin America had been capitalist since the days of conquest, that backwardness was the consequence not of feudalism but of capitalism itself, and that inequities among nations can be explained in terms of dominant metropolises and dependent satellites. Frank resorted to an extensive rebuttal to these and other arguments through a continuous dialogue between him and others on the left, as reflected in *Latin American Perspectives.* For example, the first issue of the journal included a rebuttal to Raúl Fernández and José Ocampo who launched a vigorous attack on dependency theory and claimed that it does not explain underdevelopment, says little about imperialism and is a misapplication of Marxist theory. In the same issue, critical reviews of the Fernández and Ocampo piece were presented by Fernando Henrique Cardoso, Timothy Harding, and Marvin Sternberg. Later, in issue 4, Ocampo offered a rejoinder to critics, but concentrated his attack on Cardoso and especially Frank. In issue 5, Barbara Tenenbaum evaluated Frank's historical explanation in terms of Mexico from 1821 to 1856 and concluded that his view of the bourgeoisie during that period was incorrect and tended to obscure reality. In issue 6, Fernández and Ocampo applied their ideas to the Colombian situation and argued that underdevelopment there was the consequence of the low level of capitalist development in the face of persistence of the feudal and semi-feudal forms of agricultural production. Finally, in issue 9, Frank provided a rebuttal to Ocampo's earlier criticism.

This debate seems not to have convinced contributors to abandon their interest in dependency, and indeed the pages of the journal were permeated with various views and applications of the theory. The majority of published articles represented one or another interpretations of dependency; conspicuous examples included pieces by Rodolfo Stavenhagen (issue 1), Richard Feinberg (issue 2), Juan Corradi and Monica Peralta Ramos (issue 3), Juan Felipe Leal (issue 5), Kenneth Erickson and Patrick Peppe (issue 8), and Peter Evans and Theotônio dos Santos (issue 9).

Given such interest, it is not surprising that a second effort to assess the ideas of dependency and the relationship between dependency and Marxism was presented in issue 11 (1976) of the journal, in particular in essays published by Agustín Cueva and Timothy Harding. Cueva systematically criticized Frank for abandoning Marx's notion of capitalism and equating capitalism with money economy; Rodolfo Stavenhagen for substituting a focus on exploitation and class conflict for a system of national and regional contradictions; Dos Santos for confusing the worldwide expansion of capitalism with economic growth in the periphery; Cardoso and Falleto for mixing developmental and Marxist frameworks, and Marini for differentiating classical from dependent capitalism. He concluded that "there is no theoretical space within which to locate a theory of dependency." At the same time, he argued that the concept dependency is not dead; "It isn't, and no one has tried to deny its existence for it represents a salient feature of our societies. The many studies which have been made on it are still relevant and will continue to be relevant. What has perhaps stopped being relevant is that something called a theory of dependency" (issue 11: 15-16).

Harding attempted to assess such criticism in the light of the contributions to *Latin American Perspectives* from 1974 to 1976. He showed how the original Economic Commission on Latin America (ECLA) ideas were representative of the effort by the national bourgeoisie in Latin America to establish autonomous capitalist development in the face of imperialism but that the multinationals moving into Latin America were rapidly taking over the new industrialization. This led Dos Santos and others to criticize the ECLA thesis and promote the idea of new dependency. The early dependentistas also sought independence from the sterile ideas of the Latin American communist parties, in particular the two-stage thesis that the working class should support the national bourgeoisie in the initial effort to build capitalism and later to promote the second stage of socialist revolution. Concerned about the postponement of the socialist revolution and with the reformist programs of the communist parties, the more radical dependentistas, according to Harding, "were returning to the Marxist view set forth by Lenin and Trotsky which analyzed imperialism as having spread capitalism throughout the world, but not permitting the local bourgeoisie to develop strength in the underdeveloped areas" (issue 11: 4). Harding also noted Dos Santos' observation that the nationalist movements of the early sixties coalesced the radical bourgeoisie with the revolutionary working class in the drive for national liberation and democracy for all; in part, this accounted for confusion, for example, as Marxist terminology on imperialism was fused with a bourgeois theory of nationalist development.

Turning now to a third assessment of dependency and Marxism, several trends can be noted. First, the weaknesses and problems of bourgeois dependency theory are all too apparent in North American social science. The ideas of dependence have permeated the mainstream of this social science as U.S. academicians have tended to apply them indiscriminately to their empirical research. Generally, the origins of the ideas and their relationship to Marxism are ignored, and this has led to new confusion and jargon. It is not the purpose of this issue to focus on this problem, but it will suffice to say that in U.S. academic circles the sloppy work based on the superficial aspects of dependency tends to turn many of us away from the essential questions. Second, the debate over dependency in this journal has continued with the strong criticism of dependency theory and its advocates. Some Marxists, in line with Lenin, have argued that the dependentistas are not Marxists and that the concept of dependency distorts an explanation of progressive capitalism in backward countries; William Bollinger, Elizabeth Dore, and John Weeks represent this position in issue 14. Some Marxists sympathetic to Lenin, Mao, and Stalin, such as Fernández and Ocampo, believe that dependency ideas ignore a theory of imperialism and that backwardness in Latin America can be attributed to the persistence of feudalism or its remnants in contrast to the idea that capitalist development causes underdevelopment. Some Marxists, following in the thought of Trotsky, such as Michel Lowy in issue 7 and George Novack in issue 9, observe that variances in capitalist growth around the world are due to uneven and combined development; thus writers like Ernest Mandel tend to use dependency to describe the patterns of growth and backwardness that resulted from the combination of feudalism and other precapitalist modes of protection with capitalism. Finally, some Marxists continue to work with ideas of dependency and to defend their earlier theory. While Frank and Cardoso have abandoned the effort, Frank having turned to world systems theory of Immanuel Wallerstein and Cardoso to new attempts to speak of autonomous capitalist development, Marini (1978) insists on combining dependency within a Marxist-Leninist framework, and Bambirra (1978) and Dos Santos (1978) reaffirmed their belief in the new dependency. Their influence upon Latin American and North American radical and Marxist writing continues to be evident in this journal; for example, the majority of essays in issue 21 ("Views of Dependency").

It is clear also that in the early 1980s the debate over dependency persists. Many writers, both North American and Latin American, continue to incorporate dependency into their Marxism. Dale Johnson and Joel Edelstein are very explicit about this in the current issue while many of the proponents of dependency theory, especially the Brazilians Bambirra, Dos Santos, and Marini represent major intellectual influences throughout Latin America and especially in Mexico where they have resided for nearly a decade. For this reason, it was decided to invite the editors of the journal as well as major protagonists in the debate to write essays around a number of questions relating dependency to Marxism, among them: Is dependency compatible with a theory of Marxism and with revolutionary thought in general? Does dependency theory merely reflect the needs of competitive capitalism in the face of monopoly capital in countries where the capitalist mode of production has not yet become dominant? Is dependency relevant to a Marxist or Marxist-Leninist critique of imperialism? Does it help to explain the relations of production in the transition to socialism?

The essays which follow represent outstanding contributions to the debate. They are organized into three sections. One comprises a review essay by Ronaldo Munck, who updates and critically examines literature since the founding of the journal. Another contains seven position papers. Contributors to this section were asked to write briefly on one or more of the questions above. There are also three lengthy essays, each an overview that assesses debate over dependency and Marxism in an insightful manner. These essays challenge the reader to transcend past issues and discussion around dependency and to apply Marxism more concretely to the experience of contemporary Latin America.

## SUMMARY OF THE ARGUMENTS

The identification and succinct summary of positions and theoretical lines may assist the reader in engaging with the diverse essays of the present collection. If these essays were classified in terms of allegiance to ideas about dependency, then Joel Edelstein and Dale Johnson offer strong defenses, while other contributors agree that questions of dependency in the past have assisted students in study of Latin America, but that a new focus is now necessary. David Barkin, for example, suggests that emphasis on the internationalization of capital is the most productive framework. James Dietz and Norma Chinchilla support a modes of production analysis. Colin Henfrey is critical but sympathetic to this modes of production analysis and insists on relating a theory of imperialism to exploited classes. James Petras places attention on class and state relationships. Thomas Angotti criticizes dependency theory as idealist and leading to reformist solutions; thus attention must be directed to the role of imperialism in underdevelopment. John Weeks also denounces dependency theory, calling for a theory of world economy that emphasizes capitalist accumulation on an international level. Gary Howe locates the genesis of dependency in seventeenth century mercantilist thought, whereas Carlos Johnson traces the idealist and populist notions associated with dependency to the nineteenth century Russian Narodniks. I now turn to a summary of arguments in the seven position papers.

### Locating Dependency in Marxist Analysis

Joel Edelstein identifies and criticizes two types of dependency theory. One type incorporates a bourgeois nationalist conception of dependency and is inherent in the work of Raúl Prebisch and the ECLA. This theory ignores the labor process in the formation of classes and class struggle and is static, idealist, and unable to guide the working classes toward a socialist revolution. The other theory, based on a radical conception, challenges the bourgeois notion that capital and technology from the advanced capitalist nations to the backward nations destroys feudalism and leads to capitalist development.

This theory shows that Latin America was shaped largely by the needs of the center and by participation in the world system. While radical theory may explain dependent capitalism, its weakness is apparent in its emphasis on circulation and neglect of the labor process, especially the labor theory of value in a Marxist view of history. Edelstein indicts left sectarian critics who equate this radical theory with the bourgeois nationalist variant of dependency theory. They fail to recognize, he argues, that dependent capitalist development in Latin America is different from industrial capitalist development that Marx appropriately analyzed in England and Northern Europe. Thus while the radical dependentistas offer no general theory and thus do not compete with Marxism, they provide concepts for a special theory of understanding social formations in an expanding world capitalist system.

Dale Johnson admits that dependency theory has tended to exaggerate an analysis of exchange rather than production relations, but he sees no serious alternative, very little theoretical development, and insufficient substantive research beyond some of the work on dependency. He agrees with Edelstein that writings on dependency exposed the weaknesses of reformist nationalist approaches, discredited the tenets of modernization theory, and also that these writings offered a response to some inadequacies of traditional Marxism. Dependency writers, he believes, revealed the mechanisms used by metropolitan bourgeoisies to appropriate surplus and emphasized a view from the periphery rather than the center as evidenced in most studies of imperialism. At the same time, he acknowledges deficiencies in dependency writings: the stagnation thesis associated with the idea of development of underdeveloped appeared to preclude prospects for socialism; emphasis on external aspects obscured attention to local class struggles; foreign penetration tended to be explained in terms of conspiracy rather than as the practice of transnational corporate capital in a new stage of monopoly capitalism and imperialism. Finally, he suggests that dependency is more than a perspective than a theory, and he calls for a balanced approach to the study of production and circulation and for a dialectical analysis of internal and external aspects in the study of concrete relations of social forces and class analysis.

## From Dependency to New Approaches

Many of the contributors to this issue agree with Edelstein and Dale Johnson that past attention to dependency has stimulated interest in Marxist analysis of Latin America, but they suggest that contemporary investigation may also be enhanced by new approaches.

Norma Chinchilla and James Dietz affirm that dependency theory has contributed significantly to Marxist analysis of development and underdevelopment. Such theory challenged orthodox Marxist theory by addressing new questions and offering new categories for analysis, but it did not adequately conceptualize the terms development and underdevelopment. Dependency writers tended to relate their perspective to the capitalist mode of production while ignoring apparent precapitalist relations of production. They also were unable to differentiate dependent capitalism from nondependent capitalism in Latin America. Critics of dependency have argued that imperialist penetration of Latin America creates conditions for a mature capitalism and the destruction of feudalism and precapitalist relations of production, but, argue Chinchilla and Dietz, this perspective also is flawed. Thus, an alternative approach, the modes of production analysis, appeared within Marxist thought. Three premises are evident in this approach: each national economy is seen as a concrete social formation comprising two or more modes of production; stages of development of different modes of production are articulated within any social formation; and the development is understood as capitalist development which is always underdeveloped. In contrast to Barkin's internationalization of capital approach, the mode of production analysis focuses directly on the national economy. While acknowledging the impact of international monopoly capital on social formations in the Third World, Chinchilla and Dietz suggest that attention to mode of production allows for attention to internal processes such as the reproduction of capital through its articulation with other modes in the social formation. This may permit analysis of class alliances and struggles ignored in dependency studies.

James Petras also focuses on class but argues that the process of capital accumulation must be looked at globally within a framework of class and state relationships. He recognizes the significance of a world capitalist system, but he delineates the faults and weaknesses of a world systems theory which is seen as a derivative of dependency theory. He shows how theorists have distorted understanding of capitalist accumulation by using categories that obscure specific relations and processes that shape historical development; how their emphasis on external relationships leads to difficulties in analyzing capitalist development in terms of class conflicts between labor and capital. Petras emphasizes the social relations of production rather than dependency. Investigation of class relationships, both at the internal and international levels, allows for analysis of class and state relationships and of core capital within the class structure of peripheral societies.

David Barkin, for example, believes the dependency school appropriately questioned the causes of underdevelopment, but suggests the most useful framework for examining this issue is that of internationalization of capital. This framework necessitates examination of the laws of capitalist accumulation and attention to social relations in the capitalist mode of production. His approach shifts analysis from the nation-state to the international political economy. For instance, Marx's attention to the three currents of capital (money capital, productive capital and commodity capital) might be extended to the international level. Thus, one weakness in some dependency analysis (emphasis on the nation-state) can be overcome. He illustrates his approach by reference to Mexico where he notes that national decision making has combined with international capital to "internationalize" the domestic economy, resulting in greater unemployment, immiseration of masses of people, and denationalization — all consequences of concern to dependentistas. He also sees this approach as useful to popular struggles on a local level. Thus, a theory of internationalization of capital can be linked to concrete structural changes in particular situations.

*Incompatibility of Dependency and Marxism*

While some contributors see the compatibility of dependency and Marxism and others desire to move analysis in new directions, two writers reject dependency altogether.

Thomas Angotti identifies two strategic lines in dependency theory: one is "rightist and reformist" and represented by Amin and Cardoso, while the other is ultra "left" and calls for worldwide socialism as the solution to underdevelopment and is represented by Frank. Both lines, Angotti argues, divert attention from the socialist revolution and fail to advance the anti-imperialist movement. Dependency theory offers a critique of dualism, distinguishes between core and periphery, analyzes unequal exchange, and emphasizes the dependent relationship of the bourgeoisie on external forces, but, according to Angotti, a Marxist interpretation of these propositions would reveal them as idealistic. Therein lies the major methodological error of dependency theory and an explanation as to why the theory pays scant attention to stages in the revolutionary process, changes in the mode of production, and the class struggle. Dissatisfied with Marxist critics of dependency theory, in particular with Charles Bettelheim for his "anarcho-syndicalist" outlook and Robert Brenner for his "idealism," Angotti believes that Marxists must offer a critique of dependency as well as affirm the role of imperialism in development in order to promote unity in the anti-imperialist movement.

Distinguishing sharply between Marxist theory and dependency theory, John Weeks emphasizes capitalist reproduction as the basis of the world economy. His central position is that dependency theory lacks both empirical verification and theoretical validity. In summarizing the theory of dependency, he looks at the view of capitalist development established in the writing of Paul Baran and André Gunder Frank who showed that uneven development was the consequence of advanced nations appropriating and accumulating wealth or surplus product while countries losing that surplus stagnated into underdevelopment. Weeks relates this line of thought to a critique of the unequal theory found in the writing of Amin, Emmanuel, and Mandel. Materialist theory of accumulation differs from dependency theory in that accumulation on an expanding scale is the consequence of the progressive development of productive forces rather than of a redistribution of a surplus among societies. He extends his discussion to world economy and the theory of imperialism which he defines as "the theory of the accumulation of capital in the context of the struggle among ruling classes." In summing up, he states first that accumulation is the consequence of particular capitalist social relations in a society, and, second, that most direct investment of capital flows among the developed countries rather than from developed to underdeveloped areas as hypothesized by dependency theory.

*Toward a Theory of Imperialism*

The three lengthy essays in another section of this issue elaborate on many of the positions, ideas, and criticisms found in the brief position papers, offer serious criticisms of dependency theory, and suggest direction which Marxist analysis should take in the study of Latin America. I now turn to a brief summary of the argument in each of these essays.

Colin Henfrey initiates his discussion with a critical overview of ECLA's reformist structuralism and dependency. Both theories, he believes, attempted to reformulate an understanding of underdevelopment, set out to analyze class relations and struggles, and were responses to the crisis of Marxist thought after Stalin. Henfrey distinguishes between two dependencies: the stagnation model of Frank and the structural historiography of Cardoso and Faletto. In a review of these dependencies, he offers an assessment of the various strands of thought, the underlying issues of contention, and the relationship of theory to Marxism. For example, he draws out the differences in the prolonged debate between Cardoso and Marini, then shows how Marini identifies with Frank but, unlike Frank, attempts to place emphasis on production rather than circulation. He concludes that the debate is circular and its terms "more assertive than investigative." Given the lack of class analysis in studies of dependency, Henfrey turns to an examination of modes of production and their implications for comparative study of Brazil and Chile. First, he examines the work of John Taylor "which criticizes Frank's problematic but reproduces its generality"; then he looks at Laclau's critique which "encourages a reductionist use of the concept for labeling local modes of production"; and finally he delves into the historical use of modes of production in the work of Carlos Sempat Assadourian, Roger Bartra, and Agustín Cueva. Second, he concludes that mode of production analysis is limited because it has little to say about class relations beyond the capitalist mode; it emphasizes the economic, thereby losing sight of superstructural elements in an analysis of working classes; and it is limited by its concern with structure rather than movement. Thus, although the mode of production approach offers the possibility of more precise analysis, it suffers from some of the limitations that affected dependency theory. The problem before us, therefore, is to resolve "the task of relating a theory of imperialism to the histories of the exploited classes, not in dependent capitalism, or articulated modes of production, but in Latin American social formations."

Carlos Johnson attempts to demonstrate that while radical dependency theory appears to stand both as a body of socialist revolutionary thought and as a Marxist-Leninist critique of imperialism, in reality this theory is idealist and ideological and falls short in any theoretical relevance to socialist development or transformation and thus tends to substantiate capitalism in the less developed countries. Dependency theory also fails to adequately address international economic exchange relations, to explain relations between capital and labor, or to offer a path toward socialism.

Johnson posits the thesis that concepts like dependency reflect the idealist, populist thinking associated with theory about capitalist development which can be traced to the nineteenth century. The Russian Narodniks, for example, advocated socialist and revolutionary objectives, yet relied on petty-bourgeois analysis by noting the need for foreign capitalist markets in order to gain surplus value and by recognizing the impossibility of establishing capitalism in Russia at that time. Johnson notes that the theses of developmentalism promoted by ECLA during the 1950s were both a response to imperialism and an attempt to move the area toward autonomous capitalist development. The result was that some local ruling classes sought greater involvement in the process of capitalist accumulation. When these classes failed to halt imperialist extraction of capital, critics like Cardoso resorted to a mixture of structural functional and Marxist concepts to attack the notion of progress inherent in the developmentalism of ECLA. Johnson finds in these concepts an ideological justification in favor of the needs of competitive capitalism in the face of imperialism. He discounts bourgeois applications of dependency theory and focuses particularly on efforts to incorporate dependency into a theory of Marxism. He acknowledges that Lenin, Trotsky, and other Marxists used dependency in their writings; dependency like the word class was drawn from the thought of bourgeois political economists of their times, but the term dependency was not the essence of the method of materialist reasoning and explanation used by Lenin and Trotsky. In contrast, Marxist-Leninist dependency theorists such as Marini and Dos Santos represent the class needs of local ruling classes that favor greater national accumulation of surplus value. Johnson faults these and other writers for failing to analyze the principal relations of capital accumulation and class struggle and for such erroneous theses as identifying consumption with capital accumulation, statically dividing surplus labor from necessary labor, or overemphasizing the degree of exploitation of the labor force. Further, he indicts the dependentistas for emphasizing exchange relations and circulation of capital rather than the relations of production. In summary, dependency theses are simply a product of capitalist class needs for accumulation and bourgeois ideological reasoning. They do not offer, he believes, an analysis of socialism and international economic relations but instead obscure materialist explanation through ideological forms of theoretical interpretation.

Gary Howe dismisses dependency theory because it deviates from the classic theory of imperialism, especially in its attention to exploitation among nations rather than classes and its emphasis on circulation rather than production. Howe illustrates with reference to Brazil where the relevancy of dependency theory was called into question in the face of the collapse of efforts to form an alliance of the bourgeoisie and the working class to promote national autonomous development. Both alliance and theory failed in the face of foreign capital penetration, resulting in rapid expansion of Brazilian industry; furthermore, the working class, skeptical of the bourgeoisie's drive toward national development, withdrew, thus sharpening the struggle between capital and labor. Howe argues that Marx did not systematically address the unequal development of productive forces and relations; a Marxist theory of the internationalization of capital, especially in the less developed parts of the world where industrialization is slow and large populations exist within precapitalist relations of production, has not been fully elaborated. Lenin, he says, examined the export of capital "within a remarkably nationalist frame of reference." Howe then looks at two periods of imperialism: the nineteenth century, with emphasis on primary production for export from the periphery, and the period 1914 to 1945, with the internationalization of production as represented by the multinational corporations. The first period was characterized by absolute surplus value through intensification of labor and extension of the working day, while the second period led to dominance of a system of relative surplus value and the development of new forces and relations of production in the core. New contradictions appeared in the reorganization of the international system of production, resulting in the emergence of mass labor organization in the transition of one form of imperialism to another through a period of world wars and fascism. Thus, concludes Howe, both dependency theory as well as most theories of imperialism have not advanced analysis of the international capitalist system in the contemporary period. What is needed is analysis of unequal development of the relations of production with attention to "the reproduction of the capitalist mode of production through the integration of different systems of production in the *global, social* system of production and realization of surplus value."

## CONFRONTING THE PROBLEM OF DEPENDENCY AND MARXISM

In view of these arguments, I now turn to an examination of some theses which emanate from the questions initially asked contributors. My discussion sifts through all the essays that follow in an effort to synthesize various perspectives. As the reader approaches these articles, it might be useful to keep these questions in mind, so as to determine to what extent the various contributors have attempted to respond.

What about the relationship of dependency to a theory of Marxism? The idea of dependency is suggested in the writing of Marx. In chapters 24 and 25 of the first volume of *Capital*, Marx describes the relationship between rich and poor countries. In chapter 20 of volume three he states that merchant's capital "functions only as an agent of productive capital . . . Whenever merchant's capital still predominates we find backward nations. This is true even within one and the same country . . . " (Marx, 1967, III: 372). Kenzo Mohri (1979) writes that until the late 1850s Marx strongly believed British trade and industrial capital would destroy monopolistic societies and establish the material foundations of Western capitalism in Asia; this view is evident in a passage from the *Communist Manifesto*, in his writings on India (in 1853), and in numerous passages from *Grundrisse* (1857-1859). Mohri argues that Marx shifted ground in the middle 1860s, in particular in his writing on the Irish question; one passage in chapter 15 of the first volume of *Capital* resembles the idea of development of underdevelopment: "A new and international division of labor, a division suited to the requirements of its chief centers of modern industry, springs up and converts one part of the globe into a chiefly agricultural field of production, for supplying the other part which remains a chiefly industrial field" (Marx, 1967, I: 451). Mohri concludes that Marx was moving toward a view in which British free trade was transforming the old society into the world market system so that "the resulting transformation of this society would determine a course of development of its economy and a structure of its productive powers completely dependent upon England" (Mohri, 1979: 40).

Lenin also referred to the idea of dependent nation and periphery. In *Imperialism: the Highest State of Capitalism*, he stated : "Not only are there two main groups of countries, those owning countries, and the colonies themselves, but also the diverse forms of dependent countries which, politically, are independent, but in fact are enmeshed in the net of financial and diplomatic dependency . . . " (Lenin, 1967, I: 742-743). Cardoso suggests that Lenin provided the first systematic analysis of capitalist development in backward nations when he "formulated with simplicity what would be the core of the dependency analyses" (Cardoso, quoted in Palma, 1978).

A systematic review of the writings of Marx and Lenin may demonstrate support of contemporary dependency theory. Gabrial Palma (1978) devoted some attention to such a review but concluded that approaches to dependency have not really succeeded in building a formal theory and assessment of concrete situations of dependency. Carlos Johnson suggests that Lenin took the concept of dependent nations from bourgeois political economists but that he was guided by materialist reasoning and theoretical analysis. Gary Howe is correct in his view that Marx had not fully developed any systematic analysis of dependent relationships, believing that dependency theory was not based on formulations by Marx. Although Joel Edelstein and Dale Johnson agree that no general theory of dependency has emerged, they believe that the past work on dependency must be used as a foundation for future investigation. Henfrey, Barkin, Chinchilla and Dietz, and Petras all believe that theoretical analysis will profit from new directions, while Weeks insists on a restoration of classical materialist theory in a Marxist tradition.

Does dependency reflect only the needs of competitive capital in the face of monopoly capital in countries where the capitalist mode of production is not dominant? Carlos Johnson answers affirmatively by illustrating his position with a critical analysis of Cardoso and Marini. Howe effectively relates dependency to the failure in Brazil to establish a national alliance of bourgeoisie and working class to promote autonomous national development. The question is not directly addressed by other contributors, but most I suspect, would recognize the political implications of class alliances that obscure recognition of class enemies.

What of the significance of dependency for analysis of class and class struggle in Latin America? A decade ago specialists were insisting that theory and investigation incorporate a class analysis. Yet today there remains a dearth of such work. The mode of production approach suggests the possibility of empirical study on the class relations of production. Class analysis using other approaches has been suggested. In general, there is agreement that dependency theory has not yet contributed significantly to the study of social classes in Latin America.

Finally, has dependency theory provided any developmental solutions for Latin America? The contributors would answer negatively. Dependency theory served the purpose of questioning old and static formulations, especially in bourgeois thinking but also in questioning rigid ideas emanating from the Stalinist period and the Communist International's models of underdevelopment and class alliance. The latter models incorporated a unilinear perspective of feudalism and capitalism and called for alliances with the national bourgeoisie. As Munck suggests, even the Communist Party of Mexico recently recognized that dependency theory had confronted these old schema of the Comintern and the Latin American communist parties. It is also clear that dependency theory was conceived as a response to the inadequacies of theories of imperialism in explaining the impact of capitalism on domestic structures of the less developed countries. Most contributors would agree, however, that dependency theory has not provided us with any new theory of imperialism. Nor has it demonstrated any way to solve the problems of capitalist exploitation. Likewise, it seems not to offer any strategy of achieving socialism, and it has not been used to analyze relations of production in the transition to socialism.

In summary, while many contributors acknowledge the fact that questions of dependency stimulated new questions and interesting analysis of Latin America, there is also agreement that past work has suffered from many problems. Those interested in dependency have recognized that no general and unified theory exists and that confusion over terminology has diverted investigation away from central concerns. The criticisms raised in the present issue and elsewhere are numerous. It has been argued that some theories of dependency distort the thought of Marx and Lenin. Idealism and ideology permeate the writing on dependency. Some versions of dependency focus on the needs of competitive capital and thus appear to be supportive of the dominant classes in Latin America. Dependency may divert attention from the impact of imperialist penetration or overlook the importance of precapitalist social formations. Dependency theory may emphasize static categories so that dynamic and dialectical analysis is not possible. Class analysis, for example, is often lacking due to stress on relations of exchange rather than on relations of production.

Given these criticisms, all the contributors suggest that theory and investigation must advance. Some, such as Carlos Johnson and Weeks, urge a return to classical Marxist conceptions of international capital. Others, like Dale Johnson and Edelstein, believe that Marxist formulations do not necessarily lead to adequate analysis of the contemporary world capitalist system; and thus, new concepts and theory building may correct this deficiency. Barkin refers to the need for and approach to the study of the internationalization of capital. Dietz and Chinchilla write on the usefulness of the modes of production approach, while Henfrey argues that we must go beyond such analysis toward work on imperialism and class struggle. Petras reinforces this position, while Howe stresses relations of production, and Angotti is concerned about class alliance and political strategy in the struggle against imperialism. It seems clear that the task in the decade ahead necessitates not only familiarity with the classical Marxist texts and theories of imperialism but the development of theory and investigation that benefits from close examination of relations and modes of production, specifically class analysis of social formations that allows attention to state-class relationships and the impact of the internationalization of capital.

# REFERENCES

Amin, Samir
   1976 *Unequal Development: An Essay on the Social Formations of Peripheral Capitalism,* New York: Monthly Review Press

Bambirra, Vania
   1978 *Teoréa de la dependencia: una anticrítica,* Mexico City: Ediciones Era

Cardoso, Fernando Henrique
   1972 "Dependency and Development in Latin America," *New Left Review,* 74 (July-August), 83-95

   1980 *As idéias e seu lugar: ensaios sobre as teorias do desenvolvimento,* Petrópolis: Cadernos CEBRAP (33), Editora Vozes

Dos Santos, Theotônio
    1970 "The Structure of Dependence," *American Economic Review*, LX (May), 231-236

    1978 *Imperialismo y dependencia*, Mexico City: Ediciones Era

Frank, André Gunder
    1966 "The Development of Underdevelopment," *Monthly Review*, XVIII (September), 17-31

    1967 *Capitalism and Underdevelopment in Latin America: Historical Studies of Chile and Brazil*, New York: Monthly Review Press

Laclau, Ernesto
    1971 "Feudalism and Capitalism in Latin America," *New Left Review*, 67 (May-June), 19-38

Lenin, V. I.
    1967 *Selected Works*, 3 volumes, Moscow: Progress Books

Marini, Ruy Mauro
    1974 *Dialéctica de la dependencia*, 2nd ed. Mexico City: Ediciones Era

    1978 "Las razones del neodesarrollismo (respuesta a F. H. Cardoso y J. Serra)," *Revista Mexicana de Sociología* (XL), 57-106

Marx, Karl
    1967 *Capital: A Critique of Political Economy*, 3 volumes, New York: International Publishers

Mohri, Kenzo
    1979 "Marx and 'Underdevelopment,' " *Monthly Review*, XXX (April), 32-42

Palma, Gabriel
    1978 "Dependency: A Formal Theory of Underdevelopment or a Methodology for the Analysis of Concrete Situations of Underdevelopment?," *World Development* (VI), 881-924

Quijano, Aníbal
    1971 *Nationalism and Colonialism in Peru: A Study in Neo-Imperialism*, New York: Monthly Review Press

Rodney, Walter
    1972 *How Europe Underdeveloped Africa*, London and Dar es Salaam: Bogle-L'Ouverture and Tanzania Publishing House

Thomas, Clive Y.
    1974 *Dependence and Transformation: The Economics of the Transition to Socialism*, New York: Monthly Review Press

Warren, Bill
    1973 "Imperialism and Capitalist Industrialization," *New Left Review*, 81 (September-October), 3-44

# 2

## DEPENDENCY, MODES OF PRODUCTION, AND THE CLASS ANALYSIS OF LATIN AMERICA

by
*Colin Henfrey**

### THEORY AND CONTEXT: THE LOSS OF PRAXIS IN APPROACHES TO LATIN AMERICAN DEVELOPMENT

For a quarter of a century Latin America has been the fulcrum of development theories. From the Economic Commission on Latin America's (ECLA) reformist structuralism to the dependency perspective and analyses of modes of production, each radical reformulation of the Latin American dilemma has ushered in a new approach to underdevelopment in general. The reason for this is clearly contextual. By the mid-twentieth century the region effectively represented the "highest stage" of underdevelopment and its attendant contradictions, economic, political and social. This made it a natural source for theories based on an originally innovating but now generally accepted premise: underdevelopment is not a traditional state, nor a stage in a standard development process, but a distinct historical condition for which neither bourgeois nor Marxist theories of unilinear evolution afford explanations or solutions (Frank, 1971: 27-30).

The experience of the structuralist reforms of the 1950s and 1960s was the catalyst of this new thinking. Their contradictions were a mirror of the Latin American situation. On the one hand, they embodied a notion that Latin American history was shaped by the international division of labor and unfavorable terms of trade (Furtado, 1970). On the other hand, they were a last attempt to realign this history with a standard model of capitalist development through Keynesian forms of intervention: state planning, import substitution industrialization and agrarian reform. The radical inference of their failures, in Brazil and Chile particularly, was that history could not just be rerouted through the existing state apparatus. If significant change were to be achieved, this history had to be broken out of by revolutionary means and in the revolutionary direction which Cuba was already pioneering.

Hence both the main post-structuralist approaches set out, at least in principle, to examine class relations and struggles. From the premise that

*The author is a member of the Center for Latin American Studies and department of sociology at the University of Liverpool.

Latin America's development is conditioned by the world economy (Dos Santos, 1976: 76), dependency aspired to offer: "A foundation for analysis of class struggle and strategies to promote class struggle . . . (leading) . . . to the restructuring of societies, a restructuring which limits capitalism and promotes socialism in the seeking of a new and better society" (Chilcote, 1974: 21). The subsequent discussion of modes of production, by its very nature, has the same implications. From criticizing dependency writers for their insufficiently Marxist analysis of class formation and relations (Bartra, 1976: 7), it went on to examine the region's class struggles "within the framework of definite modes of production, without the theoretical knowledge of which the very class structure becomes incomprehensible" (Cueva, 1978a: 19).

As attempts to reformulate underdevelopment, both these approaches were responses to the general crisis of Marxist thought in the aftermath of de-Stalinization. Dependency took issue above all with the evolutionary approach to history as a linear succession of modes of production; it was this which had molded the thinking and strategies of the Latin American communist parties into their "reformist" alliances with supposedly national bourgeoisies, against "semifeudal" oligarchies in partnership with imperialism. This critique of linear historiography, foreshadowed in Baran's contention that underdevelopment has its own morphology (Baran, 1973: 265-401), was shared by dependency writers as disparate as Frank and Cardoso and Faletto. In contrast, the modes of production approach has its background in the historical debates on the rise of Western capitalism between writers such as Dobb and Sweezy (in Hilton et al., 1976), and also in French structuralism with its more philosophical grounding (Foster-Carter, 1978). Here the main concern, most notably of Althusser and Balibar (1970), was to counter the theoretical roots of the economic determinism and evolutionary approach to history which had influenced communist parties' thinking during the Third International. This background explains the primarily conceptual focus on the definition of modes of production and their theoretical components of its Latin American exponents like Laclau, Assadourian, and Bartra. However, in the Latin American context, the application of such concepts to the shortcomings of dependency theory also revealed a concern for praxis. In denying that Latin America was a continent of capitalist underdevelopment and thus ripe for socialist revolution, as so many dependency writers argued, these modes of production analysts were reflecting no less on the relation between such assumptions and the failure of the 1960s guerrilla movements in Latin America (Cueva, 1978a: 13).

The paradox is that, despite this background, these theories of Latin America have been curiously far removed from praxis in the sense of producing class analyses germane to revolutionary programs. Most dependency writers' theoretical concepts are little more than instrumental to their overriding generalizations on capitalist "dependence" or "underdevelopment"; they assert much more than they examine the conditions for socialist revolution. By contrast, in modes of production analysis the concrete data tend to be secondary; all too often they are just illustrative of "correct" conceptual definitions of capitalism, feudalism, and their alleged articulation as the key to Latin American societies. The debate between Frank and Laclau,

for instance, which still holds the center of this stage, bears little obvious relation to the substance of the class struggles now ranging from the Southern
Cone to Central America. This paper is therefore addressed to the questions
which follow from this apparent impasse. What reduced this debate to little
more than a schematic confrontation between these contending generalities?
And has this obscured alternatives within both dependency and Marxism
which might have been more complementary for the class analysis of Latin
America and for Marxist development theory in general, as a "philosophy of
praxis"?

## THE DICHOTOMIES OF THE DEPENDENCY CONCEPT: REVOLUTIONARY THEORY OR METHODOLOGY?

The conception of this debate as one between Marxism and dependency
theory (Foster-Carter, 1974; Kay, 1975: preface; Taylor, 1979: 71-98) raises one
obvious set of problems: is dependency in fact a theory or a number of
competing theories, or even conceived by some people as such, but by others
as something other than theory? And if there is such variety within the
dependency perspective, which version of it attracts so much comment, in the
Latin American context and beyond it, and is it really representative?

That dependency is multi-stranded has been noted by many Latin
Americanists (O'Brien, 1975; Harding, 1976; Cardoso, 1977; Palma, 1978).
However, less effort has been made to locate the key distinctions within it
and evaluate them by clear-cut standards, the most salient of which from a
Marxist standpoint is their implications for a class analysis. It is partly this
lack of clarification which has led to the quite unwarranted assumption in
overall development theory that Frank is dependency's typical exponent and
hence to its being counterposed with more conventional Marxist analysis.
Such attempts as Latin Americanists have made to distinguish within the
dependency genre have been on three quite different counts. Of these, one is
informative but uncritical, the second significantly misleading, and the third
neglected but fundamental for a reappraisal of its potential relationship with
Marxist theory.

The first is in terms of its "formulations," which Chilcote (1974: 13-19) distinguished, with their main protagonists, as follows: Frank's development of
underdevelopment; Dos Santos' new (contemporary) dependency; the relations between dependency and development (primarily Cardoso); and imperialism and dependency (mainly Quijano, in relation to the work on imperialism of Magdoff, O'Connor and others). Though informative, these categories
gloss over quite fundamentally distinct approaches. For instance, both Frank
and Cardoso deal inseparably with the past and the present, but in ways em-
bodying conflicting conceptions of the very nature of dependency analysis.

As to what this is, Chilcote is cautious. He describes dependency simply
as "a framework for the analysis of development and underdevelopment"
(Chilcote, 1974: 21). However, others are less reserved. The second and
dominant tendency is to take for granted that dependency is a would-be
theory, or group of theories; and then to distinguish them in terms of each
one's overt political message, rather than by whatever mode of analysis it
uses in order to achieve it. The best known example of such classification is

probably O'Brien's critique of dependency theory or theories. Here it is tacitly assumed from the outset (O'Brien, 1975: 7) that dependency amounts to "theory," yet unclear why and whether it is more than one theory, and if so, how to judge between them. The initial classification is in terms of each writer's relative affinities with structuralist and/or Marxist theory; but the clearest and correlated criterion is then stated to be the empirical one of "perspectives for political action" (O'Brien, 1975: 11). On this basis, Marini, Dos Santos, and Frank are assigned to a Marxist status and Sunkel and Furtado to a structuralist one; several others — Cardoso, Quijano, Ianni, and Fernandes — are put midway between them. However, O'Brien gives no clear indication of whether these differences really matter, since he ultimately dismisses dependency as a homogeneously circular perspective without offering any substitute for it. In his conclusion, the political criterion is clearer, as Cardoso in particular appears to be shifted to a structuralist reformist status, on the grounds of his seemingly nationalist leanings (O'Brien, 1975: 24-25). The same subjective criterion is echoed in Myer's branding of Cardoso's work as counterrevolutionary, on the grounds of its alleged neglect of the significance of class struggle (Myer, 1975: 41).

In practice the yardstick used in such cases is each writer's interpretation of the "new," contemporary dependency. Here the demarcation is between those who see it as a cul-de-sac of dependent capitalist stagnation, implying "fascism or socialism" and thus an immediate clear-cut case for revolutionary class struggle (Dos Santos, 1970a: 236), and those who credit this capitalism with a certain dynamic, or expansive capacity. This latter view has what tend to be read as more conservative implications: the possibility of a struggle for "national" interests, perhaps on a democratic basis. For instance, O'Brien counterposes Frank and Cardoso on this question (O'Brien, 1975: 22-23), which is also the one on which Myer stands in revolutionary judgement on Cardoso. This distinction between their empirical positions on the "new dependency" is perfectly accurate. What is much less tenable on any but a superficial reading is that each approach is correspondingly more or less Marxist and "revolutionary." O'Brien, for instance, acknowledges that Cardoso declines "to derive in a mechanistic way the political and social consequences of dependency" (O'Brien, 1975: 19). How then can Cardoso be judged on the basis of his apparently nationalist message as distinct from the unexamined way in which he employs the dependency concept? In Myer's case this judgement rests on little but slogans. Cardoso's sin is his neglect of "the revolutionary response which has proved successful in China, Vietnam, Korea, Cuba and earlier in Russia" (Myer, 1975: 47). But is what makes any particular analysis revolutionary or counterrevolutionary its assertion or denial of the existence of the unspecified conditions for some universal revolution, or the concrete assessment of the conditions for particular forms and stages of struggle in specific historical situations? Since the latter is clearly the case, is it a new "revolutionary" *theory* which Marxists need for Latin America, as if Stalinism had somehow stifled the original one in perpetuity, or a means of applying existing theory — while recognizing that no theory is static — to the varied and changing specifities of Latin American social formations?

It is this difference between dependency as a would-be theory of underdevelopment with fixed political implications or as a merely investigative comparative-historical method which provides the third key distinction within it. It is one which Cardoso particularly both emphasizes and employs. Recently, for instance, Cardoso (1977) identified his and Faletto's work (Cardoso and Faletto, 1969) as within the Latin American Marxist tradition of examining the structural history of specific situations of dependency. He contrasts this approach, and its roots in the work of praxis-oriented Marxists from Mariátegui to Caio Prado Jr., with dependency as an over-generalized, formal theory of underdevelopment. It is mainly for ideological reasons, which Cueva (1976) has also examined in detail, that the latter and its "revolutionary" message are much more readily consumed in a radical North American market rather than in Latin America.

This distinction as well as the potential hazards of Cardoso's more pragmatic approach were spelled out in a seminal debate with Weffort. The latter pointed much more clearly than most of the later critics to dependency's propensity to slip from a class to a nation perspective, whereas the focus of a Marxist analysis of underdevelopment should be the nexus between imperialism and the class structure within the nation. In Weffort's view, dependency was therefore a superfluous and dangerous theory. In stressing the improbability of autonomous, national capitalist development, it obscured the potential for alternative forms of capitalist growth in "dependent" economies. In addition, it treated the dependent state as the independent variable or agent of the ties with imperialism, whereas these and any challenge to them — even in terms of the "national question," or priority of national interests — must fundamentally be based on class forces (Weffort, 1971). Significantly, though, Cardoso's reply affirmed that these comments were complementary with his own heuristic concept of dependence. As he and Faletto had understood it, dependency was not proposed as a theory, but as an empirical device: as a methodology for specifying the locally variable patterns of class formation and political structure in successive phases of imperialist expansion. Their focus, in short, was on "concrete situations of dependency"; and this was a matter of identifying substantive historical variables from *within* the theory of imperialism which Marxism already provided. Insofar as the nation-state was concerned, the purpose was simply to examine it as the political sphere of dependence; it was not an explanatory principle to take the place of a class analysis (Cardoso, 1971).

Here clearly we have the nub of the question of whether dependency, and more importantly which particular version of it, is more or less compatible or at odds with a Marxist understanding. How then do these rival conceptions of it compare in their scope for a class analysis of the contemporary "new dependence," since it is this which underlies the polarized assessments of them?

## THE IMPLICATIONS OF THE TWO DEPENDENCIES:
## DEPENDENT DEVELOPMENT OR STAGNATION?

There is certainly some truth in Myer's charge that Cardoso's less categorical assessment of the contemporary situation involves little class analysis or deliberation on the class struggle. However, the constructive question, to which Myer's answer is just ideological (Cardoso is a counter-revolutionary), is *why* is this analysis lacking. Does the alternative conception of dependency as a theory of underdevelopment provide an answer to this question by dealing more satisfactorily with the class dimension of the new dependence? If not, should dependency be abandoned, as many of its critics would certainly argue (Cueva, 1978a: 14), in favor of the more frankly Marxist analysis of modes of production in Latin America? My contention is that such sweeping judgement is in fact quite indiscriminating, especially by the standards of political praxis: that in overlooking the crucial distinction between the respective specificity and generality of the two approaches, it conceals the former's considerable relevance — despite its conceptual limitations — to the lack of such specificity in most Marxist analysis of underdevelopment.

For Frank, whom Cardoso cites as his target in debating the nature of the new dependence (Cardoso, 1972: 94), there is nothing essentially new about it. His assessment of it is simply a function of his notion of continuity in change (Frank, 1971: 36-38), whereby each phase of imperialism is a further development of underdevelopment in continuing the appropriation of surplus from the satellite to the metropolis (Frank, 1971: 30-36). This reaffirms the incapacity of the dependent bourgeoise to initiate significant change, which can therefore only be achieved by means of the socialist revolution (Frank, 1969: 371-409). Though this is a matter of "class struggle," the classes involved are unspecified, as are the conditions, except in terms of a general "crisis." Cardoso, however, sees the new forms of imperialism and dependency as the key to any formulation of how actually to overcome them (Cardoso, 1974: 43). The increasing rate of direct investment, particularly in manufacturing, is historically distinct from imperialism as it was characterized by Lenin, in being geared predominantly to the expansion of the internal market (Cardoso, 1972: 88-90). In therefore entailing at least a degree of prosperity within the dependent economy, this implies a certain dynamism — a combination of dependence and development, which stagnation theorists by definition regard as mutually exclusive. Since this process is qualitatively new, it is also producing a new structure with distinct political implications. While dependent development may not be general to Latin America, Cardoso concludes, it is certainly an existing situation, of which Frank's development of underdevelopment affords no possible understanding.

Frank, though, is essentially the historian of the stagnation model. It is particularly with Marini that Cardoso has conducted a prolonged debate on current developments in Latin America. While Marini identifies with Frank's model quite significantly for political reasons (Marini, 1973: 18), he is at pains to transfer its focus from circulation to production. In his view, the objective limitation of dependent capitalism lies in its inability to take the key step towards the process of self-expansion: the transition to accumulation on the basis of relative rather than absolute surplus value. His basic argument is as follows. With its products realized in the metropolis, the traditional export economy had no need of an internal market. It therefore based its accumulation essentially on "overexploitation" — not on lowering the cost of labor-power by increasing productivity but on lengthening the working day and intensifying the use of labor-power, paid typically at below its value (i.e., the cost of its reproduction) since workers' consumption played little part in the circuit of dependent capital. Hence industrialization is still limited by a severely restricted internal market; it is therefore highly dependent on exports, ensured partly by the "sub-imperialist" domination of weaker neighbors. These contradictions are intensified by the "marginality," or underemployment, entailed in such capital intensive production. In all, dependent capitalism is a cul-de-sac: its structural foundations preclude its becoming self-sustaining (Marini, 1973).

While there are many more strands to this argument, Cardoso's and Marini's main differences from the standpoint of a class analysis are as follows. For Marini class formation is given by the "laws" of *dependent* capitalism, whereas for Cardoso there are no such laws specific to dependency. There are merely historically structured types of concrete situations of dependence, in which the new patterns of imperialism (which is where the laws of capitalism, and capitalism as a whole, are located) will take root to different degrees determined by the composition of social relations. These may or may not eventually permit the expanded reproduction of capital (the production of relative surplus value) in specific cases of dependency, but among the determinants of this there will certainly be political variables: the potentially autonomous role of the state, the nature of the ruling class, and so on.

In practice though, the debate is circular and its terms are essentially Marini's — economistic, generalized and more assertive than investigative. The actual evidence is selective, with Marini (1978: 80-83), for instance, emphasizing the growth rate of industrial exports, regardless of its modest base and the general increase in manufacturing, while Cardoso stresses the latter and plays down the realization problem. Rather than developing different approaches, their exchanges become ideological. Marini (1978: 99) castigates Cardoso as "the shield bearer" of the bourgeoisie, since he appears to be disputing the case for socialist revolution; and Cardoso replies that Marini's position of advocating armed struggle is voluntarist, ineffective, and dangerous (Cardoso and Serra, 1978: 51-53). The contrasting precepts and politics of the two positions are so overt — the relative emphasis on forces or relations of production and on sheer revolution or pragmatism — that most "Marxists," as Myer's case illustrates, will choose between them a priori. However, from the standpoint of praxis, the issues are qualitatively different. Which approach is potentially more effective for an understanding of class formation? And if it is only potentially effective, what accounts for its limitations in practice?

Within the limited terms of the debate, the evidence is certainly in Cardoso's favor. Their controversy is increasingly focused on Brazil, where armed struggle has proved ineffective and the economy entered the eighties still with an 8 percent rate of growth (*Latin America Regional Report,* January 2, 1981, Brazil, RB81-01: 1). Yet what matters more is the evidence that Marini's basic "problematic" — his formulation of the issue in terms of economic contradictions with necessary and universal sociopolitical inferences — blocks any concrete analysis of the class struggle a priori. Thus one question which he puts to Cardoso in support of his argument is as follows: if the dynamics of contemporary dependence are empirically conditioned, as Cardoso suggests, by concrete structural variations precluding standard inferences, how did overexploitation become general not just to Brazil but to countries with stronger trade union movements, like Uruguay, Argentina and Chile? And does this not clearly imply the case for a revolutionary "struggle to the death between bosses and workers" (Marini, 1978: 98-99)? The obvious reply is: but is overexploitation a remotely adequate representation of the complex modern historical relations between labor and capital in all these cases? And can one therefore draw such conclusions, at least insofar as they seem to imply that the "new dependence" everywhere involves the conditions for advanced class struggles? Why, for instance was the new dependence so much less easily implemented in Argentina than in Brazil? Or, in obvious contrast with both of them, is anything like it occurring in Chile, with its marked de-industrialization since the overthrow of the Popular Unity (Henderson, 1977)? Is Marini, in giving such priority and inexorability to the economic, not underrating the very class struggle — or rather, class struggles — with which he like Myer expresses concern? Do classes themselves not bring their own specific history and agency to all such struggles? What else could explain these differing effects in particular countries or social formations of whatever general tendencies there may be at the economic level? Do these differences not in fact preclude any but empty generalizations — and Marini's is no more than that — as to the nature of future struggles?

In part then the issue at stake is one which lies at the heart of Marxist thinking: the relations between base and superstructure and the very nature of class itself, as more or less economically determined, and hence as the object or agent of history (Thompson, 1978; Anderson, 1980). Thus at one point Marini charges Cardoso with overturning the main tenet of Marxism as he understands it: the dominance of the forces over the relations of production. In giving priority to the latter, Cardoso "sociologizes" Marx (Marini, 1978: 68). Yet Marini's position is distinct even within the contentious premise of such economic determinism. Not only does he see laws of movement as overwhelmingly determinant, he also treats their contradictions — such as the realization problem or the relative surplus population (the "marginality" which he stresses) — not as those of the capitalist mode of production, i.e., as general tendencies expressed in differing degrees and ways according to the particular context. Instead he locates them categorically in a distinct dependent capitalism. Thus he sees them existing not just as tendencies in the abstract but, necessarily, in the concrete; they acquire an inexorable, invariable presence in all Latin American *social formations.* This conflation in "dependent capitalism" of two concepts of such different status as mode of production and social formation, which Marini therefore rarely uses, is intrinsically anti-analytic. At a stroke it pre-empts the complementary theoretical scope of the former concept and the flexibility and specificity afforded by that of social formations. These lie, first, in its connotations for the autonomy of political and ideological from purely economic forces, and second, in the notion of their interplay to make the process of class formation unique to specific social histories, which preclude the reduction of class struggles to "modes," let alone to one notional mode of production such as dependent capitalism.

In obscuring any such specificity, for instance of the class formation of Brazil compared to that of Chile, this confusion of analytic levels suggests that Marini's main concern is not with such substantive matters. Rather than being analytic, his overexploitation model is ideologically determined. In effect it is just a post-hoc theory of armed struggle as an unspecified class one. What it involves is not class analysis, but the inversion of its tacit target - the communist parties' implicit denial of the conditions for revolution in any of the region's social formations. In reply Marini is asserting, on the contrary, that such conditions are universal; he then constructs an appropriate theory at the level of these supposed conditions, not at a theoretical distance from them. Thus he reproduces the intrinsic premise that Latin America — "dependent capitalist," instead of the communists' "semi-feudal" — is homogeneous; the "laws of dependent capitalism" then provide him with much the same charter for this ideological standardization as did evolutionary modes of production for the Latin American communist parties.

Hence even if his model affords some insights, their expression as "laws " blocks their empirical application and possibly fruitful implications. For instance, overexploitation may be a much more valid concept for characterizing relations of production in the case of Chile than of Brazil, to which Marini seems compelled to apply it in order to deny the latter's dynamics and its complex political implications. Or, to take another instance of the concealment of concrete implications by the pursuit of general laws: if labor-power, as Marini contends, is paid for at below its value (i.e., the cost of its reproduction), how then is it actually reproduced? That is, how do workers and their families subsist, and with what specific implications in terms of relations of production? Marini's answer, based on São Paulo — atypical, for its industrialization — is that where one person per family once worked, two now typically do so, both overexploited but able between them to support the family (Marini, 1978: 91): there is simply an increase of capitalist overexploitation. Now either this rather weakens the case for the inelastic labor market, implicit in his notion that marginality or underemployment, like overexploitation, is inherent in dependent capitalism, or else it suggests that marginality is producing wage goods at below their value outside the capitalist sector to help reproduce its labor power and hence its over-exploitation (Oliveira, 1972). This obviously raises a set of questions about the dynamics of class formation — the linkage of simple commodity production with capitalist accumulation (Scott, 1979) — which Marini's undifferentiated picture of dependent capitalist class formation can scarcely accommodate in general, let alone as something which may vary from one social formation to another (Roberts, 1978: 134).

How successful then is Cardoso's quite different proposition of examining the new dependency inductively, not as evidence for a fixed theory-cum-schema, but as a "concrete situation"? The implicit danger of such an approach is that of exchanging the determinism and generalizations of Frank and Marini for merely empirical descriptions; these may be much more accurate and yet fail to interpret what they describe in the absence of a clearly guiding theory and related analytic concepts. These are very much the qualities of Cardoso's account of dependent development (Cardoso, 1972). Empirically it demystifies Frank's and Marini's generalized schema; yet its own implications are rather uncertain. In the absence of any clear means of *explaining* dependent development in Brazil, in terms of all aspects of class relations, its trajectory remains unclear — its origins, its contradictions, and most important its possible outcomes — as do its comparative implications for other Latin American countries. The main contradiction is identified as intra- rather than inter-class: dependent development differentiates each class into an internationalized fraction linked with the dynamic sector, and another outside it which is "marginalized" by this sector's monopoly of resources. Cardoso is careful to explain that this is not a dualist analysis, but a "new differentiation" of the unity of social relations. The political alternative to which he points is not the implicitly reformist one which most of his critics attribute to him. Rather, it raises the "national question," in the sense of calling for mobilization to re-integrate the marginalized sector through policies geared not just to national but, specifically, to popular interests. Not only does this mean a radical break with the pattern of external domination, it is also explicitly dissociated from the notion that a national bourgeoisie can provide the leadership for this process (Cardoso, 1972: 95).

What Cardoso fails to indicate is what class or classes will generate it. In effect he identifies little more than its ideological characteristics — its equation of national with "popular" interests. Hence rather than being conservative, his conclusions are merely indecisive. What they lack is the means of anatomizing dependent development in such a way as to answer the ensuing questions of social agency, alliances, and programs, which are basically those of class formation. The theoretical vagueness is particularly marked. Cardoso just states that a number of authors — Baran and Sweezy, Magdoff, O'Connor and Mandel — provide the means for updating Lenin's theory of imperialism to take into account the new importance of the dependent internal market. Yet these authors' theories are very varied. For instance, Baran's concept of surplus has an essentially national focus and little to do with class relations in the accepted Marxist sense (Culley, 1977). Mandel's approach, on the other hand, though contentious, is much more clearly Marxist. Its main emphasis on the rate of profit (Mandel, 1975: 74-107) does point to class formation and relations as the nexus between imperialism and "concrete situations of dependence." Within such a perspective, which Cardoso infers but does not pursue, the sorts of questions which ensue are as follows. Once the general theory of imperialism and capitalist expansion is identified, what specific structural relations between labor and capital *in Brazil* created the conditions in the 1960s for implementing the current model of capital accumulation? What historical factors lay behind them? What have been the structural consequences of this process since the 1960s? Do they point to a possibly new class basis for developing the national question? What accounts for these structures in Brazilian history, in the sense of the variables underlying the formation of the bourgeoisie, the state, and the working class or classes? If the former is judged to have had its day, the latter will now be particularly important, as will the variables affecting the scope for a working-class dominated alliance among the petty bourgeoisie, the peasantry, and the "marginal" sector. Could such variables provide the methodology for a comparative structural history of class formation and dependence which might, for instance, identify the key contrasts between Brazil and Chile and how they affect their respective options?

Dependency's omission of such questions suggests the incapacity to pose them in class as distinct from "national" terms, which Weffort (1971) originally alleged. Yet there is an alternative hypothesis: that it has simply failed to do so. As is shown by Cardoso's debate with Marini, the alternative search for a generalized model and autonomous theory of dependence — at heart, an ideological one — appropriated the terms of discussion, stunting the much more methodological, concrete, and analytic option. Hence the striking features of dependency writing as typified in this debate are its overemphasis on the external, its economism at the expense of an understanding of the *social* relations of production, and its repetitive generality, with the lasting dearth of substantive case studies which Chilcote noted at an earlier stage (Chilcote, 1974: 20). Yet the few exceptions, like Torres-Rivas' (1969) analysis of Central America, do show that the concept when used heuristically can shed some light on specific class struggles. Why then has it generally failed to do so, even when aimed at specificity, as in the account of "dependent development"?

The answer to this question lies in the uses of dependency as historiography. Here the contrast between the respective approaches of Frank and Cardoso and Faletto, though rarely discussed, is central to the question of the relations between Marxism and dependency.

## DEPENDENCY AS HISTORIOGRAPHY: CONCRETE SITUATIONS AND CLASS FORMATION

No less than the stagnationists, Cardoso and Faletto looked to the past for some understanding of the current dilemma which the existing linear theories of neither ECLA nor the communist parties seemed to be capable of providing (Cardoso, 1977: 8-11). However, while Frank addressed this problem as one of finding a new theory (Frank, 1971: 15), what Cardoso and Faletto noted was that the crisis of the new dependence took different forms in particular countries. In both Brazil and Chile it led to an economic impasse and spelled the eventual transformation of the sociopolitical order. Yet Mexico seemed to be undergoing a more stable transition to the new dependence. From this they concluded that the crucial difference must be political since it was the post-revolutionary state, with its corporative-integrative effects, which most clearly distinguished Mexico from the other Latin American countries (Cardoso and Faletto, 1969: 7-9). Hence dependency's theory was not the issue. This already existed in the Marxist approaches to imperialism, which a number of authors had already updated (Cardoso, 1972: 87). Rather, the task was methodological (Cardoso and Faletto, 1969: 11-38): to identify systematically the sociopolitical variables which had shaped the distinctive and changing boundaries of Latin American countries' responses to imperialism's successive phases. It is these which differentiate between "concrete situations of dependence." The crisis of the new dependence, for instance, lay in the specific contradictions between the new forms of imperialism and pre-existing political alignments (Cardoso and Faletto, 1969: 144-160). Correspondingly it is the role of the state, with its increasing autonomy, which makes dependent development possible, despite its intrinsic contradictions (Cardoso, 1974). Equally it is to the political level as a "prime mover" that Cardoso is looking, however opaquely, for some way out of these contradictions (Cardoso, 1972). Though neither Cardoso nor his critics have spelled out its uncertain implications, this priority of the political is the key to his and Faletto's notion of dependency as a historical method for dealing with concrete situations. As such, it is equally the key to both its scope and its limitations in relation to Marxist theory.

Their schema of comparative "structural history" is now available in English (Cardoso and Faletto, 1979) and has also been summarized by Kahl (1976: 155-170). It pivots on the variations in Latin America's export phase of "development toward the outside," from the mid-nineteenth century onwards: it was these which governed the potential responses of different Latin American countries to the crisis caused by the Depression (as they see it, the "moment of transition"). In countries where the main export commodity was primarily under local control (the "national control of the means of production"), a relatively organic ruling class with strong economic and social roots was reasonably able to retain control, establish new alliances, and develop the internal market for import substitute manufactures from the 1930s to 1950s. Differences within this category, between Argentina and Brazil, for instance, were a function of the same variable: the relative structural cohesion of the Argentine oligarchy as compared to the fragmentation of Brazil's. This compelled the latter to make adjustments to the role of the state and the new urban "masses," which only occurred in Argentina much later and more traumatically under Peronism in the 1950s. In "enclave" economies, by contrast, where the means of production (mines and plantations) were directly controlled by foreign capital, the ruling class by definition was relatively inorganic — a political intermediary for an insulated export sector with few internal ramifications, economic, political, or social. In such cases the impact of the Depression was economically more acute, in the absence of diversification and internal capital accumulation, while the social basis for responding to it was much less structurally resilient; hence the consequences were more far-reaching. Where a certain amount of local control of the financial and commerical sectors had created new urban middle classes (typically in mining economies like Chile's), these came to establish a significant presence in the relatively autonomous state apparatus — autonomous in the relative absence of an economically ruling class. Where such heterogeneity was lacking — for instance, in the plantation economies of many Central American countries — the crisis of the Depression resulted in a generation of caudillos (Cardoso and Faletto, 1969: 39-101). The varied postwar trajectories of different Latin American countries, Cardoso and Faletto suggest, were structured by these historical backgrounds, above all by their political forces, alliances and oppostitions, which the new dependence is now reshaping (Cardoso and Faletto, 1969: 102-166).

The success of this schema in identifying and interpreting empirical data is arguably greater than that of the rest of dependency writing put together. Of course, this in itself may make it "non-Marxist" to the Marxists, for whom empirical study is by definition "empiricist" and nonscientific, and also to those for whom history is "real" but allows no empirical variations, conforming instead to the patterns entailed in one revolutionary line or another. To such gurus and sects one need only reply that Marx throughout his political writings (Marx, 1973-1974) considered the empirical an object of study; and that above all what he studied it for was not its fixed lines but the *variations* of state and class formation and conjuncture in the expansion of capitalism in Germany and France especially. The problem of Cardoso and Faletto's work lies not in the object of study they define, with its open-ended implications — on the contrary, this is their contribution — but in complex aspects of how they approach it; it is these which frustrate the incipient scope of their historiography for interpreting and explaining the present. This weakness lies in a cluster of problems at different levels: their theoreticization of the political in relation to the economic; an ensuing conceptual ambiguity, particularly regarding class; and a consequently restricted focus of increasing significance through time (which is why their historical analysis is more convincing than their analysis of the present) on the ruling rather than the exploited classes. The essence of all these problems, however, lies in a single basic one: their failure to see their key variable of internal control/enclave economy as a matter not merely of control but of the *types of capital* involved, from which the political differences ensue, as a function of varied class formation.

First, though, the extent of their embryonic "epistemological break" is worth noting. Unlike Frank, not only do they reject *all* linear theory, they also begin their analysis not in the sphere of circulation (be it exchange or underconsumption, on which Frank and Marini respectively focus), but in production and accumulation. It is from the control of the means of production, with its consequences for the specificity of internal capital accumulation and concomitant state and class formation, that they take their point of departure for distinct "situations of dependence;" initially at least, it is clearly such matters which underlie their much emphasized political variables.

However, the first major problem is that the nature of these relations between the political and the economic and the reasons why they should imply the dominance of the political are not theoretically examined. Their essence can be stated as follows. On the one hand, the export economy, internally or externally controlled, is by definition disproportionately subject to the external market: hence in either case, in different ways, the "economic center" is absent from the dependent social formation. To this extent the political becomes dominant by sheer default — the ruling class rules disproportionately through the political mechanisms of its relations with other classes, rather than through economic ones, which it controls either incompletely or scarcely at all in the export sectors (in internally controlled and enclave economies respectively). On the other hand, and this is the point which Cardoso and Faletto scarcely touch on, the *capital* involved, which is shaping the exploited classes partly independently of who controls it, is typically industrial in the one case and merchant capital in the other; thus the social relations of production entailed in the centrally formative export sectors tend in the one case to be capitalist and in the other noncapitalist, albeit in varying ways and degrees. (At best one is looking initially for the parameters, or ideal types, of social formations.) In the light of this fundamental distinction, the dominance of the political is a somewhat different matter in each case: in the one, a function of the absence of the capitalist class per se, in the other, of social relations of production which, being less typically capitalist, are reproduced largely by ideological and political rather than economic forms of coercion. It is these distinctions, I would suggest, particularly as they effect the formative relations of the exploited classes, which foreshadow the contemporary differences between such cases as Brazil and Chile.

However, Cardoso and Faletto do nothing to theorize this dominance (or dominances) of the political in the history of dependent social formations. Instead they tend merely to assume it empirically, with increasingly confused consequences. In effect, the internal becomes the political — as opposed to the primarily political expression of latently economic variables — and the external the economic; the priority of the political within the dependent social formation is no longer a function of the latter's specific economy and class relations but an assumed priority. In short, it ceases to be a Marxist and turns into a Weberian notion. From this theoretical ambiguity it is only a short conceptual step to seeing the political — as Cardoso and Faletto increasingly do — as a matter of relations between indeterminate groups and forces instead of between determinate classes. And since until the modern period, the exploited, as distinct from the ruling classes, have little visible political presence, the empirical effect is not just that they are temporarily missing from Cardoso and Faletto's historical schema; more importantly, one loses sight of the very roots of their formation in its ideological and political as well as its economic aspects. Thus once they become political actors, particularly from the Depression onwards — though others have argued convincingly that this active presence goes back much further (Cueva, 1978a: 18; Weaver, 1976: 24) — Cardoso and Faletto are without the means of discerning their potential practice in a politics which, in any case, has not been handled as a level of class but only of vaguely group relations. Their theoretical and empirical weaknesses are thus fundamentally interdependent in that their conceptualization of class is inadequate for specifying the exploited classes as objects of study in dependency as they conceive it: that is, according to Cardoso's reply to Weffort, as the complementary and concrete expression of a Marxist theory of imperialism (Cardoso, 1971; 1972).

A textual analysis of this process, whereby a potential perspective for class analysis fails to develop, would call for an article in itself; the book is certainly deserving of it, but this is not the present purpose. The effects, which are the immediate issue, are to limit the field of understanding to the obviously related subjects of dominant "groups" and the role of the state in Latin American social formations. In the case of Brazil, while the ruling class was a relatively organic one (characterized by internal control of the means of production), it was also heavily fragmented as the poles of the export economy shifted from sugar to gold and then to coffee (Furtado, 1963) before manufacturing became predominant, resulting in the deepening autonomy of the state, especially after the Depression and indeed right down to the present day (Cardoso, 1974), though in no sense did this undermine the fundamentally bourgeois control of it, even within a populist framework. In Chile, by contrast, the primarily political ruling class (characterized by external control of the means of production from the late nineteenth century onwards) has long since derived its class existence from control of what was a fundamentally autonomous state. The Chilean state, however ultimately bourgeois, was a much more open terrain of class struggle, resulting in the unique political rise of the Popular Front in the 1930s-1940s and later in the strategy and the contradictions of the Popular Unity.

So much for the "moment of transition," and its immediate aftermath in the nationalist and populist period. By the time we reach the present, the picture is much less specific. What Cardoso and Faletto now stress is the difference between Mexico and the other countries — a difference in their capacities for a smooth transition to dependent development at the level of the state and the ruling classes. They take little note of the striking contrast in the forms of the crisis of this transition in the countries most familiar to them, where class relations were much less stable but in different ways — again, Brazil and Chile. In Brazil the crisis had already led, through the dissolution of the populist alliance (not just between fractions of the bourgeoisie, but with the organized working class), to the subordination of labor to what was to be the outstanding example of the new model of accumulation, or "dependent development." In Chile, in the absence of such an alliance and with the autonomy of the labor movement, the crisis of Frei's reformism, which Cardoso and Faletto observed, was leading directly to the Popular Unity's electoral victory of 1970. By Marini's standards this makes little difference — Chile would soon be the scene of the same overexploitation. However, for a concrete class analysis, not just to explain this chapter of history but in order to understand the present in terms of contrasting class relations, these differences are clearly crucial. The reason why Cardoso and Faletto neglect them is that the main variable involved is now precisely the one precluded by their increasingly Weberian concepts: the quite different formation of the working classes and indeed of all the exploited sectors in the cases of Brazil and Chile, both structurally and in their political practice. This accounts for Cardoso's limited scope for explaining or drawing political conclusions on dependent development in Brazil, since this aspect of class formation, I would argue, has been the main condition for it, and in Chile's case the main obstacle to it.

The details of this argument, as one which is equally precluded by an overemphasis on modes of production, are spelled out in the concluding section. What is worth adding is that the grounding of this weakness in Cardoso and Faletto's basic concepts is evident elsewhere in Cardoso's writing and that it clearly explains the vagueness of his political formulations. For instance, where he does discuss the nature of the workig classes (Cardoso and Reyna, 1968), he continually emphasizes not their specificity as classes classes (the autonomy of Chile's or the patrimonial roots of Brazil's) but the general, economic, and descriptive distinction between their integrated and marginalized fractions, in the "modern" and the "traditional" sectors. This implicit assumption of the existence of a suborned labor aristocracy in the auto industry and so on, for which even the immediate economic evidence is now uncertain (Humphrey, 1979), by definition excludes the political: the extent to which class practice may not be just economically, but ideologically and politically determined by historical aspects of class formation in the face of deepening contradictions. Hence Cardoso's general formulations of political alternatives for Latin America have been vague and overtly "bourgeois" by omission in-failing to give weight or specificity to the part to be played by popular forces. It is this which foreshortens his political conclusions, rather than making them reactionary. In the current conditions of Brazil — the strength of the state apparatus, the continuing expansion of capitalism and the ground which the working class is still covering towards independent self-organization — his posing of an alternative in terms of "national interests" (Cardoso, 1972) is a quite rational starting point with a perfectly respectable ancestry in the Marxist concern with the national question (Lowy, 1976). Its progressive potential, which Myer (1975) dismisses so automatically, will clearly depend on its class basis — on how far the new working class movement, induced by recent Brazilian industrialization, will determine its political direction and will do so not just in its own interests but also in those of the "marginal" and rural strata which constitute its potential allies. The fact that the democracy which Cardoso is now advocating (1975) will necessarily be bourgeois does not in itself preclude the conditions for developing some such alliance and program. What he omits to specify is the historical foundation and class components of this alliance and the ways in which the contradictions of Brazilian development may carry it forward. One need hardly point out that in this respect, far from updating Lenin's analysis, he fails precisely in the tasks which Lenin undertook in his analysis of capitalist development and overall class formation in Russia (Lenin, 1974).

However, the virtue of this emphasis on concrete situations of dependence is that it does at least prompt such questions. Though limited, this is in marked contrast to Frank's "revolutionary theory," whose development of underdevelopment schema belies any such social agency or specificity a priori. The central theoretical issue involved — Frank's emphasis on circulation, so that market links and the transfer of surplus make Latin America capitalist from its historical inception — has long since and often been pointed out (Laclau, 1977; Assadourian, 1971; Booth, 1975; Kay, 1975; Culley, 1977; Weeks and Dore, 1979). It is therefore hardly worth reviving. What is arguably more significant is the critics' concentration on Frank (and thus on dependency as a would-be theory) and their dwelling on this obvious theoretical issue rather than on Frank's *metatheory* and its substantive consequences: on his telescoping of all reality into a single exclusive schema in which quasi-theory and doubtful data are simply conflated; and his preclusion of concrete analysis which his critics also tend to neglect in their use of the modes of production concept. In looking more briefly at Frank's work, since it has so much less to offer, I will therefore deal mainly with two points: (1) the logic of his historiography as one which precludes any specificity and (2) the way in which criticism of him, in neglecting this substantive issue, foreshadows the same empirical weakness in the modes of production concept which his critics propose as an alternative to dependency theory.

## FROM DEPENDENCY TO MODES OF PRODUCTION:
## FRANK AS AN OBJECT OF CRITICISM

The most notable aspect of Frank's work, considering how little it actually says about Latin American situations, is the attention which it has attracted. While Cardoso and Faletto's book took a decade to be translated, *Capitalism and Underdevelopment in Latin America* was available in Spanish a year after its publication in English and was seen as central to the debate on the Latin American dilemma (Assadourian 1978: 20). The main reason for this is one which also underlies its limitations: its ideological connotations as a debate with the communist parties (Frank, 1974), whose evolutionary strategy had already been called into question by the making of the Cuban revolution. Frank in effect was the would-be historian to Debray's *Revolution in the Revolution*. Yet even this political significance was something of an intellectuals' illusion. As Cueva (1978a: 13) points out, and as one can see from Guevara's writing (Guevara, 1969: 200-201), Frank's outright denial of feudal traits in Latin America was inconsistent even with most of the guerrilla movements' thinking. The main reasons for his impact lay in the cultural and ideological climate of the late 1960s and 1970s. On the one hand, he offered (and continues to offer) a simplistic "revolutionary" message of the kind which helped fill the lasting vacuum resulting from de-Stalinization. On the other, he provided a ready target for the way in which the French structuralists were criticizing such reactions as threats to the essential rigor and discipline of Marxist thinking. By their standards, his notion of underdevelopment was a travesty of epistemology or the way in which theory should be constructed; and within this, his conceptualization of capitalism in Latin America was directly at odds with the weight which they gave to the understanding of modes of production in the interpretation of history. In part, then, it is Frank's very critics who have inflated his importance, to the exclusion of the more constructive conceptualization of dependency afforded by Cardoso and Faletto. This in itself is indicative of how the debate between Marxism and dependency has been more concerned with generalities than with the substantive investigation of the Latin American past and present. However, within the Marxist critique, there are significant variations. Their significance lies in the way they foreshadow the degrees to which modes of production analysis is directed to such substantive ends, as opposed to the mere theorizing or labelling of class formation.

Within overall development studies, the posing of this debate as one between Marxism and dependency theory, especially as represented by Frank, is epitomized by Foster-Carter (1974, 1978). In strongly advocating the latter, he sees its "neo-Marxism" as a healthy reversal of orthodoxy. This he identifies not just with the Stalinist tradition, but the "paleo-Marxist" Eurocentricity running right from Marx to Lenin, which contributed little in theory or practice to the major fact of modern history — the success of Third World revolutions based on the primacy of praxis. Those opposed to the "open-mindedness" of such new revolutionary thinking, especially the structuralists with their concern for the "scientific" sanctity of Marxist concepts, "merely ensure that what they choose to call Marxism will have nothing to do with what happens in the world" (Foster-Carter, 1974: 94).

There is clearly an indisputable case for reconciling Marxism with history, from which structuralists have indeed divorced it no less than Stalin in their different way (Thompson, 1978). Yet Foster-Carter's arguments slur over many points too central to warrant dismissal as "paleo-Marxist," especially with reference to class analysis. After all, the term neo-Marxism still claims legitimacy by Marxist standards. The restriction of these to the realm of action comes close to ruling out theory per se, not just paleo-Marxist orthodoxy, as the weapon of praxis. For all Foster-Carter's appeals to history, have such neo-Marxist emphases as those on "morals" and "revolution" (Foster-Carter, 1974: 90-92) in fact contributed to its making? On the contrary, the evidence links such notions of their independent agency with vanguardism, failure, and setbacks (as in Latin America in the sixties) on account of their substitution of theory. As Anderson (1980: 85-86) has pointed out, there are good reasons why most Marxists question such moral agency in history, since its outcome is typically voluntaristic. If there is a Marxist ethic, it lies not at this subjective level but in the materialist understanding and activation of class forces, however distorted this may have been in the Marxism of the Third International (Claudin, 1975). One might argue, in contrast to Foster-Carter, that where Third World praxis has been successful, it has still been for the traditional reason that its key has lain (for example, in Cuba) in discerning class meaning within such categories as the nation or "internal colonialism," which dependency tends to substitute for it, and not in reducing theory to them. Although many such indeterminate categories are accentuated in Third World settings, the issue from a Marxist standpoint is not whether they are more or less important than questions of class formation, but the relationship between them; not whether to use a class analysis, but how to do so in Third World contexts. What Foster-Carter's account of this in neo-Marxist writing conveys is not a contextual sensitivity but its conceptual and empirical weakness (Foster-Carter, 1974: 87-90). Its central feature is its negativism — its rejection of the two categories of the "national, progressive bourgeoisie" and "feudalism" at the periphery. Thus dependency theory's typical history of class formation is an ideal-type *non*-history — not one of which classes have formed and how, and the relationships between them, but of those which inevitably failed to do so on account of external, negative, and historically unchanging forces like the "appropriation of surplus." This is complemented by such theory's opaqueness about the classes — the proletariat, "lumpenproletariat," and peasants — which it casts as agents of revolutionary change. To criticize this analysis is not to deny the central importance of such revolutionary alliances. On the contrary, what it calls into question is the scope of neo-Marxism for defining them at all exactly; for assessing the conditions for revolution as distinct from shouting its commitment to it; for producing strategies with a class basis, as opposed in the Latin American case to a blueprint *foquismo* which totally lacks one.

It is precisely this lack of scope for any class analysis which consistently characterizes Frank's work. Rather than simply misinterpreting all class relations as "capitalist," as his critics typically suggest, he attaches so little importance to them that he fails to characterize them at all. The question of why class formation in Chile and Brazil should vary, for instance, is ruled out a priori by his schema of the "capitalist development of underdevelopment" (rather than "capitalist" class formation), despite his overtly dealing with these specific countries and their histories. In practice the schema serves merely to prove one point of quasi political economy: the continuous appropriation of surplus from the satellite to the metropolis, in which classes are not only passive but merely incidental actors. At one extreme, local bourgeoisies are by definition "dependent" and "lumpen," by virtue of their association with metropolitan domination, regardless of their varied and changing forms and of their tasks as ruling classes in specific totalities of class relations. The only variation on this theme is the notional nineteenth century alternative of a would-be autonomous bourgeoisie which is swept aside by the onward march of the "development of underdevelopment" (Frank, 1971: 80-123). At the other extreme, the exploited classes are simply asserted to be the expression of the same universal process. They are "fully incorporated into, and indeed the necessary product of an underdeveloped capitalist metropolis-satellite economy" (Frank, 1971: 136) — as if the sheer fact of their being the product of an essentially unitary history conveyed how they are "incorporated," i.e., their identity as classes. Even when Frank turns to what are potentially specific matters of class formation, in dealing with the "Indian problem" (Frank, 1971: chapter II), with the history of Northeast Brazil (Frank, 1971: chapter IV), or quite explicitly with "class structure" (Frank, 1969: 393-402), it is only the single, continuous assertion of the "commercial determination" (Frank, 1971: 300) of all Latin American social relations, not their actual nature, which still concerns him. Nor do Frank's responses to his critics advance his analysis in this direction. For instance, in acknowledging Dos Santos' comments on the lack of internal class analysis in Capitalism and Underdevelopment (Frank, 1974: 97), he claims to have incorporated it into his second major work, Lumpenbourgeoisie, Lumpendevelopment. In reality there is no sign of this, though. The "dependent" nature of the bourgeoisie, which he insists is a class phenomenon, is simply the reiteration of its standard, merely economic, and inexorably subordinate external relations (Frank, 1970: 23-31). "Class" appears in the subtitle, alongside "dependence" and "politics," but nowhere in the ensuing analysis, in the sense of substantive instances of class formation, relations, or struggles.

To be fair, Frank is much less distinct on this count from most Latin American dependency writers than their criticisms of him acknowledge. By definition, if dependency is seen as a standard determining condition, and typically one of stagnation, the investigative analysis of class formation is precluded. Thus Marini's "over-exploitation" is no less the product of a standardizing and arbitrary approach to history; its main difference from Frank's is that it only goes back to the nineteenth rather than the sixteenth century (Marini, 1973: 16). Nor does Dos Santos, for all his comments, get much closer than Frank to a class analysis, despite his emphatic recognition of the specificity of the "new dependence" (Dos Santos, 1970a). His schema of Latin American history (Dos Santos,1970b) is hardly less exclusively geared to external and economic ties, and to "groups" and "forces" as a function of them, as distinct from internal, class relations; hence like Frank and Marini, he can only argue for the same indiscriminate foquismo, rather than any specific class strategy (Fausto, 1971). Even Quijano, who is often seen as an exponent of class analysis (Chilcote, 1974: 18), becomes involved in the same dilemma. His examination of Peru (Quijano, 1971), for instance, does nothing to explain the idiosyncrasies of the radical military regime nor to assess the consequences of the Peruvian experience of it; instead it simply explains it away as just another mechanism of adjustment to the new dependence. His study of marginality (Quijano, 1974) has much the same one-dimensional quality. Though dealing directly with class formation, all it offers is a standard and exclusively economic model of marginal labor's subordination to the dominant monopoly sector. Again, there is no indication of whether the class composition of marginality may not well vary from one social formation to another, be this in terms of the local history of the relative surplus population, or of different accumulation processes in contemporary Peru and Brazil, for instance — a speculation which is certainly encouraged by the different patterns of political behavior in Peru's *barriadas* and Brazil's *favelas.*

As regards dependency's incapacity as a "theory" of underdevelopment to produce an effective class analysis, Frank is therefore not unrepresentative. What then are the specific steps which impose this constraint on his understanding? And which of them most concern his critics who are working towards a more Marxist analysis? In fact, the motor of his argument, just like Marini's, is not primarily its conceptual "errors," but its ideological determination in opposition to the strategies of ECLA and the communist parties. Its essential logic is simply the reversal of each component of their similar thinking. The result is that Frank remains within the same epistemology or theoretical construction of the issue in terms of autonomous capitalist development. Where they see disarticulation between a modern and traditional or capitalist and semifeudal sector, Frank simply asserts the integration of a homogenously "capitalist" system. Where they see national bourgeoisies as the agents of a capitalist "stage," Frank sees only lumpenbourgeoisies as the intermediaries of underdevelopment. Their unilinear modelling of history to suit the case for a bourgeois alliance is not challenged by Frank with a different way of thinking about Latin American history. Instead, he offers an equally linear, albeit bi-linear model of history — one of capitalist development and underdevelopment, with the latter no less predetermined by his equally homogeneous goal of a simultaneously anti-imperialist and anticapitalist revolution.

In this reproduction of linearity, Frank's mode of analysis falls fairly and squarely on the Stalinist side of Marxist thinking, as distinct from that of pre-Stalinist writers from Marx himself to Mariategui, for whom the analysis of capitalist expansion was not a matter of standard models or preconceived political "lines," but the application of a central theory to the concrete analysis of social formations. In principle, then, there is nothing new about Frank's approach or its basic weakness — its endemic conflation of theory and substance, or what the structuralists distinguish as "objects of thought" and "real objects." Nor are its concepts the central factor, indeed they are hardly concepts at all in the sense of ways of using a theory for *asking questions* about reality. Hence his entrepreneurial ability to borrow others from his critics, like "class struggle" and "accumulation," for incorporation at least in his titles. His very concept of concepts is such that his actual analysis is almost immune to them. Those used to prove his basic schema — the "capitalist" appropriation of surplus from the satellite to the metropolis — are simply supplementary to it. They are ideological molds for reshaping the raw material of history in the single preordained direction which *depends* on taking circulation as the exclusive determinant of political economy, and thus in Frank's view of class formation, or more precisely, nonformation. Any notion of "surplus appropriation" by classes, rather than nations or regions, would necessarily have raised such questions as local capital accumulation and the relations of production entailed in generating the surplus. These would have made it impossible for Frank to ride rough-shod over the variations between Latin American social formations and their possible implications for the dynamics of the new dependence — the issues which Cardoso and Faletto hint at, despite their conceptual limitations, and which render socialist revolution a far more complicated matter. As it is, Frank's model slams the door on asking such questions from the outset. Hence his in-capacity to incorporate the conceptual comments which, by the same token, he can simply borrow like so many labels. Were he to incorporate them in practice, the concrete results would be incompatible with the ideological end goal which also comprises the point of departure for the circle "in the realm of pure thought" which he traces towards his own lumpen-revolution.

From a Marxist standpoint the conspicuous flaw which most exercises Frank's many critics is his conception of capitalism in both its theoretical and historical aspects. To prove his thesis, he defines it in terms of market relations, then applies it indiscriminately to the whole of Latin American history. One might well ask why his revolution was not forthcoming in the sixteenth, let alone in the twentieth century. At first sight the obvious solution is the one Laclau (1977) offers: a more Marxist concept of modes of production in terms of the development of the productive forces, the ownership of the means of production, the mode of appropriation of surplus, and so on; and a recognition that different modes can coexist historically, without this implying their separation (as in the dualist conception) or their identity (as Frank had argued). In practice though, if the purpose is that of analyzing class formation, the modes of production panacea raises two complex sets of questions. First, how is it to be applied? What notion of the relationship between base and superstructure is entailed? Is it just a historical paradigm or one with reference to the present? What modes of production are at issue apart from the capitalist mode itself? In what sense can different modes co-exist in a single accumulation process, and what is their relative significance for relations of production and class formation? And secondly, how sufficient is the concept? Is a social formation to be understood simply in terms of the combination of modes and the interrelations of their various "levels" — the economic, the political, and the ideological? Can we infer from this alone the totality of class relations, including, for example, the nature of the state or the working class in a given instance? Or is more entailed in pin-ning down the specificities of history?

In all these respects the use of the modes of production concept as the heir to dependency has varied, and these variations are closely reflected in the different critiques of Frank's "theoretical" version of it. At the risk of over-schematizing, each use is partly a response to a different stage in Frank's progression from his initial problematic (his reified notion of underdevelopment), to his operative concepts (the "capitalist appropriation of surplus from satellite to metropolis," and so on), and finally to his handling of history in terms of such specific matters as the alleged inverse correlation between growth and ties to the world market (Frank, 1971: 35). These differences of critical focus are important because neither of the first two uses of modes of production escapes these beginnings, with their distance from substantive issues. The structuralist response to Frank's first step in his underdevelopment problematic has the intrinsic limitations of a substitute "grand theory" of history. The conceptual response to the second one retains much of Frank's economism and his mere labelling of social phenomena. It is only when modes of production analysis is directly addressed to empirical history, or "stage three" of Frank's thinking, that it both orders and investigates data, not least because it no longer attempts a total explanation of them. Instead it affords a framework for looking at specific patterns of class formation without excluding variables, such as the agency of the state, which are not directly given by it. In many ways these distinctions are parallel to those within the dependency perspective, between exclusive generalization and more heuristic investigation. Hence this latter use of modes of production is much more open to the issues suggested by Cardoso and Faletto's approach, especially the nature of the state and the specificity of popular movements — in short, the key elements of class struggles, which neither of the first two deployments of modes of production can encompass.

This is not to suggest the discovery of yet another panacea for the Marxist analysis of development. On the contrary, the precedents for taking modes of production as a starting point rather than the object of analysis lie in the pre-Stalinist approaches to capitalist expansion and social formations, without "lines" or labelling or "theoretical practice," by writers like the early Lenin and Trotsky. The future of Marxist analysis in any field, development included, lies primarily in whether it can move on from schematic critiques of the Third International, both ideological and theoretical, to the study of the substantive issues facing contemporary socialist movements: the changing and locally variable nature of capitalist expansion on a world scale; the specificity of the capitalist state and processes of class formation in instances of this expansion into historically varied settings; the handling of political paradigms such as the "permanent revolution" as concrete hypotheses rather than dogmas, as in Gramsci's consideration of its applicability to Italy; the concern with superstructure on the part of Gramsci and Mariategui, and the sense of class agency and conjuncture which once maintained a continuum between concepts as abstract as modes of production and moments of praxis as political as the writing of the "April Theses." In short, the need is neither for "neo" nor "paleo," but for "neo-classical" Marxism. In concluding, I will therefore examine the trends in both the critical and analytic uses of the modes of production concept, and their implications for the comparative class analysis of Brazil and Chile.

## MODE OF PRODUCTION AND SOCIAL FORMATION: THE CLASS ANALYSIS OF LATIN AMERICA

First I will consider Taylor's work, as an instance of the structuralist "grand theory" of history which criticizes Frank's problematic but reproduces its generality. I will then take Laclau's conceptual critique which, despite its pioneering role, encourages a reductionist use of the concept for labelling local modes of production; and finally I will look at the investigative historical use by Assadourian, Bartra, and Cueva, which seems to me much more suggestive for purposes of class analysis.

While the structuralist analysis is the most recent, it derives a logical priority from its apparent aspiration to provide a total theory of history. It is hardly surprising that its exponents, in their emphasis on the distinction between the theoretical and empirical or "objects of thought" and "real objects" (with the former conceived of as "scientific"), should concern themselves with Frank's first step: his view of dependency as a condition requiring a "theory" of its own, an opinion which he shares with most dependency writers apart from Cardoso and Faletto. Thus for Taylor (1974) Foster-Carter's contention, that dependency and related approaches provide a new body of theory appropriate to the realities of underdevelopment, is a "sociological fantasy." Its assumption is that the real object of Third World societies produces the theory. On the contrary, Taylor argues from an evidently structuralist viewpoint, theory's scope for dealing with realities depends on its autonomy from them, its scientific universality as Althusserian "theoretical practice." It is precisely this universality which gives Marx's theory of modes of production its scope for dealing with *all* realities, including those of underdevelopment or "peripheral capitalist social formations" — realities which Frank reduces to his single underdevelopment model, for lack of any such key distinction between real objects and objects of knowledge. While this stems from his circulationist concepts like those of surplus appropriation by regions and nations rather than classes, its roots lie deeper in Frank's ill thought-out "problematic": his basic construct of underdevelopment, which derives from Baran's same circular vision (Taylor, 1979: 71-98). Other structuralist critics have pursued this question of how Frank's "knowledge" is produced. In Leys' view his "underdevelopment theory" is ideologically conceived in emphasizing depredation rather than exploitation and structure, and teleological in being constructed by antithesis with the notional model of autonomous metropolitan development (Leys, 1977). As the fruit of such a misconception, a "theory of underdevelopment" is scientifically "impossible" (Bernstein, 1979: 91). Phillips (1977: 19-20) puts this more practically. Not only is it unable to deal with the questions of major concern to Marxists, like the scope for further capitalist expansion and class formation in Latin America, but its frame of reference, in the presence or absence of a notional autonomous development, prevents it from even asking such questions, since it is not focussed on what *is* occurring.

To dismiss such comments as structuralist abstractions, as does Foster-Carter (1979), evades the issue. There is nothing abstract about arguing that Frank's thinking prevents one from asking questions about Latin American social formations. The question is whether the substitute for it is more directed to substantive enquiry. Taylor certainly maintains this to be his objective in using the modes of production concept. He carefully distinguishes his own position from the "formalism" of Hindess and Hirst (1975), who question in principle the possibility of "objects of thought" appropriating "real objects," or of theory as a means of empirical study (Taylor, 1979: 163-171). His concern is precisely with the "contemporary concrete situation in peripheral social formation[s]," in terms of "the *specific* effects of the *different* forms of capitalist penetration experienced by Latin American societies" (Taylor, 1974: 8, 11, italics mine). The results in his book, which rests heavily on a would-be reinterpretation of the Latin American evidence, are therefore a potential test of whether such concrete understanding is afforded by even a non-"formalist" version of the structuralist theory of modes of production.

At its source, this seems somewhat unlikely. The structuralist conception of modes of production (Balibar, 1970) is clearly an advance on the Stalinist notion of their literal existence as linear stages in the one-way historical determination of the superstructure by the base. Instead they are seen by Balibar as essentially theoretical constructs: the thought "dynamics" rather than the literal forms of history, with their ideological and political levels determined only "in the last instance" by the economic. Though this is dominant in the capitalist mode, it determines the dominance of other levels in the forms of surplus appropriation specific to other modes of production — the political in the feudal mode, and so on. Moreover with this autonomy it follows that each particular level enjoys its own "historical time," or diachronic freedom of movement. Hence any social formation may involve not only distinctive modes of production but the interpenetration of their levels — e.g., the partial reproduction by one mode's ideology, say, of another's particular social relations. If one thinks of such cases as Brazil, with its lasting "patrimonial heritage" from a noncapitalist background, this is obviously a suggestive concept. However, the transition from this mode of thought to such a concrete interpretation of history, as presented in Balibar's seminal statement, is in practice problematical, as the former has such exclusive priority. His whole project of conceptualizing the dynamics of specific modes of production (particularly the capitalist mode) is presented as a self-contained exercise in defining "objects of thought," not applying them. How they relate to actual history is a question which Balibar constantly assigns to a different plane for separate and subsequent consideration. In addition, the notion of the dynamics of each mode of production as self-contained necessarily inhibits the identification of any relationship between them. How then can one "think" the transition from one mode of production to another, or correspondingly, their "articulation," which structuralists identify as the key to Third World social formations?

These problems dog Taylor's sweeping attempt to theorize Latin American history at the "real" level of social formations. Specifically, he sets out to assess the constraints of pre-existing modes of production on the expansion of the capitalist mode and the relationships between them; but given the absence in the structuralist matrix of any effective mediation between modes of production as objects of thought and social formations as real objects, the latter at best are merely reflections of juxtapositions of the former. The sum of the Latin American reality — as distinct from the realities promised by Taylor — is seen as the obstruction of the capitalist relations of twentieth century imperialism, by the persistence of a feudal mode installed by merchant capital in previous phases of expansion.

The problem is not whether this is valid, but how much it actually tells us. Its only specificity lies in the contrast with Southeast Asian formations, where a different contradiction arises from merchant capital's interaction and hence imperialism's encounter with the Asiatic, not the feudal mode. However, this by definition imposes a single abstract mold on all Latin America's structural history. No less than Frank's, the picture is one of social formations reduced to, and therefore as homogeneous as, the concepts applied to them (in Taylor's case, the capitalist and feudal modes of production). Hence this conceptual differentiation (in contrast to Frank's mere capitalism) does little to interpret such obvious differences as those between Brazil and Chile. The "Spanish and Portuguese penetration of Latin American social formations" (Taylor, 1979: 188-192) is homogeneously depicted in terms of a predominance of merchant capital and control by a feudal oligarchy, which obstruct the expansion of capitalism into agriculture right down to the present. In the closely examined case of Chile (Taylor, 1979: 261-262), the failure of the structuralist reforms under Frei is just one more expression of this contradiction. There is nothing, despite this subsection's title, "The Class Structure of Third World Social Formations," to suggest why such a specific class force as the Popular Unity should have emerged from this contradiction in the case of Chile. Such factors as might help explain it — the early predominance of industrial capital in the mining sector, for example — are at a level of specificity which tends to elude the structuralist concern with the inner logic of modes of production in overreaction to their previous reduction to "real" as distinct from theoretical objects. Instead of historicized ideas, they become an idealization of history, which is far from providing interpretations of "contemporary concrete situations" (Taylor, 1974: 8). Moreover, even the general relation between the two "modes" involved is uncertain, apart from the notion of capitalism being somehow obstructed by feudalism. Such social formations are described as "transitional" — but to what and how is quite unclear from this account of the contradiction between their component modes of production, since it gives little indication of the forms of their articulation as distinct from their mere coexistence. Hence one gets no impression of a trajectory, let alone of specific trajectories, but only of a single, suspended history. Will the capitalist mode become generalized, and if so, is the current contradiction of anything more than passing importance? Or is it permanently obstructed, and with what political implications? In Taylor's account, there are no mediating concepts like accumulation and class formation between the two worlds of "thought" and "real" objects to help in answering these questions. Class relations and indeed the whole of history appear to be *given* by modes of production. One is reminded of Rancière's critique of this perspective as one in which structure itself is determinant and classes are therefore not merely nonagents, but hardly even the ingredients of history in any remotely specific way (Rancière, 1974). Such theoretical practice seems far from pertinent to the politics which Taylor charges both Frank and Foster-Carter with obscuring (Taylor, 1974: 20-21).

Laclau expresses a similar concern with Frank's lack of concrete inferences and his crude political conclusions but attributes them much more directly to his conception of capitalism (Laclau, 1977: 27). Drawing mainly on the Dobb and Sweezy debate on the roles of productive and market forces in the rise of Western capitalism (in Hilton et al., 1976), he observes that Frank's emphasis on the latter as the key to capitalism's expansion is no less historically confusing than Sweezy's. To define the capitalist mode in terms of production for profit and market relations is to take it right back to antiquity, not just sixteenth century Latin America. Essentially Frank is confusing capitalism with capital — i.e., production with exchange — and the homogeneity of a mode of production with the heterogeneity, or various articulated modes, to be found in economic systems. His urge to show that underdevelopment is linked with capital accumulation by no means demonstrates or depends on the former's being of a capitalist nature. "To affirm the feudal character of relations of production in the agrarian sector does not necessarily involve maintaining a dualist thesis." On the contrary, production for the world market has involved the strengthening of noncapitalist relations in Latin America, as in Eastern Europe's "refeudalization." Even today "peasant proletarianisation . . . is very far from being concluded . . . and semi-feudal conditions are still widely characteristic of the Latin American countryside" (Laclau, 1977: 32). Far from their being mutually exclusive, the interplay between capitalism and feudalism at the periphery, as a source of cheap wage goods and raw materials, has helped counteract the tendency to the former's falling rate of profit.

Though this lesson in Marxist historiography does clarify Frank's conceptual confusion, its own empirical implications and even its conceptual ones are uncertain. While Laclau is careful to avoid the impression of offering a universal model as distinct from a way of looking at history, he leaves open the question of what modes as concepts infer for empirical relations; and this implicitly fosters the danger of the former's reduction to the latter by those who follow in his footsteps. Empirically, his broad historical perspective still leaves one to speculate on the problems of what noncapitalist relations persist and where and to what degree and with what long-term implications. Are they still essentially semifeudal, or are other types now more characteristic, not just in the countryside but in the cities? And conceptually, what makes them noncapitalist? Though Laclau alludes mainly to noncapitalist "relations," he does seem to equate them with the persistence of various modes of production as such (Laclau, 1977: 40) and not just with the workings of the capitalist mode in social formations at the periphery. With the latter now generally dominated by a capitalist accumulation process, this apparent inference that other modes can still reproduce themselves within it seems questionable and perhaps misleading as to the real nature of such relations.

Laclau's postscript disowns such reification of modes of production as empirical objects (Laclau, 1977: 48-50). Yet his outward posing of the problem as one of their historical conjunction, as distinct from their use as theoretical concepts for dealing with concrete class formation, encourages such literal searches for them. He criticizes one such labelling process in Ciro Cardoso's (1974) identification of specifically colonial modes of production, but several others occur in his name. One is that of sticking a pin in the point at which social formations "become capitalist" — 1930 in the case of Chile, according to Steenland (1975: 54). In which month? One is inclined to wonder. And more seriously, does this reveal anything of substance about the Chilean social formation? Ironically, Steenland is using this labelling, and even admitting to the term (Steenland, 1975: 55), to support the Frank/Marini "line" for direct socialist revolution, which Laclau himself (1977: 27) began by deriding. Thus the wheel of his purely conceptual critique can be brought full circle, albeit crudely, for want of an adequate indication of how to apply it empirically, i.e., to specific class formation. The opposite extreme of this labelling is the "mode around every corner" genre, in which each distinct relation of production is taken to denote a different mode. Long (1975), for instance, finds an almost infinite number of them in a short outing in the Andes and within single rural households as well, so that in effect the former concept is simply dissolved into the latter.

Quite clearly at this empiricist level — the inverse of Taylor's tendency to subordinate data to abstraction — the concept has lost all interpretative value. It is also purely economic, which means the exclusion of its other aspects and an overly-formal interpretation of even its economic dimension. If modes either "exist" or cease to exist, and relations reflect one mode or another, then the latter's components can obviously no longer be disaggregated. Hence the potentially informative notion of the distinct historical times of the various "levels" of a mode of production is lost altogether, along with its otherwise subtle implications for processes of class formation. For instance, one can no longer conceive, within this concept of modes of production as indissoluble "real" wholes, of a precapitalist ideology persisting in shaping contemporary relations between labor and capital in Brazil. Not only does this mean that the only form of articulation which is considered by Laclau and others is economic, it also tends to mean that the mere economic form of "articulated noncapitalist relations" — the form in which surplus is appropriated, as distinct from such matters as the labor process — is taken as defining their essential class meaning. Identified with a "mode" of their own, not just for economic but restricted economic reasons, such relations are seen as necessarily semifeudal or whatever. Even in economic terms, this overlooks the argument that the fact of their articulation with a capitalist accumulation process may make the form of appropriation a mere "form of exploitation" (Banaji, 1977: 5-9) which masks essentially capitalist relations — and does so in potentially varied ways, as this process itself is by no means standard. This is far from being a matter of mere words. May not peasants in such circumstances — like the lengthening of their working day in response to increasing productivity in the capitalist sector of agriculture — be all but formal "proletarians" (Roseberry, 1978)? And may this not govern their consciousness? For instance, are they always more concerned to reproduce their existence as peasants than with a hunger for employment? (Juan Martínez-Alier, unpublished note, cited by Laclau, 1977: 31). In which case, and for many other reasons, is the modes of production concept per se of much contemporary use at all, except as a mere starting point for raising questions about class formation — a necessary but far from sufficient condition for any concrete Marxist analysis?

There is nothing novel in this suggestion that social formations as the object of study can only be understood incipiently in terms of the modes of production concept, for all Marx's understanding of it as the "innermost secret" of social relations. Laclau's postscript acknowledges this also; and indeed it is Balibar whom he cites to bring out the point of this distinction —

only social formations, which are not just sites for the abstract dynamics of modes of production, are a real object of transformation, as "the only one which really implies a history of class struggle" (Laclau, 1977: 48). The problem is that where modes of production become an exclusive theory of history, they tend to pre-empt this consideration in precluding specific variables of a lower level of abstraction to mediate between the theory and the raw material of class struggles. Of these, perhaps the most important are the accumulation process, the state, and the patterns of class formation and also of differentiation among the dominated classes within the capitalist and noncapitalist sectors. It is here that the precedents are provided by the classic Marxist analyses of imperialism at the periphery, and indeed of earlier capitalist expansion. The idiosyncrasies of the capitalist state in the absence of fully bourgeois hegemony are, after all, Marx's main concern in the bulk of his political writings (Marx, 1973-1974). Both this and the specific formation of the proletariat in Russia — its recency and concentration, in a given accumulation process — were major features, in Trotsky's view, of that country's "peculiar" development and its political contradictions (Trotsky, 1967: 21-32). The differentiation of the peasantry as the product of this particular history was of similar concern to Lenin (1974). And in the Latin American context it is hardly a coincidence that those who have succeeded somewhat in relating the modes of production concept to the dynamics of class struggle have taken history as their point of departure and looked to the concept to illuminate it, not vice versa.

Much of this work, in the volumes edited by Assadourian (1974) and Bartra (1976) and in Cueva's *El desarrollo del capitalismo en América Latina,* is highly historical and rather fragmented; in the first case some of it is also embroiled in the "colonial modes of production" concept (Garavaglia, 1974; Ciro Cardoso, 1974). However, there are emphases in it which do help to elucidate class struggles in terms of the interpenetration of imperialism and specific formations, in ways not wholly incompatible with Cardoso and Faletto's dependency perspective. The conception of Latin American development which these writers share is not its uniqueness in Marini's sense of a process having its own laws, but rather its particularity, as a certain expression of the general laws of capitalist development (Cueva, 1978a: 14). Assadourian (1978: 22), for instance, is concerned with the weakness not just of Frank's concepts, but of their effects, "in underplay[ing] the specific dynamics of social phenomena, emptying of substance and history a much more complex reality." Thus Frank's case for the inverse correlation between growth and metropolitan ties, and the very dichotomy on which it rests, between "independent" and "under" development, bear no relation to this historical specificity or complexity — for example, to the fact that Chile's growth during the seventeenth century European depression was still based on exports to Peru (Frank's intermediate "metropolis"); or that Balmaceda's "Bismarkian" policies in the late nineteenth century were no less export-oriented (Assadourian, 1978: 25-27). Frank's autonomous development is simply idealist in ignoring the lack of the material and social conditions for such a process; the motor of his alternative history is the bourgeois one of mere intention, and the evidence for even this is doubtful (Assadourian, 1978: 22, 27). At the same time Assadourian, though using the modes of production concept and recognizing feudal traits in much of Latin American history, is reluctant to characterize as feudal a process governed by merchant capital. No history is a mirror of modes of production. While these provide a conceptual framework, the key to Latin American societies lies in the variations within their common "historico-genetic" basis of economic subordination (Assadourian, 1978: 31).

Cueva (1978b) widens this view of the region's history, as one with its own distinct dynamics, to the same comparative horizons as those of Cardoso and Faletto. Though critical of dependency theory for overlooking modes of production and their implications for class formation, he acknowledges that dependence is a "salient feature of our societies" (Cueva, 1976: 16). In their export-led economies, the effects of primitive accumulation are transferred to the metropolitan center: their transition to capitalism stems from late nineteenth century imperialist expansion. Their "particularity" therefore lies in their typically liberal oligarchic and incomplete bourgeois revolutions. Their Junker-type path to the limited development of capitalist relations in agriculture and also of the internal market means that the capitalist state which holds this particularity together — an emphasis shared by Cardoso and Faletto from their Weberian perspective — can hardly be bourgeois-democratic. In this context democratic tasks have always been those of popular forces; their implications, as Cuba shows, are therefore more socialist than bourgeois. Hence Cueva, like Assadourian, stresses the need to study the popular sectors (Assadourian, 1978: 32; Cueva, 1976: 14). It is not external factors which structure and distinguish Latin American histories, but the class struggles engendered by the development of their productive forces; and these are variously conditioned by precapitalist, servile and slave, relations. The articulation of modes of production which shapes this general trajectory is expressed concretely as class relations involving wide variations on it — the "singularity" of social formations within Latin America's "particularity" (Cueva, 1978b: 65). It is these specific class relations which explain historical development. The reorientation of Brazil and Chile to industry and the internal market after the Depression, for instance, might seem to support Frank's market thesis as to the inverse correlation between outward ties and inward development. In fact, in Brazil the seeds of this were planted in the 1920s with the crisis of the oligarchic state; and in Chile it only really occurred in the late 1930s to 1940s at the instigation of the class forces which came to power in the Popular Front. Argentina's industrial development, both before and after the Depression, follows a trajectory similarly rooted in the changing balance of class relations rather than external factors. In addition, like Cardoso and Faletto, Cueva notes that only Mexico has sustained balanced growth since the 1940s; but this exception is accounted for not by the nature of the state itself, but by Mexico's being the only case (except the frustrated one of Bolivia) of the rupture of oligarchic power from within its substantially precapitalist foundations. It was not a set of political arrangements nor a concerted bourgeois program, but the peasant basis of the revolution which paved the way to Cárdenas's launching of a Bonapartist development process (Cueva, 1978b: 162-178).

For all this, Cueva's analysis of the modern period is disappointing. Although it brings out the key role of the state and popular democratic issues, it loses sight of the variations between different Latin American countries and ends in a descriptive vein more characteristic of dependency writers. The main symptom of this is that like these writers it fails to examine the specificity of Latin American popular movements, despite locating them more clearly as agents of potential change — as the "history-making classes" (Assadourian, 1978: 32). This weakness suggests a number of counts, with respect to class analysis, on which even the most substantive use of the modes of production approach is wanting, when it is treated as a sufficient, as distinct from a preliminary, coordinating theoretical construct. On the one hand, it tends to be imprecise about noncapitalist relations, insofar as they differ in form or essence from typically servile feudal relations. On the other, in itself it offers no clear guidance to each working class's singularity as a function of the particular histories of labor-capital relations, Cueva's problem lies in the limited categories which the modes of production perspective affords him — essentially slavery, feudalism, and the capitalism which he acknowledges as "dependent," so long as the capitalism is substantive and the dependence just adjectival (Cueva, 1976: 14). Yet as Bartra (1976: 13-16) observes, and as Cueva (1978a: 17) concedes without managing to incorporate, the main concrete form of articulation between the capitalist and noncapitalist sectors in twentieth century Latin America is simple commodity production in all its varieties, rural and urban. Though empirical studies have stressed its importance (Oliveira, 1972; Scott, 1979), it seems to be neglected in theoretical and comparative ones for not corresponding to a mode of production — an intrepretation which Bartra (1976: 13) confirms in suggesting confusingly that it is one — no less than dependency writers abjure it with the noncategory of "marginality." Inevitably this limits the understanding of actual or potential popular movements — not in the sense of arguing for the revolutionary nature of the peasantry or "lumpen–proletariat" (itself a sweeping misnomer for varied relative surplus populations), but in the sense of analyzing their specific histories and contradictions with particular patterns of accumulation. For example, in Castells' estimation (in a rare attempt at a class analysis of a crucial political conjuncture) the Popular Unity's central problem lay in the failure to build an alliance between organized labor and the small peasants, the *minifundistas* (Castells, 1973: 188). Yet Steenland's modes of production taxonomy of Chile's history negates this issue by defining the society as capitalist since 1930 and thus unproblematically set on a straight line to socialism (Steenland, 1975: 51). Hence his tendency to argue politically that the Popular Unity's problem lay merely in its lack of a firmly socialist direction (Steenland, 1973). The gap between modes of production analysis and praxis as possible class practice in specific totalities of class relations could hardly be better illustrated.

However, there is also a sense in which this judgement on Steenland's part is less unwarranted than unexplained, and this reveals an additional weakness of exclusively modes of production analysis with reference to the proletariat. Whatever the immediate problem of the minifundistas' class nature and practice, it was the Chilean working-class movement which lacked an appropriate answer to it. The pertinent question, though, is why? The appropriate answer is not to be found in the revolutionary/reformist dichotomy which renders the problems of socialist strategy one and the same in all situations but in the potential and specificities of this working class's political practice. The conventionally circular political answer which Frank (1974, for instance) untiringly reproduces is "communist party reformism," but this does nothing to prove the scope for a more revolutionary program. A marginally more precise answer might be that the practice of the Chilean working class movement was petty-bourgeois dominated (Petras, 1978: 204-227); but this too is just another slogan unless explained specifically in terms of the Chilean social formation. At this much more substantive level one would want to account in the first instance for the traditional autonomy of working class politics in Chile, in such marked contrast to those of Brazil with their ideological susceptibility to the corporative state apparatus. Within this one would then look for the roots, within this class's material history, of the tension between its socialist and anti-imperialist ideologies. No class struggles occur on the standard lines implied in the "right or wrong" type post-mortems on the Popular Unity experience. They occur as class practice — retrogressive, progressive, or revolutionary, if revolutionary conditions exist (Debray, 1977: 310-311) — within *historically specific totalities* of class relations. It is this which puts contemporary struggles beyond the analytic range of a purely modes of production approach without any further conceptual equipment for the specificity of social formations. Having identified their basis in a subordinate capitalism and articulated modes of production, it then has little to say in itself about substantive class relations within or beyond the capitalist mode — least of all about contemporary relations now that this mode is dominant, and their substance is therefore largely conditioned by its accumulation process, whatever their purely formal nature.

In part this omission is similar to the one attributed by Sofer (1980) to dependency writers' analyses of the Latin American working classes: the neglect of class formation "as a historical process situated in a particular context . . . [which] has its own national characteristics and is limited by the specificity of struggles which emerge from and become a part of traditions, value systems, ideas and concrete modes of organization" (Nun, 1976: 51, cited by Sofer, 1980: 170). Such precision, which dependency analysis loses by over-emphasizing the external, is obscured in that of modes of production by its emphasis on the economic, that is, on the particular form in which surplus is appropriated. If this imperception of the "superstructural" limits its analysis of the working classes, it is even more of a constraint on that of the noncapitalist sector, where "classness" is by definition much more determined by social history than by economic forms of coercion. Yet this neglect of the superstructural is not the only problem involved, since the E.P. Thompson approach to class, which Sofer (1980: 168 and 176) is explicitly advocating, does seriously underestimate its economic-historical aspects (Anderson, 1980). On htis account, as Banaji (1977) has shown, and despite its basic economism, the modes of production analysis of even economic relations is limited by its formalism — its concern with structure rather than movement, or "modes" as distinct from accumulation within the capitalist mode, which will govern the effects of articulation and also vary from one case to another. For both these reasons (its economism and its formalization of the economic) the modes of production approach to class struggles tends to be limited a priori to its generalized if valid statements on the role of the state and the popular sectors. Hence it loses its specificity not only for gauging their possible outcomes (for example, in El Salvador in comparison to Nicaragua) but also for explaining the present in terms of the balance of class forces.

To take the cases of Brazil and Chile to illustrate these issues briefly, I argued above that Cardoso's specifying approach does identify some of the empirical conditions for "dependent development" in Brazil, which are lacking in the case of Chile; yet it also prevents him from looking beyond the state and the dominant block in each case for a more comprehensive explanation in terms of overall class relations, for which modes of production only provide a general conceptual and historical framework. It is these historically specific relations, especially of the working classes, which account for the very different patterns of peripheral capitalist development in contemporary Brazil and Chile.

Not only was pre-coup Brazil endowed with a strong and autonomous state apparatus in which popular interests were represented, though always clearly subordinated to those of capital in general, but above all it had a working class whose formation and traditional political practice exposed it wholesale to the imposition of the new model of accumulation based on the increasingly authoritarian and intensive exploitation of labor. The historical break in its formation, initially by European immigrants and later by internal labor flows from the backward Northeast to the bouyant South (rooted in the patrimonial, precapitalist background of the Northeastern fraction of agrarian export economy) provided the social basis for the Brazilian corporate state and its populist politics under Vargas. All these left the Brazilian working class, as the structuralist reforms collapsed in the sixties, without anything like the self-organization which opened such different vistas in Chile. Here the working class's political autonomy had almost the opposite foundations: the long-standing proletarianism engendered by the industrial capital of the copper and nitrate mining economy; the continuity between these roots, its experience of mass redundancies before and after the Depression, its urbanization in the 1930s, and the disillusionment of the Popular Front; its exclusion, rather than co-option, by a system of labor legislation established by a comprador bourgeoisie with whom its relations had long since been more political than economic. This singularity of the working class, which made the Popular Unity possible, was not dispelled by its defeat, and therefore remains a specific restraint to peripheral capitalism in Chile.

Hence the distinctive qualities of the Chilean model under the junta, in such contrast to Brazil's "miracle": the calculated deindustrialization, quite literally destroying the working class in its material existence; the dismantling, in all but its repressive aspects, of the weakly autonomous state apparatus (in terms of its class characteristics) which the working class movement had penetrated; the much more evident orientation, conforming more closely to Marini's picture, to the external market — a pattern almost opposite that afforded by Brazil's combination of a substantial internal market, a historically malleable working class, and an extensive precapitalist sector to cheapen the cost of laborpower and complicate the tasks of the popular movement. Combined with the rather different dynamics of the internatioinal economy in the late 1960s and the 1970s, these differences proved decisive. Yet at the same time the very dynamics of dependent capitalism in Brazil have spelled new contradictions in the shape of an increasingly autonomous and radicalized labor movement. Similarly, in the precapitalist sector, the dynamics of this specifically Brazilian accumulation process have had equally acute material and sociopolitical implications — for the autonomous frontier peasantry, for instance, as a fraction which is quite distinct in ways unnoticed in the literature from the one which previously helped to shape the working class's "clientelism." It is on the basis of such elements that any significant popular program is likely to be constituted, in circumstances much too specific for the relegation of the national question to the sphere of merely bourgeois interests. In Chile, on the other hand, the autonomy of the popular movement is given, and the space available to it in a bourgeois democratic framework would seem to be historically exhausted, both economically and politically, with radically different implications. What these may be in either case is not the subject of this paper. What it has sought to establish is the appropriate sphere for such issues, not in predetermined political schemas or merely theoretical reformulations, but in the effective understanding of potential class practices and conjunctures, which depends on the further conceptualization and concrete analysis of social formations.

Frantz Fanon once stated that Africa's great problem was its lack of theory. In the case of Latin America it is tempting, but dangerous, to suggest the reverse. The real problem is how to bring theory to bear (and particularly the theory of imperialism) on the raw material of social histories. Otherwise they will be made without it, as has been the case with most modes of production as well as dependency analysis. González Casanova (1979), for instance, in the one recent contemporary history of Latin American class struggles makes almost no reference to either of them. One can arguably learn more about Chile's or Brazil's popular movements from Elias Lafertte's autobiography or the novels of José Lins do Rego than from either of these two approaches. It seems likely that in the coming decade Latin Americanists and Latin Americans in Latin America especially will be mainly concerned with this task of relating a theory of imperialism to the histories of the exploited classes, not in dependent capitalism or articulated modes of production, but in Latin American social formations. If this too provides a precedent for overall development studies, it will perhaps bring them closer this time to being a "philosophy of praxis."

## REFERENCES

Althusser, Louis and Etienne Balibar
  1970 *Reading Capital*, London: New Left Books

Anderson, Perry
  1980 *Arguments Within English Marxism*, London: Verso

Assaudourian, Carlos Sempat
  1971 "Modos de producción, capitalismo y subdesarrollo en América Latina," *Cuadernos de la Realidad Nacional* (CEREN) (Santiago, Chile), March (also published on pp. 47-81 in Assadourian et al., *Modos de producción en América Latina* and in 1978 in English in *Two-Thirds*, I [first quarter], 20-33)

  1978 (see Assadourian 1971)

Assadourian, Carlos Sempat et al.
1974 *Modos de producción en América Latina*, Cordóba, Argentina: Cuadernos de Pasado y Presente (40)

Balibar, Etienne
1970 "The Basic Concepts of Historical Materialism," pp. 199-308 in Althusser and Balibar, *Reading Capital*, London: New Left Books

Banaji, Jairus
1977 "Modes of Production in a Materialist Conception of History," *Capital and Class*, 3 (Autumn), 1-44

Baran, Paul
1973 *The Political Economy of Growth*, London: Pelican

Bartra, Roger
1976 "Sobre la articulación de modos de producción en América Latina," pp. 5-19 in Bartra et al., *Modos de producción en América Latina*, Lima: Delva Editores

Bartra, Roger et al.
1976 *Modos de producción en América Latina*, Lima: Delva Editores

Bernstein, Henry
1979 "Sociology of Underdevelopment versus Sociology of Development," pp. 77-106 in Lehmann, David (ed.), *Development Theory: Four Critical Studies*, London: Cass

Booth, David
1975 "A.G. Frank: an Introduction and Appreciation," pp. 50-85 in Ivar Oxaal, Tony Barnett, and David Booth (eds.), *Beyond the Sociology of Development*, London: Routledge and Kegan Paul

Cardoso, Ciro
1974 "Sobre los modos de producción coloniales de América Latina," pp. 135-159 in Carlos Sempat Assadourian et al., *Modos de producción en América Latina*, Córdoba: Cuadernos de Pasado y Presente (40) (also published in 1975 in English in *Critique of Anthropology* [4-5], 1-26)

Cardoso, Fernando Henrique
1971 ¿Teoriá de la dependencia o análisis de situaciones concretas de la dependencia?," *Revista Latinoamericana de Ciencia Política*, I (December), 402-414 (also published in 1971 in Portuguese in *Estudos CEBRAP* [1], 25-45; and in 1973 in Cardoso, *O modelo político brasileiro*, São Paulo: Editôra Civilização Brasileira)

1972 "Dependency and Development in Latin America," *New Left Review*, 74 (July-August), 83-95

1974 "As contradições do desenvolvimento associado," *Estudos CEBRAP*, 8 (April-June), 41-75

1975 *Autoritarismo e democratização*, São Paulo: Paz e Terra

1977 "The Consumption of Dependency Theory in the United States," *Latin American Research Review*, XII (3), 7-24

Cardoso, Fernando Henrique and Enzo Faletto
1969 *Dependencia y desarollo en América Latina*, Mexico City: Siglo XXI (also published in English as *Dependency and Development in Latin America*, 1979, Berkeley and Los Angeles: University of California Press)
1979 (see Cardoso and Falleto, 1969)

Cardoso, Fernando Henrique and José Serra
1978 "Las desventuras de la dialéctica de la dependencia," *Revista Mexicana de Sociología*, XL (E), 9-55

Castells, Manuel
1973 "La teoría marxista de las clases sociales y la lucha de clases en América Latina," pp. 159-190 in Fernandes, et al., *Las clases sociales en América Latina*, Mexico City: Siglo XXI

Chilcote, Ronald H.
1974 "Dependency: a Critical Synthesis of the Literature," Latin American Perspectives, I (Spring), 4-29

Claudin, Fernando
1975 The Communist Movement: from Comintern to Cominform, London: Penguin

Cueva, Agustín
1976 "A Summary of 'Problems and Perspectives of Dependency Theory'," Latin American Perspectives III (Fall), 12-16

1978a "The Modes of Production Concept in Latin America," Two-Thirds, I (First Quarter), 13-19 (also published in 1976 in Spanish, pp. 20-36 in Bartra et al., Modos de producción en América Latina, Lima: Delva Editores)

1978b El desarrollo del capitalismo en América Latina, Mexico City: Siglo XXI

Culley, Lorraine
1977 "Economic Development in Neo-Marxist Theory," pp. 92-117 in Barry Hindess (ed.), Sociological Theories of the Economy, London: Macmillan

Debray, Regis
1977 A Critique of Arms, London: Penguin

Dos Santos, Theotônio
1070a "The Structure of Dependence," American Economic Review, LX (2), 231-236

1970b Dependencia y cambio social, Santiago: Universidad de Chile, Cuadernos de Estúdios Sócio-Económicos, (II)

1976 "The Crisis of Development Theory and the Problem of Dependence in Latin America," in H. Bernstein (ed.), Underdevelopment and Development: the Third World Today, London: Penguin (originally published in 1969 in Spanish as La crisis de la teoria del desarrollo y las relaciones de dependencia en América Latina, Santiago: Siglo XXI)

Fausto, Ayrton
1971 "La nueva situación de dependencia y el análisis socio-política de Theotônio dos Santos," Revista Latinoamericana de Ciencias Sociales, 1-2 (July-December), 198-211

Foster-Carter, Aidan
1974 "Neo-Marxist Approaches to Development and Underdevelopment," pp. 67-105 in Emanuel de Kadt and Gavin Williams (eds.), Sociology and Development, London: Tavistock Press

1978 "The Modes of Production Controversy," New Left Review, 107 (January-February), 47-78

1979 "Marxism Versus Dependency Theory? A Polemic," University of Leeds, Department of Sociology: Occasional Papers (8), mimeographed

Frank, André Gunder
1969 Latin America: Underdevelopment or Revolution, New York and London: Monthly Review Press

1970 Lumpenburgesia: Lumpendesarollo, Santiago: Editorial Prensa Latinoamericana

1971 Capitalism and Underdevelopment in Latin America: Historical Studies of Brazil and Chile, London: Pelican

1974 "Dependence is Dead, Long Live Dependence and the Class Struggle," Latin American Perspectives, I (Spring), 87-106

Furtado, Celso
1963 The Economic Growth of Brazil: a Survey from Colonial to Modern Times, Berkeley: University of California Press

1970 Economic Development of Latin America: a Survey from Colonial Times to the Cuban Revolution, London: Cambridge University Press

Garavaglia, Juan Carlos
1974 "Introducción," pp 7-21 in Assadourian et al., Modos de producción en América Latina, Córdoba, Argentina: Cuadernos de Pasado y Presente (40)

González Casanova, Pablo
 1979 *Imperialismo y liberación: una introducción a la historia contemporánea de América Latina*, Mexico City: Siglo XXI

Guevara, Ernesto "Ché"
 1969 "Cuba, Exception or Vanguard?," pp. 196-206 in John Gerassi (ed.), *Venceremos! Speeches and Writings of Che Guevara*, London: Panther

Harding, Timothy F.
 1976 "Dependency, Nationalism and the State in Latin America," *Latin American Perspectives*, III (Fall), 3-11

Henderson, Barrie
 1977 "The Chilean State After the Coup," *Socialist Register* (Annual), 121-142

Hilton, Ronald et al.
 1976 · *The Transition from Feudalism to Capitalism*, London: New Left Books

Hindess, Barry and Paul Hirst
 1975 *Pre-Capitalist Modes of Production*, London: Routledge and Kegan Paul

Humphrey, John
 1979 "Auto-Workers and the Working Class in Brazil," *Latin American Perspectives*, VI (Fall), 71-89

Kahl, Joseph
 1976 *Modernization, Exploitation and Dependency in Latin America: Germani, González Casanova and Cardoso*, New Brunswick, New Jersey: Trans-Action Books

Kay, Geoffrey
 1975 *Development and Underdevelopment: a Marxist Analysis*, London: Macmillan

Laclau, Ernesto
 1977 "Feudalism and Capitalism in Latin America," in his *Politics and Ideology in Marxist Theory*, London: New Left Books (previously published in 1971 in New Left Review, 67 [May-June], 19-38, and in Spanish in 1974 in Assadourian et al, *Modos de producción en América Latina*, Cordóba: Cuadernos de Pasado y Presente (40)

Lenin, V.I.
 1974 *The Development of Capitalism in Russia*, Moscow: Progress Publishers

Leys, Colin
 1977 "Underdevelopment and Dependency: Critical Notes," *Journal of Contemporary Asia*, VII (1), 92-107

Long, Norman
 1975 "Structural Dependency, Modes of Production and Economic Brokerage in Rural Peru," pp. 253-282 in Ivar Oxaal, Tony Barnett, and David Booth (eds.) *Beyond the Sociology of Development*, London: Routledge and Kegan Paul

Lowy, Michael
 1976 "Marxists and the National Question," *New Left Review*, 96 (March-April), 81-100

Mandel, Ernest
 1975 *Late Capitalism*, London: New Left Books

Marini, Rui Mauro
 1973 *La dialéctica de la dependencia*, Mexico City: Ediciones Era

 1978 "Las razones del neodesarollismo (respuesta a F.H. Cardoso y J. Serra)," *Revista Mexicana de Sociología*, XL (E), 57-106

Marx, Karl
 1973-1974 *Political Writings* (volumes 1-3, ed. David Fernbach), London: Pelican

Myer, John
 1975 "A Crown of Thorns: Cardoso and the Counter-Revolution," *Latin American Perspectives*, II (Spring), 33-48

Nun, José
 1976 "Workers' Control and the Problem of Organization," *LARU Studies*, I (October), 41-64

O'Brien, Philip
  1975 "A Critique of Latin American Theories of Dependency," pp. 7-27 in Ivar Oxaal, Tony Barnett, and David Booth (eds.), *Beyond the Sociology of Development*, London; Routledge and Kegan Paul

Oliveira, Francisco de
  1972 "A ecónomia brasileira: crítica à razão dualista," *Estudos CEBRAP*, 2 (October), 3-82

Palma, Gabriel
  1978 "Dependency: a Formal Theory of Underdevelopment or a Methodology for the Analysis of Concrete Situations of Dependence?," *World Development*, VI (7-8), 881-924

Petras, James
  1978 *Critical Perspectives on Imperialism and Social Class in the Third World*, New York and London: Monthly Review Press

Phillips, Anne
  1977 "The Concept of Development," *Review of African Political Economy*, 8 (January-April), 7-20

Quijano, Aníbal
  1971 *Nationalism and Colonialism in Peru: a Study in Neo-Imperialism*, New York: Monthly Review Press

  1974 "The Marginalised Pole of the Economy and the Marginalised Labour Force," *Economy and Society*, III (November), 393-428

Rancière, Jacques
  1974 *La leçon d' Althusser*, Paris: Gallimard 1974

Roberts, Bryan
  1978 *Cities of Peasants: the Political Economy of Urbanisation in the Third World*, London: Edward Arnold

Roseberry, William
  1978 "Peasants as Proletarians," *Critique of Anthropology*, III (Spring), 3-18

Scott, Alison MacEwan
  1979 "Who Are the Self-employed?" pp. 105-132 in R. Bromley and C. Gerry (eds.), *Casual Work and Poverty in Third World Cities*, Chichester, England: John Wiley

Sofer, Eugene F.
  1980 "Recent Trends in Latin American Labor Historiography," *Latin American Research Review*, XV (1), 167-176

Steenland, Kyle
  1973 "Two Years of Popular Unity in Chile," *New Left Review*, 78 (March-April), 3-25

  1975 "Notes on Feudalism and Capitalism in Chile and Latin America," *Latin American Perspectives* II (Spring), 49-58

Taylor, John G.
  1974 "Neo-Marxism and Underdevelopment: a Sociological Phantasy," *Journal of Contemporary Asia*, IV (1), 5-23

  1979 *From Modernisation to Modes of Production: A Critique of the Sociologies of Development and Underdevelopment*, London: Macmillan

Thompson, E.P.
  1978 *The Poverty of Theory and Other Essays*, London: Merlin Press

Torres-Rivas, Edelberto
  1969 *Procesos y estructuras de una sociedad dependiente (Centro-America)*, Santiago: Ediciones Prensa Latinoamericana

Trotsky, Leon
  1967 *The History of the Russian Revolution* (3 volumes), London: Sphere Books

Weaver, Frederick Stirton
  1976 "Capitalist Development, Empire and Latin American Underdevelopment: an Interpretative Essay on Historical Change," *Latin American Perspectives*, III (Fall), 17-53

Weeks, John and Elizabeth Dore
1979 "International Exchange and the Causes of Backwardness," *Latin American Perspectives*, VI (Spring), 62-87

Weffort, Francisco
1971 "Notas sobre la teoria de la dependencia. ¿Teoria de clase o ideología nacional?," *Revista Latinoamericana de Ciencia Política*, I (December), 389-401

# 3

# DEPENDENCY THEORY AND THE PROCESSES OF CAPITALISM AND SOCIALISM

*by*
*Carlos Johnson\**

In this article, dependency theses are considered to be a product of the struggle between different degrees of capital accumulation, specifically between monopoly capital and competitive capital. The principal levels of analysis concern the theoretical reasoning behind dependency constructs, the interpretation of capital/labor relations, and socialist development in terms of dependency itself. A brief review is made of the economic theses postulated by the *dependentistas* and those advanced by the Russian Narodniks of the nineteenth century in order to demonstrate that the basic postulates of dependency theory reoccur throughout capitalist history.

In spite of the relationship of dependency theory to capitalism and imperialism and its theoretical irrelevance to socialist development, dependency theory is presented by many contemporary authors as a body of socialist revolutionary thought and, specifically, as a Marxist-Leninist critique of imperialism. This paper, however, aims at showing that when dependency theory is applied to socialist transformation, it assumes a historically regressive meaning for the socialist process itself. In such cases, dependency theory represents an ideological substantiation of capitalism in countries where capital/labor relations are not yet dominant and reflects the class needs of competitive capital in the face of monopoly capital. Finally, it is argued herein that dependency theory addresses itself to the most superficial aspects of international economic exchange relations (e.g., changes in the magnitude and forms of the production of surplus value). Because of this, dependency theorists fail to explain capital/labor relations, much less socialist transformation and development. Dependency theory itself, therefore, requires explanation in terms of capital/labor relations in order for us to understand its historical and sociopolitical meaning for class struggle.

The ideological practice of considering word-concepts *to be* the social relations themselves has long been characteristic of idealists and critical idealists alike. In *The German Ideology,* Marx and Engels (1964) clearly

*The author is at the Instituto de Investigaciones Social, Universidad Nacional Autónoma de México (UNAM). This article originally appeared in a similar version in Carlos Johnson, "Dependency Theory and the Capitalist/Socialist Process", Working-Papers Series, Center for Developing-Area Studies, McGill University, January 1979, 36pp.

distinguish the basic elements characteristic of idealist thinking. Furthermore, they explore certain critiques which, in spite of being presented as supportive of socialism, in fact, merely represent a critical form of idealist thought. The persistent uproar about dependency theory (Cardoso, 1976) reveals the nature of recurring forms of ideological thinking; dependency theory is held to be a theoretical framework for interpreting not only capitalist and imperialist economic relations but international socialist economic relations. Dependency theory is mainly concerned with the analysis of capital/labor relations at the level of international exchange relations. However, because of the superficiality of dependency as a conceptual relation, many ideologues of capitalism and imperialism are able to use the word "dependency" in favor of capitalist-imperialist needs and, furthermore, to employ it in analyzing socialist relations (consult Gilbert, 1974: 107-123, for an initial critique of such an application). Dependency itself is thereby considered a phenomenon characteristic of certain undeveloped and underdeveloped countries and not a specific form of socioeconomic relations of production and appropriation in class terms.

Many critics today accept dependency theory as (or as having once been) a valid interpretation of capital/labor relations. Leys (1977: 92) states: "It is becoming clear that 'underdevelopment' and 'dependency' theory is no longer serviceable and must now be transcended." Such a Hegelian notion of transcending dependency theory rests upon Leys' interpretation of what dependency theory represents in terms of class relations. Dependency theory, inasmuch as it reflects theses regarding particular class needs, will not be transcended *in abstracto* until the class needs themselves, upon which dependency theses rest, are materially eliminated (i.e., the appropriation and accumulation of surplus values at the level of international exchange relations). In this way, some critics (Gilbert, 1974) object only to the lack of relevance of dependency theory to international, socialist economic relations.

The fact remains, however, that neither dependency theorists, nor their critics have abandoned the idealist terminology and formulations of bourgeois ideology. Dependency theory itself fails as a dialectical-historical-materialist analysis of socioeconomic relations, be they precapitalist, capitalist, or socialist. In order to exemplify such contentions, we shall first review the dependency theses in terms of capital/labor relations and then evaluate the concept of dependency as applied to international, socialist economic relations. We shall proceed in this manner because the relationship of ideological forms of reasoning to capital/labor relations must be examined before discussing the significance of the historical process of socialism itself.

## DEPENDENCY THEORY: AN INTEGRAL PART AND PRODUCT OF CAPITAL/LABOR RELATIONS

Throughout class history, class needs have undergone constant change in relation to different modes of production and to appropriation of surplus and accumulation of capital (Marx, 1964). Slave relations of exploitation gave way to feudalism, feudalism succumbed to capital/labor relations, and now capitalism is progressively being consciously replaced by socialist and communist relations. Such changes in class history constitute the process towards classless relations in society. They reflect the transition from societies based on *social* production and *private* appropriation to societies founded on modes of *social* production and *social* appropriation. We shall develop our analysis of dependency theses and their significance to capital/labor relations and the socialist process at the general level of social production and private class appropriation, which serves as the material basis of capitalist accumulation. This level represents the general expression of what Marx termed the contradiction of class societies, that is, the contradiction between socialized production and capitalistic appropriation (Marx, 1974). Class history entails the process of the elimination of specific forms of private class appropriation, which currently signifies the elimination of capitalism itself as a system of social relations.

These modes of production and forms of property (appropriation and accumulation), *in relation* to subsequent capital accumulation, develop from and give rise to concrete class needs. Among these *needs* are the control of the means of production, particular forms of private class appropriation, the subsequent enforcement of property rights, and control of the social product. From these needs arise still others with respect to the subsequent moments of the process. These needs are related to commodity exchange relations (exchange of surplus products or surplus values) as a function of accumulation itself (capital concentration and centralization). Control of the social product refers to the control and ownership (appropriation) of the means of production and/or the control and ownership (appropriation) of the commodities (surplus value) socially produced. For, in fact, at this stage of capitalist relations and under certain conditions, it is of little importance to the capitalist whether he actually owns (in capitalist terms of property) the factory and machinery as long as he controls, owns, and is able to appropriate the social products thereof, allowing for capital accumulation of surplus values — the capitalist's material base of reproduction.

Those needs related to producing ideological *theses* to substantiate the specific class forms of appropriation and accumulation, though less visible, are of equal importance. Dependency theses are one example of how specific classes formulate ideological discourse on the needs of capital appropriation and accumulation within the context of the struggle for control of capital production at the international level.

In the face of the imperialist theses of *developmentalism* espoused during the 1950s by the Economic Commission for Latin America (ECLA), some sectors among the local dominant groups fought for greater participation in the process of capital accumulation. We are referring to the work of such analysts as Aldo Ferrer, Celso Furtado, (1969a, 1969b, 1970) Raúl Prebisch, Osvaldo Sunkel, and Maria de Conceição Tavares, to cite only a few of the more significant theorists of developmentalism (some of whom now employ the concept of dependency). The work of these authors mainly emphasizes the ideological concepts behind the dichotomy of modern and traditional societies, viewing growth and industrialization as a way out of underdevelopment for Latin America. Even though the critics of developmentalist thought attempt to avoid the dualist expressions of modernization, the essentially idealist form of reasoning remains intact in their work. Consider, for example, the following quote from André Gunder Frank (1971a: 97), one of the initial critics of developmentalism: "The polar contradiction metropolis-satellite of capitalism runs throughout the entire world capitalist system, from its macro-metropolitan centre to its most micro-peripheral satellite." In opposition to the idealist modern-traditional conception of social reality, we now find the critical-idealist conception of metropolis-satellite. (The latest contemporary example of such dualist reasoning is found in the North-South conception of world economic relations.)

Development-underdevelopment theses in Latin America initially represented a critique of U.S. imperialism and an ideological substantiation of capital accumulation on the part of the local dominant classes.

> All this has led Latin America, after breaking away from the limitations of the colonial period, to a *dependent capitalism* based on the export sector. The tracks left by an exporting colonial regime establishes the parameters for a "liberated" Latin America. Not only because a *large share of our surplus* was being taken away from us, but fundamentally because our socioeconomic structures were *dependent* and the liberating revolutions did not engender change at the foundations of these structures, dominated as they were by the *criollo* oligarchy (Dos Santos, 1970b: 44; translation and emphasis mine).[1]

The local dominant classes fought to retain larger portions of the surplus values they had already appropriated from the working class in their respective countries. That surplus value was being significantly reduced through "unfavorable terms of trade" on international markets and by imperialist practices of financial domination (e.g., loans). One author calculated that for 1965, the "spoils extracted from the peoples of the Third World" in general, "through the deterioration of their terms of trade," were estimated at $4,500 million dollars. And, if one adds an outflow of capital of $6,000 million and an additional $1,500 million for shipping costs, then for that one year alone the total drain is almost $12,000 million (Jalée, 1969: 117). In this sense alone, one can understand the nationalistic overtones of the dependency theses and their validity as a strictly Latin American phenomenon of social science theory-building. It is significant to note, however, that although theories of underdevelopment and dependency are generally represented as explaining Third World phenomena, similar theoretical interpretations issue from countries such as Canada (Pearson, 1970). This occurs, again, not because of specific geographical location, but because such theories reflect the specific needs of competitive capital (national, local dominant classes) in the face of monopoly capital (imperialist classes). Pearson's (1970: 7,13,14,17,19,41) own interpretation of Latin American relations with capitalism summarizes the view that dependentistas offered during the same period.

The inability of local dominant classes in Latin America during the 1950s and 1960s to halt imperialist siphoning-off of capital to the United States, and thereby to retain a significant portion of the surplus value produced by their working classes, created diverse reactions in political and academic circles. Attempts were made to break with the abstract concepts. Critiques were made of the developmentalist vocabulary of modernization. Initial critical reactions resulted in hybrid sociological analyses of a predominantly structural functionalist nature combined with Marxist concepts of dialectics (Cardoso

---

[1]Throughout the text all translations from Spanish have been made by Carlos Johnson.

and Faletto, 1967). Another early attempt on the part of critical-idealism to struggle against the development-underdevelopment dichotomy without basically criticizing the accepted values of economic growth per se, was carried out by André Gunder Frank (1966). The use of the concept of structural dependence can be found as early as 1963 in analyses dealing with the Caribbean area (consult Norman Girvan, 1973).

Dependency concepts, constructed as an ideological antidote to the developmentalist language used by ECLA, surfaced as a spontaneous critical reaction to the general concept of development-underdevelopment (Dos Santos, 1970a: 37):

> This crisis of the dominant model of development in the social sciences of our times (and of the development project implicit in it) caused a crisis for that same science. It created a crisis for the very notion of development and underdevelopment and the explanatory role of said concepts. From that crisis is born the concept of dependency as a possible explanatory factor of this paradoxical situation.

It should be understood, however, that in fact there was no crisis within the imperialist class project of dominance or its ideological conception of development. These were effectively translated into monopoly capital penetration in Latin America and the resulting capital appropriation to the highly industrialized countries. The crisis that Dos Santos attributes to the social sciences in fact takes place within the project of capital accumulation of the local dominant classes and within the conceptualization by the petty-bourgeois intellectuals of national development. Monopoly capital imperialism witnesses no particular crisis at the time, for it continued to siphon off capital from Latin America. Local competitive capital was unable to put an end to this dominant relationship, hence the critique by dependency theorists.

The local dominant classes and their nationalist ideologues realized that development-underdevelopment was an ideological construct of imperialism, responding to the needs of monopoly capital investment. Development, from the imperialist perspective, merely meant the appropriation and accumulation of Latin American capital (materialized labor) for the imperialist countries and underdevelopment *in abstracto* for the Latin American nations. In spite of such efforts to formulate a critique, the imperialist terminology of development-underdevelopment was replaced by the equally ideological dichotomy of dependency-autonomy. The equally idealist concepts of nationalistic capitalist ideology were set against the idealist concepts of imperialist ideology. Such ideological wars over words are characteristic of class struggle. Outside the relativized metropolis-satellite construct, Frank (1977b), for example, has been intent on creating new words which at best are plays on words, with the author never deciding which concept he prefers: underdevelopment, dependency, or lumpendevelopment.

The word-concept "dependency" itself becomes an interpretative wild card which side-steps the difficult task of materialist analysis. Consider, for example, a few of the multiple uses of the concept of dependency found in the work of Dos Santos (1970b: 6-67): "the necessity of the theory of dependency," "the concept of dependency as a scientific explanatory category," "the international situation of dependency," "dependent structures," "mercantile dependency," "financial industrial dependency," "the history of dependency," "colonial dependency," "financial dependency," "technological industrial dependency," "the dependent system of production," "the dependent economic system," "the development of dependent capitalism." If one starts off from the general statement that the entire system of socioeconomic-political relations is "dependent," then it is understandable that all specific aspects of the system will be qualified as dependent. One can therefore speak of social dependency, economic dependency, political dependency, educational dependency, dependency in medicine and health, dependency in technology, *ad infinitum*. This, however, explains nothing. In addition to using "dependency" as a conceptual wild card, Dos Santos (1970b), much like Frank (1971b), interchanges the concepts of underdevelopment and dependency, even though at the beginning of this same work (1970b: 9), he states that there is a very real difference between the two concepts.

At a theoretical level of abstraction, the concept of dependency (as a substitute for the word "underdevelopment") is grounded on considerations about the most superficial aspects of capital/labor relations.

> *Dependency* is a situation in which the economy of a certain group of countries is conditioned by the development and expansion of another economy to which the former is submitted. The relation of *interdependency* between two or more economies, and between these and world commerce, assumes the form of *dependency* when some countries (the dominant ones) are able to expand and self-propel themselves, while the other countries (the *dependent* ones) can only do so as a result of that expansion, which can act positively or negatively on its immediate development. Either way, the basic question of dependency leads to a global situation in the dependent countries whereby they are placed in a backward position in relation to, and under the exploitation of, the dominant countries (Dos Santos, 1970b: 45; emphasis mine).

A similar definition of dependent countries may be found in Pearson:

> We should never forget, in short, that the developing peoples do not start from scratch in a new world but have to change and grow and develop within a context unfavorable to them, because in the past their position has been so largely determined by the interests of other nations. If we forget this historical context, we will not understand the problems that now exist; nor will development cooperation to solve them be likely to succeed (1970: 17).

It is quite interesting to observe the similarity of the explanations offered by a Marxist-Leninist social scientist and a former Prime Minister of an industrialized, Western capitalist country. Such similarity is itself a reflection of the direct ideological link of dependency theses to the needs of competitive capital in the face of imperialism. This occurs because dependency theorists focus on the changes in magnitude of the production of surplus value and its subsequent exchange and accumulation.

Notice, for example, the importance accorded this level of analysis by Ruy Mauro Marini (1973: 36): "What is important to point out is that, in order to increase the mass of value produced, the capitalist should necessarily rely upon a greater exploitation of labor, either through increasing its intensity, or through prolonging the work period, or, finally, by combining both of the procedures." Although in another part of his work Marini alleges that this characteristic of "superexploitation," as he calls it, is a feature of dependency (Marini, 1978: 74), the fact remains that these different procedures of labor exploitation are proper to capital/labor relations and not specific to "dependent" capitalism or "*sui generis*" capitalism, to use Marini's (1973: 14) phrases. This theoretical misinterpretation on the part of Marini exemplifies the main error committed by dependentistas; i.e., they consider features characteristic of all capital/labor relations as unique to socioeconomic formations dominated by imperialism.

The changes in magnitude of surplus value are of utmost importance to capitalists (and, in this case, especially to the local capitalists), but are of little historical significance to revolutionary socialists. Marx pointed out that,

> Ricardo never concerns himself about the origin of surplus value. He treats it as a thing inherent in the capitalist mode of production, which mode, in his eyes, is the natural form of social production. Whenever he discusses the productiveness of labor, he seeks in it, not the cause of surplus value, but the cause that determines the magnitude of that value. On the other hand, his school has openly proclaimed the productiveness of labor to be the originating cause of profit (read: surplus value) (1974, I: 483).

Marx also emphasized that the forms of exploitation are of determining value to the capitalists themselves (1974, I: 477ff).

The dependentistas ignore capital/labor relations at the level of production and appropriation and focus rather on capitalist exchange relations of circulation and distribution of commodities and capital.

> A second problem relates to the method used in the essay, which becomes explicit in the indication of the need to begin with circulation towards production, in order to then initiate the study of the circulation engendered by that production. This point, which has aroused certain objections, corresponds rigorously to the road followed by Marx. Suffice it to remember, how in *Capital*, the first sections of Book I are dedicated to problems proper to the sphere of circulation and only in the third section does Marx begin studying production; furthermore, once examination of the general questions has been completed, the particular questions concerning the mode of capitalist production are analyzed in an identical manner in the following two books (Marini, 1973: 83).

Consequently, it is no wonder with such interpretations of method that the dependentistas limit themselves at times to comparing degrees of labor exploitation, discussing whether workers in underdeveloped, dependent countries are exploited more than those in imperialist countries (see Leys, 1977: 102ff). In the first volume of *Capital*, Marx discussed the futility of such comparisons between nations and pointed out the methodological problems such a debate entails, given the historical significance of value itself.

The imperialist theses of ECLA (e.g., underdeveloped countries require foreign capital investment in order to become developed nations) were advanced in spite of the fact that more foreign capital investment and loans means absolute capital accumulation, but relative poverty for Latin America. An immediate response to such theses came in the nationalist thesis that Latin America would never develop in the same way and to the same extent as imperialist countries (Frank, 1971a: 35-36). Dependency theorists argued that developmentalists were wrong in stating that some day Latin American countries would become developed. Rather, they claimed that Latin America would remain dependent on the United States, never becoming fully developed, economically autonomous countries. Latin America, they concluded, was condemned to a life of dependency (Frank, 1971b; Dos Santos, 1970b). This counterthesis is situated at the opposite pole from the equally ideological conclusion reached by developmentalists, i.e., that Latin America will one day reach full development. For it is not a case of creating ideal concepts of development or national autonomy, which represent, for example, capital accumulation in favor of monopoly capital as against national competitive, nonmonopolistic capital. Rather, it is a case of understanding from what material base the specific mode of production and accumulation arises and in what direction it evolves in relation to the specific sociohistorical needs of capital/labor production, appropriation, and accumulation. (It should be mentioned that although both developmentalists and dependency theorists maintain their level of analysis at commodity and capital circulation and distribution, some dependentistas openly oppose imperialism and are therefore considered radical.)

Nevertheless, such simplistic ideas represent specific forms of ideological class struggle taking place between imperialists and capitalists to retain a greater share of the surplus value produced by labor. These ideological theses would require no further deliberation were it not for the fact that dependency theory (as a specific manifestation of dominant class ideology) has gained importance among many Marxists as a method of reasoning and that capitalist/imperialist ideology is dominant among social scientists and economists under capitalism. Some Marxist-Leninists are now attempting to rescue the "concept" of dependency from its structural-developmentalist characteristics. Consider Marini's comment on this point:

> There is nothing left for us to do in this brief note but to warn that the implications of superexploitation transcend the level of economic analysis and should also be studied from the sociological and political point of view. It is by advancing in this direction that we shall accelerate the birth of the Marxist theory of dependency, liberating it from the functional-developmentalist characteristics that have adhered to it during its gestation (1973: 101).

The object is to make of dependency theory a Marxist theory. Dos Santos (1970b: 9), like other dependentistas, refers to the so-called "problem of dependency within Marxism". This is a false problem. One can never emphasize enough that the superficial aspects of language are of little importance and that what is historically significant are the materialist explanations of social events. No doubt revolutions are to a great extent carried out in the language of the dominant classes, this language being turned against these classes. Something similar occurred with the concept of "class," which as Marx himself once emphasized was not conceived by him but taken from the bourgeois political economists before him. For years the concept of class was taboo for bourgeois social scientists and economists. Only recently, having worn out the concepts of social group, sector, stratum, and so forth, many capitalist ideologues are exploring the use of the concept of class once again. However, no matter what particular concept they choose, their analyses remain an essentially idealist manner of apprehending social relations in general.

In an effort to make a Marxist analysis of dependency, some Marxists have been attempting to wrench dependency concepts from the dominant ideological influence. Discussion as to whether development-underdevelopment or underdevelopment-dependency are concepts more suitable for interpreting capitalist or socialist relations is basically an ideological debate. Ideological imprecision can readily be observed in the following example of Gunder Frank's writing:

> Nevertheless, although we must not and cannot fail to recognize the progress in Latin America during that period, history has shown us that the inevitable counterpart of their progress, in the context of *(neo) colonial dependence* on world capitalism, is the development of *lumpendevelopment* in Latin America. Furthermore, the very "development" policy of the Latin American *lumpenbourgeoisie* proved to be an effective instrument of growing *dependence* and *underdevelopment*. In our century as well, the class policy of the Latin American *bourgeoisie* served the same purpose: while promoting *neoimperialist development*, it has fostered the ever acuter *neodependence* and *underdevelopment* which characterize the present period (1971b: 89; emphasis is mine).

After the diluvium of invented word-concepts, the principal issue remains the method of reasoning behind the conceptual constructs of theoretical explanation and the praxis adopted in effecting socialist transformation.

Lenin himself used the particular concepts of dependent nation and periphery (Lenin, 1970), taken from bourgeois political economists (Fraisse, 1904; Redslob, 1914). What was essential, however, in Lenin's contribution to scientific socialism (in Marx's work as well) was the method of materialist reasoning and explanation guiding the use of words, the theoretical analysis, and the socialist revolutionary praxis. And insofar as the method of reasoning is the basis of all theoretical and practical activity, it must be examined prior to any other factor. Our treatment of the dependency theses has nothing to do, then, with a concern for the word "dependency" which, in itself, means nothing; it becomes significant only within the context of an analytical interpretation of existing social relations. The essential question is not the particular word-concept itself but the ideological attempt to construct a theoretical framework of explanation that supposedly interprets social relations in terms of one specific word: "dependency" (Dos Santos, 1978).

In order to better understand this issue, we shall examine the various meanings of this word-concept at different stages of social relations and levels of theoretical abstraction. On the theoretical level, the reasoning and explanations are primary and the particular words become secondary. On the level of ideological constructs, specific words become the important elements, while the method of reasoning is ignored and deemed unimportant. Dependency theorists fight over the word "dependency" and its purity of application, never questioning their own theoretical reasoning, much less the specific class needs represented by dependency theses (Marini, 1978). Because many dependentistas avoid this issue, they are often seen as not being Marxists, even though they portray themselves as such. Analysts like Dos Santos (1970b) and Marini (1973) claim to develop Marxist-Leninist analyses in their work on Latin American social relations. While other radical dependentistas make no claim to Marxism (see Frank, 1974: 96).

Among critical-idealists, particular words become the object of extensive literary discourse, and the invention of new words permits new writings, as Marx and Engels (1964) once commented. The search for the one word that would define an entire historical period takes the following form:

> Finally, I continue to use the word "underdevelopment," a word whose etymological origins and present usage is the most shameless negation — ideological, political, economic, social, cultural, and psychological — of an accurate conception of reality. I am unable to find a substitute for this word, to free myself from this cultural colonialism. In order to make a start at replacing this word with a term which mirrors reality, if not perfectly then at least more accurately, might we not look to Adam Smith, the scholar who provided us with one of the epigraphs to this essay and who was concerned with colonialism and colonies? Might we not designate the consequences of colonialism as "lumpendevelopment"? (Frank, 1971b: 19).

Old theses, which correspond to class needs, are reformulated. Such attempts to use the concept of dependency to explain production relations (at a national and international level) reflect different class interests. In this context it is understandable that dependency theorists dislike being lumped together as dependentistas (Bambirra, 1978: 112).

Let us cite one example of such displeasure:

> To begin with, they address the thrust of the theoretical attack to an abstract entity created by North American proponents: the "dependentistas." It is difficult to be precise in globally criticizing authors and interpretations which disagree on significant points. In truth, the central part of the criticism is directed specifically to A.G. Frank, but by extension (and as far as I know this is not a valid criterion . . . ) all those called "dependentistas" fall into the same bag (Cardoso, 1974: 66).

This displeasure occurs because some dependency theorists are conscious ideologues or apologists of monopoly capitalism and imperialism (Werner, 1978). Here theses around class needs surface in the form of an argument in favor of North American interests against OPEC raises in oil prices, or proposals of policies to generate other forms of energy so that Western capitalism and imperialism may survive. Others are representatives of national capitalist needs and interests. Here class needs surface in the form of policy proposals for the renegotiation of dependency and Latin America's unfavorable terms of trade, in order to favor national capital accumulation (Dos Santos, 1970b: 126). Still others (Marini, 1969) are morally committed to international proletarianism. Here class needs surface in the form of conclusions in favor of political policies for socialist revolution through the internationalization of the workers' movements against imperialism and the national bourgeoisies.

Each of these ideological formulations of dependency theory constitutes in itself a product of class struggle, specifically, of capital/labor relations. The ideological nature of dependency theory can be better understood when it is realized that dependency theses represent a specific stage of capital/labor relations, i.e., the struggle between monopoly capital and competitive capital. Furthermore, the essential ideological theses of dependency have already been developed under diverse guises during previous historical periods of struggle among various capitalist and imperialist classes.

## DEPENDENCY THESES ON CAPITAL/LABOR RELATIONS AND CAPITALIST CLASS NEEDS

During a similar stage in capitalist history involving a struggle between monopolistic and competitive degrees of capitalist accumulation, economic theses resembling those of contemporary dependency theorists surfaced. During the latter part of the nineteenth century, the Russian Narodniks, or populists, in their interpretation of economic relations in Russia, postulated essentially the same socioeconomic theses as those currently advanced by the dependency theorists in Latin America. The Narodniks attacked monopoly capital and supported various popular policies of nationalization and "people's production" designed to encourage Russian agrarian and capital interests. Furthermore, some Narodniks proposed the direct transition to socialism through the peasant organizations called MIR.

Lenin (1974: 37-70) criticized the Narodniks, disclosing the class origins of their policies, which in historical terms represented essentially antirevolutionary, antisocialist theses, in spite of the socialist and revolutionary objectives stated by some exponents. It was just as difficult then to make general statements about Narodism (or populist theory) as it is today about dependency theory. One must review the specific theses in order to understand how each theorist treated the historical need for socialist transformation of capital/labor relations. At one level of abstraction, however, as Lenin demonstrated in his critique of Narodism, the Narodniks all made the same kind of petty-bourgeois economic analysis based on critical idealism; *in this sense,* they were all alike. In relation to specific economic theses, they too differed according to the class interests they represented.

Lenin pointed to the principal economic theses of the Russian Narodniks as: the shrinking of the domestic market; the need for foreign markets in order to realize surplus value; the impossibility of realizing surplus value at home; and, most significantly, the impossibility of establishing capitalism in Russia at that time (Lenin, 1974: 42-47). Lenin was direct in his critique of such theses:

And, furthermore, there is nothing more absurd than to conclude from the contradiction of capitalism that the latter is impossible, non-progressive and so on . . . ; . . . in short one must take the *facts* about the development of capitalism in the country; and it is not surprising that the Narodniks take the opportunity to evade these facts under the cover of worthless (and meaningless) phrases about the "impossibility" of both the home and the foreign markets (1974: 58,68).

Marxist dependency theorists today have repeated the same postulates regarding the impossibility of developing capitalist relations in Latin America. The two principal dependentistas who develop such theses using a phraseology very similar to that of the Narodniks are Marini (1969, 1973) and Dos Santos (1970b, 1971). Among the infinite number of times these authors have stated this particular thesis, consider: "Of course, capitalism based on superexploitation thwarts any possibility of autonomous development and of 'fair' labor relations, necessarily posing class struggle which opposes it in socialist terms" (Marini, 1969: 132). The implications of this statement by Marini in fact suggest that capitalism, based on regular exploitation, harbors the possibility of autonomous development and fair labor relations. Lenin (1974b) criticized the Russian populists for offering a similar interpretation: "Numerous errors of the populists come from their attempts to demonstrate that this disproportionate, leaping, frantic development is not development."

Both the Narodniks and the dependency theorists represent and reflect the class needs of local dominant classes attempting to establish forms of class production and appropriation that favor greater accumulation of surplus value in national terms. And, although the names may change (e.g., development, underdevelopment, dependency, autonomy, etc.), the essential issue remains that of control of the world production of surplus value. Radicals (e.g., Frank) and Marxist-Leninist dependency theorists (e.g., Marini and Dos Santos) who do not recognize this merely articulate those particular class needs in spite of their stated efforts to fight against those same needs.

The principal critical-idealist thesis of both the Narodniks and the dependency theorists deals with the impossibility of establishing capitalism. This thesis represents the ideological counterthesis, advanced by the dependentistas, to the imperialist thesis of developmentalism, which holds that capitalist development will take place in Latin American countries through foreign capital investment. Much like the Narodniks, dependency theorists elaborate the idea that in the face of monopoly capital (imperialism), national capitalism is in fact an impossibility in Latin America. At best, according to them, capitalism will develop in a deformed manner (González Casanova, 1967).

Dependency theorists arrive at such conclusions in much the same way as the Narodniks, i.e., through an idealist analysis of the exchange relations operating in domestic and international markets. Marini's (1973) use of the abstract category "a Latin American exporting economy" ultimately obscures, if not denies altogether, the entire division of labor within a specific socioeconomic formation, while defining the economic relations in relation to the activity of commodity exportation (exchange relations) alone. They conclude that internal markets in Latin America are virtually underdeveloped or nonexistent (Marini, 1973: 57) and that international market relations impede the realization of surplus value in those countries (1973: 86). From this point it is relatively easy to demonstrate that what the dependency theorists refer to as classical capitalism will never become a reality in Latin America. For that reason, more than a precapitalism, what exists is a *sui generis* capitalism that only makes sense if we contemplate it within the perspective of the system as a whole, at the national level, as well as, and mainly, at the international level (Marini, 1973: 14).

The Narodniks were famous for considering everything to be a problem of domestic and international markets. These levels were considered to be deformations of what a capitalist market should be, as opposed to some preconceived idea of what capitalism itself is. The dependentistas commit similar errors when they abstract capitalist relations from other countries (classical capitalism), and then try to demonstrate that that particular kind of capital/labor relation is not present in Latin America. From there it is relatively easy to arrive at the thesis concerning the impossibility of capitalist development in Latin America. Arriving at such theses is inevitable when the struggle against the idealist concept of development is carried out in an equally ideological manner. From this position, it is logical to argue that no "real" national bourgeoisie exists in Latin America, and hence, that there is no possibility for a democratic, revolutionary bourgeoisie to develop (Bambirra, 1978: 108), much less a democratic bourgeois revolution as the first stage of a socialist revolution (Frank, 1969b; Dos Santos, 1969): "Consequently", Dos Santos concludes that "the national bourgeoisies do not have the historical ability to sustain anti-imperialist struggle in our countries" (1969: 63).

Such conclusions counter not only all of Marx's analytical work on capitalist relations but reality itself, insofar as capital/labor relations are being established in varying degrees throughout Latin America. It is important to understand, then, that the process of social relations in Latin America is the product of capitalism's imperialist expansion and not of some kind of deformed capitalism (e.g., *sui generis* capitalism) or deformed bourgeoisie (e.g., lumpenbourgeoisie). A dialectical-historical-materialist understanding of this issue would initially recognize that it is not a case of capitalist "development" being thwarted or of "underdevelopment" and dependency" resulting from this situation. Rather, the perceived "deformity" represents in itself the product of class relations — capital/labor relations, to be exact.

The dependency counterthesis concerning the impossibility of capitalism actually refers to the impossibility of achieving specific *ideal* levels of capitalist production and consumption in Latin America. The dependency theorists set about to prove that (ideal) levels of production and consumption similar, say, to the levels of U.S. production and consumption will never be part of Latin Amercia's future. In the face of the capitalist-imperialist myth that development will become a reality in Latin America, the dependency theorists advance the equally naive countermyth that development will never take place in their countries. For example, one need only consider the disparate levels of income in such large urban industrial centers of Latin America as Rio de Janeiro, São Paulo, and Mexico City in order to understand that some levels of production and consumption in those areas far outweigh even those in some regions of the United States. Perceiving those urban centers and their corresponding degree of capitalist development as the result of capitalist and imperialist relations of exploitation reflects a materialist comprehension of the development of capital/labor relations throughout Latin America. The phenomena related to Mexico City, for example, of high crime rates, overpopulation (relative surplus population), marginality (specific forms of the relative surplus population), concentration and centralization of labor migration to urban areas, etc., represents the results of the growing dominance of capital/labor relations within Mexico and the breakdown of other modes of class production and appropriation. To attribute these phenomena to a concept as abstract as "underdevelopment" or "dependency" is merely another case of critical-idealist thinking, itself a phenomenon characteristic of classes in struggle. The essential question is to explain how and why capitalist relations promote and repress levels of production and consumption according to needs of surplus value accumulation.

Obviously, capitalist relations in such an ideally conceived state will not appear. Without recalling all that Marx has already stated about capital/labor relations and how one should go about identifying their presence, it may be said that the Marxist-Leninist dependentistas do not realize that their own theses interpreting Latin American economic relations are the very reflection of the presence of capital/labor relations and the struggle for control of the surplus product of labor.

In order to substantiate the main economic theses of dependency, the dependentistas focus their analyses on the changes in the magnitude of surplus value (Marini, 1973), on the exchange relations of commodities at the level of circulation and distribution (i.e., at the level of national and international markets) (Dos Santos, 1978), and on the phenomena of unemployment and overpopulation (Nun, 1969; Quijano, 1979). Other theoretical errors committed by the Marxist dependency theorists (Marini, 1973; Bambirra, 1974; Dos Santos, 1978) are identifying consumption with capital acumulation, statically dividing surplus labor from necessary labor, inverting the causes and effects of the different moments of the historical process, conceiving the wage-fund as something fixed, overemphasizing the degrees of exploitation of the labor force, putting forth the idea that salaries rise as a function of capital accumulation. These and other ideas are advanced without defining the particular relationship these phenomena have with class struggle (especially Bambirra, 1974). The dependentistas fail to analyze the principal relations within the methods of capitalist accumulation or the essential aspects of capitalist production, appropriation, and the concentration and centralization of capital accumulation. This results from a basic confusion about the essential levels of analysis; Marini (1973: 100), for example, takes the level of relative and absolute surplus value for the level of capital accumulation (i.e., constant and variable capital).

By using the forms of capitalist exploitation and circulation of commodities and capital to prove their theses, the dependency theorists ignore the complex levels of the concrete relations of capital/labor production and class struggle itself. Various critics (Cueva, 1976b: 12-16; Leys, 1977; Kalmanovitz, 1975) have already made this important point regarding the failure of the dependency theorists to recognize that it is the very classes in struggle which determine the terms of trade and the unfavorable exchange of surplus value and not iron-clad economic laws. In relating the phenomenon of dependency directly to the moment of circulation in capitalist relations, Marini (1973: 83) even attempts to substantiate this procedure methodologically by citing Marx's own work. Relations of production are completely ignored by Marini in his contention that, in *Capital,* Marx himself began his analysis with the process of circulation and not production. In fact, Marx begins his exposition (not his analysis and reasoning) with commodities and the concepts of production and consumption in order to discover and explain the source of the creative force (potential labor power) behind the production and reproduction of social relations, i.e., in order to materially prove that labor power creates value. It should be remembered that a capitalist myth during the nineteenth century was that capital created value. (This same myth persists today.)

By emphasizing exchange relations and the moment of circulation, the dependentistas are then able to speak in terms of double exploitation or superexploitation, whereby workers are supposedly exploited by local dominant classes *and* by unequal international exchange relations (Bambirra, 1978: 111). In the later case, the social products are sold on the international market by the local dominant classes at prices inferior to their value. Superexploitation is advanced to substantiate dependency theory and is conceived by dependency theorists as being *sui generis* to dependent Latin America economies (Marini, 1973: 101). Were this theoretically sound materialist reasoning, a good case could be made for demonstrating that a laborer is in fact exploited an infinite number of times and to an infinite degree when the commodity he produces is exchanged an infinite number of times on the market before being consumed, each exchange being equal to a greater degree of exploitation.

It should be understood, however, that the workers are initially exploited when their socially produced goods are appropriated by another class at the time of production itself. What happens to this materialized labor (surplus product/value) after the act of exploitation and appropriation does not directly concern the workers. Marx emphasized the need to maintain the level of analysis with respect to the determinant relations of production (capital/labor) and thereby avoid the determined level of exchange relations (circulation and distribution of capital and commodities).

The dependentistas further state that the local capitalists then attempt to regain their *loss* (Marini, 1973: 36) on the international market through greater exploitation of the worker at home. From a materialist perspective, the surplus value "lost" by the local dominant class on the international market can never be materially regained. The capitalists can only attempt to force their workers to create greater amounts of surplus value through more effective means of exploitation at some later moment in the production process. This is done in order to obtain even greater quantities of capital the *next* time they take to market the socially produced goods they appropriated. But nothing is materially regained, much less materially lost, for class relations mean precisely the exchange of "unequal" (different) surplus value. Thus, self-proclaimed Marxist dependency theorists unwittingly advance the class perspective of the local dominant capitalists who view unequal exchange relations as the cause of their losses. What is of determinant importance is the social act of the buying and selling of labor power and the resulting exploitation of surplus labor (i.e., the material base of private accumulation) and not the nature of the market relations produced by those social forces.

Dependency theory, as has already been established, is strewn with similiar idealist formulations, which by no means reflect problems of semantics. Such theses faithfully mirror the critical idealist reasoning carried out by the dependency theorists in their analyses. The particular theses reflect various aspects of the ideological perspective of the local capitalist class, i.e., a concern for what the local dominant class considers its loss in the face of imperialism's imposed unfavorable terms of trade. Such is the nature of nationalist bourgeois ideology itself. With such interpretations of international economic relations, the dependency theorist (knowingly or unknowingly) becomes the ideologue of the local capitalist's struggle against monopoly capital. The dependentistas express theoretically what the local dominant classes experience practically through their inability to obtain increasingly higher prices for their goods.

In this light, it appears as though the local capitalists are coopting the terminology and formulations of dependency theory. In fact, it is the self-styled Marxist or radical who assumes the bourgeoisie's ideological perspective, giving it theoretical form in spite of stated efforts to combat the bourgeoisie and capitalism. Using such analyses of exchange relations, the dependency theorist then attempts to substantiate the need for revolution and socialism *in abstracto* (Frank, 1971b: 154; Marini, 1973: 18). Such attempts already reflect a lack of understanding of capital/labor relations and represent spontaneous responses developed in the context of class struggle. "Radical" and "Marxist" dependentistas who substantiate revolution and socialism do so for the wrong reasons as we shall see below. The fact that they base their theses of dependency on exchange relations render their political conclusions ineffective.

Over a century ago, Marx and Engels offered a materialist analysis of the capitalist and socialist processes, effectively discrediting the existing utopian propositions for socialist change. They realized that socialism represents a stage in history whereby class relations set about eliminating the contradiction between social production and private appropriation. Capitalism and socialism, in that light, were understood to be part of the historical process, given the essential contradiction of class societies (socialized production versus private appropriation). Contrary to this understanding of social relations, some dependency theorists argue in favor of socialism and revolution as though they were mere alternatives to capitalism and not specific products of class struggle itself. Inasmuch as dependency theses are a product of capitalist class needs for accumulation and bourgeois ideological reasoning, such theses are quite irrelevant to an analysis of the transformation of capital/labor relations and still less relevant to socialist revolution. What must be emphasized, however, is how specific ideological constructs such as those enunciated in dependency theory represent spontaneous, critical forms of ideological class struggle, specifically against monopoly capital (imperialism). And, although dependency denunciations are themselves a manifestation of class struggle at the level of monopoly capital versus competitive capital, they do not represent the basis of theoretical knowledge required for transforming class societies into classless ones.

In an attempt to transcend the formulation of local dominant class needs for improving the terms of trade and renegotiating dependency itself, some Marxist dependency theorists (Marini, 1969: 160-161) speak of international proletarianism as the means to revolution and socialism. However, dependency theorists have learned their ideological forms of reasoning from other idealists. And in attempting an interpretation of labor needs, they only obscure the nature of capital/labor relations and socialist transformation.

Furthermore, no successful socialist revolutionary program has ever been built on the basis of such interpretations. Again, consult the political programs of the socialist revolutionary Narodniks in nineteenth century Russia. For a more contemporary and pertinent example, consult the political programs of such groups as the Movimiento de Izquierda Revolucionaria (MIR) before and during the Allende regime in Chile (1970-1973). The political program of the Chilean MIR was based to a large extent on dependency theses of rejecting alliances with the local bourgeoisies.

Like most forms of idealist thinking, the attractiveness of dependency theory lies in its ability to accommodate other idealist interpretations of social relations. The very simplicity of the theoretical construct of dependency permits any class to use it as a means of analytical interpretation. Any materially existing object or event may be considered dependent (independent or interdependent) on another materially existing object or event. This level of abstraction can easily be applied to international economic relations. Socioeconomic relations represent individuals and classes *in relation* to themselves and others, forming the very existence of the *social* production by men in society. Such shallow levels of abstraction, aside from avoiding the level of contradiction between social production and private appropriation, coincide with those levels reached by the ideologues of imperialism who preach the need for interdependence (Rock, 1964) and chastise, for example, the United States' current dependence on foreign oil imports (Werner, 1978). Again, it appears as though the imperialists are coopting the terminology and formulations of dependency theory, when in fact they are merely capitalizing on the dependency theorists' initial error, i.e., the attempt to construct a theoretical interpretation of social relations around one particular word-concept — "dependency."

Dominant classes promote the application of bourgeois ideology and idealist reasoning to these superficial levels of capital/labor relations inasmuch as such a practice promotes the reproduction of the capitalist system. Capitalists and imperialists enjoy a certain degree of ideological confrontation with other classes at *these* levels of analysis. They are confident when confronting specific critical idealist theses and at times even promote their dissemination. The concepts of dependence and interdependence, inasmuch as they reflect the ideological interpretations of social relations of a specific class (i.e., of competitive capitalist classes), are by no means objectionable to the capitalists and imperialists. Attempts are made to apply dependency theory *in abstracto* to other precapitalist countries outside Latin America (Amin, 1973). Furthermore, the theoretical constructs of dependence and interdependence are employed to establish antisocialist ideologies (Eckstein, 1978).

## CAPITALIST IDEOLOGICAL THESES OF SOCIALIST DEPENDENCY

Various attempts have been made to apply dependency constructs to socialist international economic relations (Ray, 1973). Some radical and Marxist dependency theorists (consciously or unconsciously) contribute to this situation because they do not consider private class appropriation *in relation* to social production. The ideological attacks made by capitalist and imperialist ideologues remain analytically superficial. For example, it is said that Cuba *depends* on the Soviet Union (Eckstein, 1978) as it once depended on the United States before the Cuban socialist revolution (Fagen, 1977), or that Eastern European countries *depend* on the Soviet Union. Obviously, dependency in this sense, carries a totally negative connotation. The ideological intent at this level (as in the attempts to apply dependency theory to Africa; for example, Ehrensaft, 1971) is to demonstrate the universality of the phenomenon of dependency, and ideally, to erase any differences between capitalism and socialism. Were dependency concepts applicable to international, socialist economic relations, one could safely conclude (ideologically, of course) that socialism is as objectionable as capitalism.

Such ideological theses are now surfacing in the latest imperialist language of the North-South question. Here, the rich nations (developed capitalist and socialist nations) confront the poor nations (underdeveloped nations), thus annulling the analytical conception of classes and the historical process of transformation from capitalism to socialism (Amuzagar, 1976; De Montbrial, 1975). In spite of such efforts at present to discuss international economic relations on the basis of a North-South dichotomy, which would supposedly place the Soviet Union alongside the United States, for example, the general content and scope of such analyses obviously concern the problems resulting from capitalist and imperialist conflict among dominant, Western imperialist powers and the dominated economies with which they have economic relations. Whether one identifies such relations as North-South, dependency-interdependency, metropolis-satellite, or modern-traditional, the level of analysis remains limited to that of relations among nations. The concrete class relations of the particular modes of production and forms of accumulation are ignored in terms of private class appropriation.

By applying the abstract, ahistorical concept of dependence to socialist relations (given the ideological class context in which it surfaced), many capitalist and imperialist class objectives are immediately fulfilled. Such objectives respond to class needs for capitalist ideological reproduction by destroying the conception of the historical process of capitalist and socialist relations. In this manner, capitalism and socialism are perceived as totally unrelated events. Capitalism is thereby maintained as a historical possibility, rather than a transitory form of class relations of exploitation. When the notion of dependence is applied to socialism in this way, such interpretations play an essentially reactionary role in socialist transformation. This is the case because dependency theorists, given their critical idealist approach, do not and cannot distinguish between capital/labor relations and socialist relations. This occurs because relations of unequal exchange appear to be the same, whether one is considering capitalist or socialist relations. By not taking their analyses to the level of the concept of "unequal" itself in relation to capital/labor relations, they merely regard the concept as corresponding to unfavorable exchange relations of surplus products and values.

One must not fail to remember, however, that although the *conception* of the historical process of capitalist and socialist relations may be ideologically distorted (that is, in the idealist's mind), the process itself continues; that is, the historical process of classes in struggle to eliminate the contradiction of social production and private appropriation continues.

The simplistic application of dependency constructs to the entire process of socioeconomic relations (be they capitalist or socialist) distorts reality, to say the least. The very superficiality of dependency as an interrelationship makes it bidirectional and not specific to one particular system of socioeconomic relations. For example, consider the concept of dependency in authors such as J.A. Hobson: "In other words, while the dependency of Great Britain on her empire was stationary, the dependency of her empire upon her for commerce was rapidly diminishing" (1971: 35). No socioeconomic formation of human relations is entirely dependent upon another, as though such formations were encapsulated entities. Such occurs with much of ideological theses resulting from class struggle. Independence is set up as an ideal type within struggle, the idea to become independent from a particular country's or class's dominance. Under the ideological scope of struggle, "dependency" becomes strictly negative in meaning, not allowing for an understanding that social relations precisely mean specific kinds of relationships, independent, dependent, and interdependent at specific moments. Within social *relations* (on any scale of individuals, groups, classes, nations, etc.), there is no such thing as independence, or dependence *in abstracto.* One must identify the specific *conditions* of those relations and not lead one to think that dependence is negative. Under socialist relations, the objective is to precisely integrate the social forces of production in relation to their needs of consumption and to eliminate private class appropriation and accumulation. Social production itself means the relationship of men producing together in society, in that sense depending upon other individuals for production purposes. But, if one uses "dependence" in an ideological sense of negative meaning alone, then this understanding of the social process is obscured. And, if one speaks at the other extreme of "interdependence" within class relations of production and appropriation, then the nature of capital/labor relations is obscured (Wallerstein, 1974). Hence, there is the need to identify the determinant factors of those relations' *conditions of existence.* From this we can further understand why the concepts themselves are quite incidental to a materialist explanation of socioeconomic relations. At one point, for example, Marx was emphatic in showing how labor (while dependent, so to speak, on selling its labor power to capitalists) is historically independent of capital in developing classless relations. Marx further emphasized the essential materialist point that the capitalist class is completely parasitic and dependent on labor for its own reproduction. Using the word "dependency" as an abstract concept applicable to a group of nations, or even to one nation (or individual) in particular, totally obscures such elementary Marxian theses. It would be much easier to explain the United States' dependence on the capital (materialized labor) and raw materials extracted by U.S. capitalists and imperialists from Latin American countries. "The return flow of capital" (Jalée, 1969: 114-120) from the Third World to the United States, for example, explicitly shows the degree to which U.S. levels of production and consumption are themselves dependent upon the capital extracted from other countries. To reverse this relationship, as some dependentistas have done and are doing at present in order to argue that it is Latin America which is dependent on the United States, is to deny their own efforts to critique imperialism.

By analytically confronting nations then, one avoids questioning the character of the production and appropriation relations at the base of those national economies while simply reviewing the more superficial movement of commodities and capital, i.e., social products and values which already represent appropriated, materialized labor. By abstractly applying concepts of dependency to international economic relations, many radical and Marxist dependentistas are themselves accused, and understandably so, of substantiating a moral apologia of capitalism and even imperialism. For example, Frank refers to critics who have accused him and other members of the radical left of being "provocateurs," "ultra-infantile leftists," "bourgeois Stalinists," and even of being "in alliance with the CIA and imperialism" (1974: 87-106).

Furthermore, because of the emphasis placed on exchange relations (the struggle for the accumulation of appropriated surplus values), little or nothing is stated regarding the specific relations within international socialist economic relations or the conscious attempts to eliminate the contradiction between social production and private appropriation and the possibility of private class accumulation. Nor is this contradiction examined within each particular socialist country. However, this is the only way any scientific understanding of the capitalist and socialist historical *processes* can be approached.

Once this point is understood, as well as the fact that the progressive elimination of this contradiction is carried out by the historical process of social relations (slave, feudal, capitalist class relations), it becomes possible to conclude that the United States is the most backward (underdeveloped) country in the world in this respect, for the United States is the most developed country in terms of its refinement of the means of private class appropriation of socially produced commodities. Cuba, on the one hand, must surely be recognized as the most developed nation in the world at this moment in history since it is bringing its forms of social appropriation into line with its degree of social production. However, considerations such as these, though empirically scientific, are not the object of our concern at present. For example, Jalée (1969: 84-89) offers data that would support such a debate by proving the dependence of the United States on the Third World; but again, such an effort would not break with the conceptual dichotomy itself.

Squabbling over which country is developed or underdeveloped, dependent or autonomous, etc., is merely an ideological exercise in critical idealism. That is, social relations are compared to a preconceived *tertium comparationis* (e.g., yearly income per capita) representing the factor to which the adjectives themselves (e.g., developed, underdeveloped, dependent) are ultimately compared. In the statistical jargon of the United Nations, for example, a *tertium comparationis* would be income per capita, the number of hospital beds in relation to population, the number of school rooms in relation to student population, and so on, *in abstracto*, outside any historical considerations concerning these very same indicators. One would use these comparative indicators to identify which countries are developed or underdeveloped. In the studies of the dependency theorists, the specific levels of production and consumption (capitalist labor exploitation) constitute the third comparative element in terms of which countries are classified as either developed or underdeveloped and dependent. With that, the notion of growth as something positive is not questioned.

The historically significant question, however, is to understand the nature of specific class relations and the overall process of social relations according to concrete sociohistorical conditions. What becomes determinant are the materialist reasons given for the very existence of the *tertium comparationis.* By failing to offer such analyses, theoretical constructs such as dependency theory reflect the very existence of class societies and the contradiction between social production and private appropriation. Neither the concept of dependency itself nor any of the particular dependency theses offer an understanding of how to eliminate this contradiction. On the contrary, dependency theory merely articulates specific forms of capital appropriation and accumulation required by given class needs. That is to say, the dependency theses reflect the existence of the contradiction. In no way do such theses analytically develop the needs of socialist transformation — even though they may recognize the historical need for such a transformation.

Within socioeconomic formations in which socialist relations exist and within the international socialist system, all specific forms of private class appropriation are not immediately eliminated at the political inception of socialism with the stroke of the constitutional pen. Moreover, new forms of private class appropriation arise that were not present under capital/labor relations. Such forms would refer to bureaucratic corruption, for example, within a socialist society. Although no longer based on appropriation of surplus products and the accumulation of surplus values resulting from the private ownership of the means of production, such forms would lead to cases of private accumulation by individuals due to their relationship to the socialized means of appropriation.

The concept of dependency can in no way explain such events because of the superficial level at which dependency theorists work. In order to achieve the elimination of private class appropriation and the establishment of socialized appropriation, socialist societies first pass through specific modes of production and appropriation and accumulation organized by the state. It is in this sense that socialism represents a transitional stage to a communist, classless organization of society. However, many critical idealists, impatient with current forms of socialist relations, view the Soviet Union's policies towards other nations, for example, as essentially the same as those of any capitalist or imperialist nation. Such ideological theses, once again, are based on a lack of historical perspective regarding the level of production and appropriation and on a misplaced concern for exchange relations of commodities (circulation, distribution, and consumption of commodities).

A classless society can be established only after social production has been developed *in relation* to the material needs of the existing social forces. The social organization that precedes this stage necessarily passes through various kinds of appropriation, precisely as a result of the existing relation of social production and private appropriation, in order to bring appropriation in line with social production (in terms of specific socioeconomic formations). Forms of private and class appropriation will still be present (as they are today in socialist and communist societies) until a total translation of social production and social appropriation is made in society; at such a time, such class concepts as social and private will themselves no longer be necessary. One may then speak in terms of production and appropriation, or simply, production and reproduction, with the specific moments (appropriation, circulation, accumulation, consumption) of the process delineated differently. Until then, however, the stages of class struggle currently witnessed in socialist societies will continue to represent conscious class efforts at eliminating this contradiction pointed out by Marx long ago. Within capitalist and imperialist countries, the current stages of class struggle will continue to signify the elimination of this contradiction through the material elimination of capitalist class relations and the class conscious effort to effect socialist revolutions.

Classless societies (for which there exists no name, as such, other than communism) are then a historical possibility *only* when the contradiction of social production and private appropriation is eliminated on a world scale. For only then will it become materially feasible to eliminate the specific forms of class accumulation (military armies, for example) and the *division of labor,* in order to establish a correspondence between manual and mental labor *in relation* to the process of socialized production and appropriation itself. A dialectical-historical-materialist analysis of class and classless relations in society must deal then with the level of social production and private appropriation first, that is, the social modes of production, labor forces and the manner in which the social product of these relations is appropriated by the producers along with the subsequent forms of accumulation. In constructing a theoretical explanation of class history and the scientific basis for classless relations, Marx restricted his analysis to this relational level. And, it is this same relational level that allows us to understand class ideologies such as dependency theory.

The dependency theorists who attempt to interpret capitalist and/or socialist relations in terms of dependency theses at the level of international economic relations completely ignore the level of analysis already attained by Marx. They suggest that present-day socialist societies already represent the elimination of class relations and not the process of elimination of such relations — hence, the ease with which ideological theses about Cuba's dependence on the Soviet Union, for example, are offered. One can only explain socialism as the historical attempt to eliminate private class appropriation in all forms on a world scale, *in relation to* and *in correspondence with* the socialized modes of production. Socialist revolutions themselves represent the first step in this direction, which is the elimination of private ownership of the means of production. This, in turn, eliminates the possibility of private appropriation and accumulation by specific individuals and classes. As history has demonstrated, socialist revolutions in themselves do not immediately establish a correspondence between production and appropriation-accumulation. Furthermore, the very existence of a world-wide system of capitalist and imperialist relations *conditions* the manner in which, and the speed with which, the elimination of specific forms of appropriation-accumulation will occur within each socialist country as well as among the various socialist countries.

In terms of capital/labor relations and socialism, the theoretical level of dependency theses cannot, in any manner, engender the political conclusions reached by the dependentistas regarding the need for revolution and socialism. The level identified by Marx concerning the contradiction between social production and private appropriation is the only level of analysis that historically demonstrates the need for socialist revolution in terms of the elimination of class forms of appropriation; this elimination is effected in order to consciously establish socialist or communist, and later, classless modes of production and appropriation. Furthermore, dependency theses cannot explain (other than idealistically, *in abstracto*) how to achieve revolution or socialism. Dependency theorists can do no more than elaborate an abstract, utopian thesis in favor of socialism and revolution, as so many utopian socialists have done before them. What is more, dependency theorists can only argue the case for specific capitalist class needs in certain countries. Viewed in this light, dependency concepts have nothing to do with socialism, much less with the elimination of private class appropriation within capitalism. On the contrary, dependency theses constitute a case in favor of specific forms of class appropriation and accumulation in response to concrete class needs during the initial stages of the establishment of capitalist relations as the dominant relations within a specific socioeconomic formation.

The dependentistas (and many of their critics, such as Leys [1977], for example), ignore the historical context of the socialist process and argue in favor of (or against) the word "dependency," as though the phenomenon represented by that concept were outside the realm of capitalist and socialist history. What appears at first to be an erratic array of political conclusions (apologies of capitalism, political reformism, renegotiation of dependency, incendiary revolutionism) is nothing more than an array of class needs for capital production and appropriation-accumulation, i.e., class struggle under capital/labor relations at the international level whereby, throughout the world, entire classes struggle against one another for the production of surplus value.

Socialism, on the other hand, represents a specific stage in the historical process of social modes of production and forms of appropriation which denotes a totally different historical period from that of capital/labor relations. However, one cannot expect critical-idealists armed with ideological concepts of time processes and material relations to recognize such differences immediately. The theorists of dependency who consciously propose to substantiate apologies of capitalism and imperialism are of little concern to us. The work of those Marxists who claim knowledge of Marx's own work on capital/labor relations and who continue to substantiate bourgeois ideology by attempting abstractly to construct dependency theory at the level of exchange relations alone will continue to be questioned as long as such analysts avoid the basic class contradiction in capitalist history.

We are well aware that dependency theses (as all class, ideological forms of reasoning) will be eliminated materially only when the social relations upon which they are based are themselves eliminated historically. While many critical-idealists are today trying to decide what dependency theory is, others are asking themselves what dependency theory was (Fagan, 1977: 22).

Little do they realize that specific ideological class theses (reflecting specific class needs) will, as long as class relations exist, remain present in the form of the Narodism of the late 1800s, the developmentalism of the 1950s, or the dependency theory of the 1960s and 1970s. However, for each historical period, such theses must be exposed to materialist analysis in order to reveal their class nature and ideological significance for class struggle. By doing this, one also reveals their irrelevance in effecting socialist transformation, thereby reaffirming the tenets of scientific socialism, that is, the very needs of socialist transformation.

Socialism requires an explanation of the historical task involving the elimination of capitalist forms of production and appropriation and the resolution of the contradiction of social production and private appropriation. This will explain many of the aspects of ideological interpretation encouraged by bourgeois thought and, specifically, by dependency theorists. In order to discuss socialism, a certain amount of order must be introduced among the ideological debates now prevalent in sociological and economic theory in capitalist countries. The dependency theses represent only one particular form of bourgeois ideology as interpreted by some well-meaning (and some not so well-meaning) social scientists under capitalism. We have attempted to demonstrate that what is referred to today as dependency theory, in any of its particular aspects, does not represent a dialectical-historical-materialist analysis of social relations. We have attempted to show why it represents various forms of critical idealist thought proper to the *presence* of class struggle, rather than to its possible elimination.

There is at present a large body of critical literature questioning dependency theses (Fernández and Ocampo, 1974; Cueva, 1976b; Castañeda and Hett, 1978) and the existence of dependency *theory*. Such critiques, (Kalmanovitz, 1975; Leaver, 1977; Sindico, 1977) which have taken some time to surface, merely reflect a growing reaction to bourgeois forms of reasoning and ideology. And, as has been the case throughout class history, ideological forms of reasoning have taken a significant toll among potential materialist thinkers. The main task, then, is to analyze socialism and international economic relations in terms of the historical process they represent, i.e., the progressive elimination of the contradiction between social production and private appropriation. In order to carry out such an analysis, however, it is necessary to create a greater awareness of existing ideological forms of theoretical interpretation which obscure a materialist explanation of socioeconomic relations. We have restricted ourselves in this paper to presenting what we consider the essential guidelines. The theoretical conception of analysis, based on dialectical-historical materialism, was established long ago in Marx's work on capital/labor relations — a specific form of class production, appropriation, and accumulation — and on his insights into the socialist process of transformation. We have restricted ourselves to attempting to explain one of the ideological formulations operating today within the social sciences, i.e., dependency theory.

## REFERENCES

Amin, Samir
    1973 "Underdevelopment and Dependence in Black Africa, Their Historical Origins and Contemporary Forms," *Social and Economic Studies* (XXII) 177-196

Amuzegar, Jahangir
1976 "The North-South Dialogue: From Conflict to Compromise," *Foreign Affairs*, LIV (April), 547-562

Bambirra, Vania
1974 *El capitalismo dependiente latinoamericano*, Mexico City: Siglo XXI

1978 *Teoría de la dependencia: una anticrítica*, Mexico City: Ediciones Era

Cardoso, Fernando Henrique
1974 "O Inimigo de papel," *Latin American Perspectives*, I (Spring), 66-74

1976 "The Consumption of Dependency Theory in the United States," Latin American Studies Association, Atlanta, mimeographed

Cardoso, Fernando Henrique and E. Faletto
1967 *Dependencia y desarrollo en América Latina*, Mexico City: Siglo XXI

Castañeda, Jorge and Enrique Hett
1978 *El economismo dependentista*, Mexico City: Siglo XXI

Cueva, Agustín
1976 "A Summary of 'Problems and Perspectives of Dependency Theory,'" *Latin American Perspectives*, III (Fall), 12-16

De Montbrial, Thierry
1975 "For a New World Economic Order," *Foreign Affairs*, LIII (October), 61-78

Dos Santos, Theotônio
1969 "El nuevo carácter de la dependencia," in José Matos Mar (ed.), *La crisis del desarrollismo y la nueva dependencia*, Lima: Instituto de Estudios Peruanos, Amorrortu Editores

1970a "La crisis de la teoría del desarrollo y las relaciones de dependencia en América Latina," pp. 147-187 in Helio Jaguaribe et al. (eds.), *La dependencia político-económica de América Latina*, Mexico City: Siglo XXI

1970b *Dependencia y cambio social*, Santiago: Centro de Estudios Socio-Económicos

1971 *La crisis norteamericana y la América Latina*, Bogotá: Ediciones el Tigre de Papel

1978 *Imperialismo y dependencia*, Mexico City: Ediciones Era

Eckstein, Susan
1978 "Cuba and the World Economy: The Limits of Socialism in One Country," World Congress of Sociology, Uppsala, Sweden, manuscript

Ehrensaft, Phillip
1971 "Semi-Industrial Capitalism in the Third World: Implications for Social Research in Africa," *Africa Today*, XVIII (January), 40-67

Fagen, Richard
1977 "Studying Latin American Politics: Some Implications of a Dependencia," *Latin American Research Review*, XII (2), 3-26

Fernández, Raúl A. and José F. Ocampo
1974 "The Latin American Revolution: A Theory of Imperialism, Not Dependence," *Latin American Perspectives*, I (Spring), 30-61

Fraisse
1904 "International Situation of the Dependent Countries of the Congo Basin," Carcassone, thesis

Frank, André Gunder
1966 "The Development of Underdevelopment," *Monthly Review*, XVII (September), 17-31

1969a *Desarrollo del subdesarrollo*, Mexico City: Escuela Nacional de Antropología

1969b *Latin America: Underdevelopment and Revolution*, New York: Monthly Review Press

1971a *Capitalism and Underdevelopment in Latin America*, London: Penguin

1971b *Lumpenburguesía: lumpendesarrollo*, Mexico City: Serie Popular ERA

1974 "Dependence is Dead. Long Live Dependence and the Class Struggle: A Reply to Critics," *Latin American Perspectives*, I (Spring), 87-106

Furtado, Celso
1969a *Dialéctica del desarrollo*, Mexico City: Fondo de Cultura Económica

1969b *La economía latinoamericana desde la conquista iberiana hasta la revolución cubana*, Mexico City: Siglo XXI

1970 *Obstacles to Development in Latin America*, New York: Doubleday

Gilbert, Guy
1974 "Socialism and Dependency," *Latin American Perspectives*, I (Spring), 107-123

Girvan, Norman
1973 "The Development of Dependency Economics in the Caribbean and Latin America: Review and Comparison," *Social and Economic Studies* (22), 1-33

González Casanova, Pablo
1967 "América Latina: la 'imposibilidad' del desarrollo," Toulouse: IIIéme Congrés International D'économie, July 24-28

Hobson, John A.
1971 *Imperialism*, Ann Arbor, Michigan: Ann Arbor Paperbacks

Jalée, Pierre
1969 *The Third World in World Economy*, New York: Monthly Review Press

1970 *El imperialismo en 1970*, Mexico City: Siglo XXI

Kalmanovitz, Salomon
1975 "Note critique: 'Théorie de la dépendance' ou théorie de l'impérialisme," *Sociologie du Travail*, LXXV (1), 78-104

Leaver, R.
1977 "The Debate on Underdevelopment: 'On Situating Gunder Frank'," *Journal of Contemporary Asia*, VII (1), 108-115

Lenin, V.I.
1970 *On the National and Colonial Questions*, Peking: Foreign Language Press

1974 *El desarrollo del capitalismo en Rusia*, Moscow: Editorial Progreso

Leys, Colin
1977 "Underdevelopment and Dependency: Critical Notes," *Journal of Contemporary Asia*, VII (1), 92-107

Marini, Ruy Mauro
1969 *Subdesarrollo y revolución*, Mexico City: Siglo XXI

1973 *Dialéctica de la dependencia*, Mexico City: Serie Popular ERA

1978 "Las razones del neodesarrollismo (o por qué me ufano de mi burguesía)," *Revista Latinamericana de Sociología* (2), 174-236

Marx, Karl
1964 *Pre-Capitalist Economic Formations*, London: Lawrence & Wishart

1974 *Capital*, 3 vols., New York: International Publishers

Marx, Karl and Frederick Engels
1964 *The German Ideology*, Moscow: Progress Publishers

Nun, José
1969 "Superpoblación relativa, ejército industrial de reserva y masa marginal," *Revista Mexicana de Sociología* (2), 174-236

Pearson, Lester B.
1970 *The Crisis of Development*, New York: Praeger

Quijano Obregón, Aníbal
1970 "Redefinición de la dependencia y proceso de marginalización en América Latina," Mexico City: Associación de Becarios del Instituto de Investigaciones Social, mimeographed

Ray, David
1973 "The Dependency Model of Latin American Underdevelopedment: Three Basic Fallacies," *Journal of Inter-American and World Affairs,* XV (February), 4-20

Redslob, Robert
1914 *Dependent Countries (An Analysis of the Concept of Original Ruling Power),* Leipzig

Rock, Vincent P.
1964 *A Strategy of Interdependence,* New York: Charles Scribner's Sons

Sindico, D.
1977 "New Left Theories of the Modes of Production," *Studies in Marxism* (I), 95-102

Wallerstein, Immanuel
1974 "Dependence in an Interdependent World; the Limited Possibilities of Transformation within the Capitalist World Economy, *African Studies Review,* XVII (April) 1-26

Werner, Roy A.
1978 "The Economic Impact of American Oil Dependency," *Current History,* LXXV (July-August), 1-4

# 4

## DEPENDENCY THEORY, IMPERIALISM, AND THE PRODUCTION OF SURPLUS VALUE ON A WORLD SCALE

*by*
*Gary Nigel Howe**

Fernando Henrique Cardoso and Enzo Faletto (1979: xxiii) have announced what has long been suspected, i.e., that dependency *theory* is no more. This should give rise to few regrets. Its well known emphasis upon relations among nations rather than among classes (cf. Roxborourgh,, 1979: 46) and its characteristic definition of modes of production in terms of circulation (Laclau, 1977: 15-50) marked it as a theory which sought to understand the dynamics of capitalism without a grasp of its basic organizational units. However, the demise of dependency theory has left a vacuum in the theory of the international capitalist system, for the turn to local class relations does not provide an alternative to the general systematics of the dependency school. Neither does the classical theory of imperialism fill the gap. On the contrary, both the theory of imperialism and dependency theory are strongly circulationist in character, and neither can come to terms with transformations in the system of division of labor. We will provide an alternative based on the global organization of the *production* of surplus value, attempting to periodize the international capitalist system in terms of internal contradictions in systems of production (in both core and periphery) giving rise to transformations in the structure of production in both areas — in a complementary fashion involving the articulation of modes of production on a global scale. What follows will attempt to provide a framework for an analysis based on contradictions within complex, unevenly developed systems of production of surplus value as well as to indicate some of the fundamental issues giving rise to the theories of dependency (especially in the Brazilian case) and imperialism as perspectives incapable of realizing in thought the changing forms of capitalist production and accumulation on a world scale.

### INDUSTRIAL EXPANSION AND DEPENDENCY THEORY

The onset of the world depression created the conditions for a significant

*The author, who teaches sociology at the American University in Washington, D.C., wishes to thank Elizabeth Kuznesof and Steven Soiffer for their valuable suggestions at an early point in the development of this essay.

expansion of industrial production in Brazil in the 1930s — an expansion overwhelmingly concentrated in traditional consumer-good industries. This expansion, however, was not based upon the political hegemony of the industrial bourgeoisie. The revolution of 1930, for example, is much better understood in terms of crisis in relations between fractions of the agrarian bourgeoisie than of the ascendancy of industrial interests (Basbaum, 1962). The period of world crisis facilitated local industrialization without putting it to the test as a *policy*. This situation was to change rather rapidly with the post-war reorganization of the international system, with the emergence of industrialization as a ' *political* problematic involving contradictory interests within the ruling class itself. Very schematically, substantial tensions developed between national industrial fractions of capital and agrarian capital producing for both foreign and national markets — a conflict precipitated by national industrial capital's necessarily confiscatory need for the surplus value extracted in the agrarian sector (cf. Baer, 1965; Oliveira, 1972). Industrial capital was itself divided, especially from the mid-1950s on. On the one hand, capital was involved in the production of elementary wage goods and organized in a relatively competitive fashion with a market determined by the real income of the working class. This capital was, on the whole, opposed to inflows of private foreign capital — a posture less explicable in terms of nationalist sentiments than in terms of the particular character of international capital, i.e., its monopoly character (Cohn, 1968: 89-90). On the other hand, a fraction of industrial capital was increasingly involved in the production of luxury goods for the middle and upper classes. This fraction was interested in diminishing the available income of the working class and in associating with foreign monopoly capital with which it could fully exploit a protected Brazilian market (Martins, 1976: 396-397).

This set of contradictory interests provided the effective basis for the brief rise to prominence of dependency theory in Brazil — framing the possibility of a brief and unstable alliance between the industrial working class and the fraction of national capital producing wage goods. It was an alliance against foreign capital built upon the historical immiseration of the working class and the threat of destruction confronting national capital in the competitive sector. That the theory of this alliance was oriented to the relations among nations rather than between classes directly expressed the trans-class character of the alliance. That it portrayed *monopoly* capital, rather than capital per se, as the exploiter clearly reflected this factor (a concern about which had been voiced in the 1920s — see Topik, 1978) and also pinpointed the specific form of the foreign threat. That industry was represented as the source of wealth and agriculture as the source of underdevelopment clearly reflected the growing antagonism between national industrial capital and agriculture in relation to economic policy (with the agrarian interests being clearly inclined toward a more internationalist position). In short, dependency theory appeared as the international ideology of populism (cf. Weffort, 1978: 165-181) — a theory as much directed to the reorganization of relations among the leading fractions of the Brazilian bourgeoisie as to the reorganization of international relations. Its peculiarities, its nationalist character, its location of exploitation at the level of international circulation rather than national production, and its fascination with industry all mark it as a creature of a period of disarray within the capitalist camp. The attempted cross-class alliances to determine a particular path of development of the productive system was opposed by significant fractions of national and international capital alike.

Two sets of factors can help to explain the collapse of dependency theory in Brazil, and both are connected to the political and economic collapse of the national alliance for development. On the one hand, the defeat of the alliance and the rapid penetration by foreign capital (Pignaton, 1973) actually accelerated the rate of Brazilian industrial expansion. The cherished idea that openness to foreign influence inhibits industrial development appeared disproved — as even some of the dependency theorists themselves were bound to admit under the rubric of "associated dependent development" (cf. Cardoso, 1973). Probably more important than this, however, was the *form* the defeat took, a form which denied the premises of the alliance's own ideology. The defeat was not one of the alliance being overcome by the internationalist fractions of industrial and agrarian capital, rather it involved the destruction of the alliance itself — from within.

## CLASS STRUGGLE AND THEORIES OF IMPERIALISM

The growth of working class political consciousness and independent organization, in part accelerated by involvement in the struggles of fractions of capital, brought to the fore the fact that the struggle was not simply one of "national development" but one of development on particular class terms. The increasing unwillingness of the working class to accept the national bourgeoisie's definition of national development led to a progressive disassociation of the two sides with the bourgeois fraction moving toward the international fractions of capital in order to maintain the minimum common prerogatives of capital. Simply, the more popular *the* alliance became, the more "national" capital inclined toward consolidation with international and monopoly capital. The illusion of national unity was shattered, and the struggle became more clearly defined. In relation to the question of national development, the struggle decreasingly took the form of a conflict between "nationalist" popular and bourgeois forces on the one hand and international and "comprador" forces on the other. Rather, it emerged as an immensely clarified struggle between capital and labor (cf. Erickson, 1977).

The tragic social and political consequences of the inevitable rupture in the developmentalist front do not have to be recounted here. The point is that it precipitated the emergence of a quite new universe of political action and ideological discourse, a universe in which *class* questions of the relation between labor and capital, of exploitation in the system of production, and of the ultimate unity of capital displaced the nationalist and circulationist problematics of dependency theory. Thus the theory collapsed with the transnational conjuncture from which it had sprung, leading to the emergence of a different sort of theory — one much more cautious about simply lining up nation against nation (as well as lining up the bourgeoisie *with* the nation), one more insistent upon paying attention to class struggles within dependent areas in determining paths of transformation of systems of production — a theory much more insistent upon the *capitalist* nature of the global system.

On the level of appearances this shift in problematic is not immediately evident. Frank (1972b: 1), for example, promised an analysis of dependency in terms of class struggle, though this was never developed. In this sense, the shift was less one involving a radical change in terminology than one involving the emergence of an emphasis upon the *primacy* of the class struggle. This shift appeared simultaneously as a crisis and an opportunity. On the one hand, the emphasis upon class rather than spacial relations would destroy the embracing systematics of the position developed by Frank (global chains of dependency). In short, the destruction of the larger theory reduced the world to its class elements (international and national). On the other, this made possible the theoretical reconstruction of the world system around quite a different theory of value and exploitation. Specifically, it made possible (even demanded) a rigorous Marxist analysis of the international system. Yet this challenge was never met. The eclipse of "classical" dependency theory gave rise to no theory at all, with the exception, outside of Latin America, of an essentially bourgeois "world system theory" (see Brenner, 1977; Howe and Sica, 1980). The result was an increasing unwillingness to discuss a general theory of "dependency" and a tendency to see the world as the product of more or less particular class struggles (cf. Cardoso and Faletto, 1979). Insofar as we see a more "Marxist" analysis develop, it remains very much within the basic terms of dependency theory itself — attention is concentrated upon the international distribution of wealth and upon new *forces* organizing the international system (not nations but multinational corporations). This inability to reform a structural analysis of the global system in which local class struggles and particular forms of organization of capital appear as the determined effect of the general global movement of capital, in short the continued particularization of the style of analysis, is not simply the product of a failure to come to terms with a general theory of capital. On the contrary, it points to major difficulties in *developing* a general theory of capital able to account for the real historical phenomena which provided substantial ammunition for dependency theory's initial assault upon the advanced world's saccharine theories of international development — i.e., the unequal international development of forces and relations of production (the slow development of industry in the periphery and the continued existence of large populations within precapitalist relations of production).

Notwithstanding the resurgence of self-proclaimed Marxist analyses of imperialism in the last two decades, the classical Marxist theory of the internationalization of capital had relatively little to say about the unequal development of productive forces and relations. With the exceptions of Luxemburg (1972: 47-150), who was unsure whether to put the issue at the level of circulation or production, and Kautsky (e.g., 1970: x-xiii), who dealt with formations internal to the advanced areas themselves, the question of the relation between imperialism and the preservation of "backwardness" not only went unanswered, it went unasked.

As we have shown elsewhere (Howe and Sica, 1980), Marx's own comments on the international system of capital did not address systematically the mechanics of international exploitation nor did he suggest that the development of such a system would of necessity involve consequences detrimental to the periphery in the long term.

Curiously enough, neither is it possible to mobilize the various theories of imperialism flourishing before and after the First World War to provide that Marxist theory of differentiation in the international system required to fill the theoretical gap left by dependency theory's demise. Even a superficial perusal of the works of Lenin, Hobson, and Trotsky reveals that the theory of imperialism did not revolve around the exploitation of the periphery, and *a fortiori,* was not about the underdevelopment of the periphery. The dominant concern was with class relations in the core and the relations among core states rather than with core-periphery relations — relating to the immiseration of the core working class (Hobson, 1938) and the military struggle among imperialist powers (Lenin, 1975). While there was some elaboration of the effects of imperialism upon the periphery, the effects charted (with the exception of some of Lenin's pronouncements to which we shall return) were quite different from those identified by post-Second World War theorists. Specifically, they were not represented as necessarily involving deepening international disparities in wealth and types of production. Rather, the economic factors giving rise to imperialism as a political system of unequal power and domination were portrayed as contributing to a relative homogenization of economic development throughout the world system — a long term perspective differing but little from that offered by Marx (Howe and Sica, 1980).

This reading of the Marxist theory of imperialism is not particularly compatible with the uses it was put to after the Second World War. The bridge was provided by Lenin himself, particularly in the *1920* preface to the German and French editions of *Imperialism — The Highest Stage of Capitalism.* There Lenin put quite a different emphasis on the export of capital. Rather than treat it as a mechanism of international equalization, it was represented as a means of exploitation within a remarkably nationalist frame of reference. Thus, Lenin gave vent to the opinion that Britain was becoming a *rentier* nation, enjoying a mounting income from abroad which allowed sections of the British proletariat to be "bought off" — to be mobilized in support of the imperialist interests of the British bourgeoisie. Using more violent imagery, he referred to "a handful . . . of exceptionally rich and powerful states which plunder the whole world simply by 'clipping coupons' " (Lenin, 1975: 3). Of course, clipping coupons cannot be said to be in itself a hindrance to capitalist development, so, to remove all ambiguity about whether imperialism actually hinders peripheral development, Lenin went on to warn of "the financial *strangulation* of the overwhelming majority of the population of the world by a handful of 'advanced' countries" (Lenin, 1975: 11, emphases mine) — an emphasis upon the repatriation of profits as a central mechanism of underdevelopment strongly restated in Baran's *Political Economy of Growth* (Baran, 1957: especially 142-150).

The major shift in emphasis between this later position and that expounded in the original edition of *Imperialism* is quite clear, and involves that process of *politicization* of the theory of the international economy (the politically motivated suppression of basic structured conflicts between classes in favor of conflict among nations) which, Arrighi (1978: 20) argues, contributed to the astonishing disarray of the left after the Second World War. This shift allowed an alliance between popular forces and national bourgeois fractions against the developed imperialist powers — but only at the expense of the erosion of the integrity of the theory of imperialism as a special case of theory of capitalist development.

As Owen and Sutcliffe observed (1972: 320-321), critiques of imperialism after the Second World War were increasingly rooted in the periphery rather than in core proletarian parties, and they reflected the class compromise necessary in the formation of united fronts against imperialism. It is important to note, however, that the ideological expression of this compromise did not, in spite of its nationalist-circulationist perspective, involve a fundamental deviation from Marxist economics as developed by Lenin. On the contrary, Lenin had subtly laid the groundwork in economic analysis for abandonment of the hitherto accepted equation of internationalization with homogenization. Politics were accompanied by a theory. Specifically, the theory of monopoly finance capital in Lenin's work opened the way for a departure from the classical theory of the international system in a manner similar to the way in which the theory of monopoly capital would later be used to justify departure from the law of value (cf. Baran and Sweezy, 1966: 3-7). The theory of monopoly capital allows a change in the rules of analysis without necessitating the repudiation of Marxist concepts. In particular, it allows representation of the historical system of productive relations in terms of the interests of a restricted group of forces. It is a theory of *capitalism* dominated by particular *capitals,* and thus it is fundamentally subjectivist in character. This inversion of the Marxist analysis of capitalism (the structure creates the part, not the part the structure) made possible an elaboration of the dependency scenario in Marxist terms — even though it would appear to contradict the propositions generated by Marx, Trotsky, and even Lenin himself. It was possible to argue that rather than leading to the establishment of manufacturing capacity in the periphery, a falling rate of profit leads, in the context of imperialism organized by monopolies, to quite the opposite result. Monopoly finance capital of the core (without the support of which no productive activity is possible) will defend the value (monopoly position and higher-than-average rate of profit) of its existing industrial investments in the core itself, prohibiting industrial development in the periphery and consigning the periphery to the role of secured supplier of raw materials. Lenin does not present his position in exactly this way, but it is a legitimate reconstruction of a Third World position. It also appears to be the unstated and undefended premise of Frank's early work, which shows itself to be less a simple direct reflection of the Latin American united front problematic than a reworking of an established (albeit undefended) theory of monopoly capital abstracted from its "crisis of capital" context, promulgated as the normal condition of the international capitalist system, and semantically metamorphosed so that what was brought into the world as *"monopoly capital"* re-emerges as *"metropolitan* capital."

The essential parallel between Leninist and dependency analyses certainly facilitated the "Marxianization" of theories of the international system in the wake of the collapse of the developmentalist alliance and the shift of international attention to the more revolutionary character of the anti-imperialist struggle in Africa and Asia in the 1960s and 1970s. However, it is by no means clear that this shift toward Lenin brings us closer to a full understanding of the historical periodization of imperialism and its dynamic. On the contrary, we would suggest that this alternative to the classical dependency theory is no alternative at all. Not only does it fail to grasp the dynamics of a world capitalist system, but it also fails to answer systematically and precisely the questions upon which dependency theory itself began to flounder: it fails to give the rudiments of an answer to why the productive structure of some areas of the Third World is changing radically. The imperialist structure of the late nineteenth and early twentieth century was, sadly, *not* the highest stage of capitalism, and Lenin gives us little indication of the essential dynamics of a stage that could not exist. Hence, in the wake of the collapse of the classical dependency paradigm, there is almost no theory. To be sure, we are now convinced that we are dealing with *capitalism*, but this capitalism is curiously amorphous, being reduced to circumstances and situations with unique local contradictions and struggles, with classes undergoing mystical metamorphoses (now "national," now "international"), with lurking multinational corporations (MNCs) striving for profits (without a theory of global surplus value) which contradict a desire (on whose part we do not know) for "development" (surely one of the least illuminating categories of historical analysis, appropriated uncritically from the ideology of fractions of the Third World bourgeoisie). This is not the exclusive problem of the analysis of the world capitalist system. On the contrary, it reflects a dominant tendency in Western Marxism since the 1920s, in which a proper rejection of economism has led (improperly) to a concentration not on the production of surplus value (surely the heart of any Marxist analysis), but on the production of legitimacy (cf. Anderson, 1976). We suggest that the problem lies not with the original theory of capital but with the particular manner it has been approached and that a theory of international differentiation and the periodization of imperialism can be excavated from the vitals of *Capital*, but only at the expense of abandoning the (bourgeois) problematic of distribution in favor of the Marxist problematic of production.

## UNEVEN DEVELOPMENT AND THE RELATIONS AND FORCES OF PRODUCTION

We will not dwell here upon the exaggerated estimate Lenin made of the role of monopoly finance capital in the "highest stage of capitalism" nor upon the problems of assuming monopoly organization at the international level in the contemporary conjuncture. It is important to note, however, that the identification of the basic differentiation among capitals in terms of their entrepreneurial organization and their position in the system of circulation of capital and commodities (monopoly position, etc.) — in short, to forms of administrative control over capital — expresses the remarkable inattention to the possibility (necessity?) of differentiating among capitals according to their position in the productive system (of surplus value). Though Hobson was no Marxist, his picture of surplus capital simply flowing abroad in a response to failing domestic investment opportunities captures a certain indifference to the practical organization of the system of production of surplus value common in the period. Equally common was the totally unproblematic character of the issue of the types of production this mobile capital would find in the periphery. In the discussion of the international leveling or homogenization referred to above, the implication seems to be that the process is one involving less the homogenization of processes of production than the homogenization of relations of production (i.e., the internationalization of capital as a social relationship) and rates of profit — with the material processes of production within which this new surplus value was produced being quite independent of the conditions precipitating imperialism (being quite irrelevant and of no consequence for the development of capitalism). The same might be said of the social conditions of production encountered at the periphery. The question of their actual form (and their relation to the crisis of capital) could be blithely ignored within the parameters of a theory committed to the idea of the eradication of all national and local differences (cf. Crisenoy, 1979, on Lenin's assumptions in *The Development of Capitalism in Russia*).

Rigorous as this indifference to material processes and use values might appear from the perspective of the theory of capital, it is quite inadequate to the task of conceptualizing capitalist expansion and transformation — not least because it is decidely un-Marxist in its representation of the functioning of capitalism. Capital is undifferentiated only from the perspective of circulation — in accordance with the law of the equalization of rates of profit. Yet it should be noted that for Marx the secret of capitalism lies not in circulation but in production (Marx, 1967a: 175-176). Further, even though Marx in *Capital* seeks a characterization of capitalist production, he does not rest his case upon a characterization of capitalist production *in general*. On the contrary, the production of surplus value appears as the result of the *articulation* of differentiated types of production: in terms of use value, the articulation between Departments I and II; in terms of production of commodities, the articulation between simple commodity production (see the case of the British bakers, Marx, 1967a: 248) and capitalist production proper; in terms of surplus value within capitalist production proper, the relation between absolute and relative surplus value; in terms of capitalist work processes, the relation between real and formal subsumption of labor. The point here is simply that the capitalist production of surplus value is a unified system (of mutual determinations), but it involves the unity of *differences*. Furthermore, it is a dynamic unity. In the process of capitalist *transformation*, the relations between these elements change (otherwise where is the reality of transformation?) in, of course, a determined fashion corresponding not only to the "laws" of development of the economy, but also to the development of the social struggle on local and global scales (cf. Mandel, 1980: 47-56). In this case, the contemporary attention to the question of articulation of modes of production (Foster-Carter, 1978) appears as but one of the articulation issues and one whose apparent simplicity may represent the conflation of all the above articulations.

Production, then, appears as a historically changing system of articulation of different systems. And we suggest that what this offers, i.e., the possibility of a dynamic, differentiated historical analysis of the development of the structure of production of surplus value, is nothing less than the real ground for an explanation of the differentiated/uneven international development of forces and relations of production identified in theories of imperialism and underdevelopment. Maintaining one of the fundamental theses of the dependentistas, the changing "location" (in terms of these differentiated systems) of crisis in the production of surplus value (which appears from the perspective of circulation as a crisis of capital as a whole) in the core determines specific kinds of transformations in both relations and forces of production in the periphery. In the last analysis, the international system is built upon the logic of the uneven development of relations and forces of production. This approach dictates that we pass from the circulationism of early theories of imperialism to a form of "productionism," arguing that every crisis in circulation/realization is the product of a historically specific contradiction in production (cf. Mandel, 1978) which corresponds to the stage of capitalist development (of forces and relations of production — under which we subsume the class struggle). The peripheral reorganization in response to core crises must reflect the specific nature of the crises giving rise to them. What we suggest then is that the logic of capitalist development on the international level involves relations of complementarity (hence differentiation) between core and periphery; that this complementarity actually takes the form of complementarity in production (which is in no way reducible to the international distribution of global surplus value as realized in profits); that the development of the international system corresponds to crises in both core *and* periphery; and that the possibility of the relative harmonization (through complementarity) of these core and peripheral contradictions arises from the essential structure of imperialism as not only a differentiated system of forces of production (including division of labor), but as a differentiated system of relations of production — a system, in short, whose very essence is the articulation of modes of production (and all that stands for as a complex, over-determined phenomenon). While circulation, as the empirical nexus of articulation, must appear dominant, production is always determinant (cf. Marx, 1966: 470-546).

Given the preliminary character of current analyses of the capitalist production process and given present limitations of space, we will seek to draw only the general outlines of the theory of the relation between capitalist crises (viewed from the perspective of production of surplus value) and the organization of peripheral production, providing the framework for a coherent analysis of the stages of development of forces and relations of production in Latin American in the last hundred years. This outline will divide the modern history of the world system of capitalist production into two phases, the first corresponding to the imperialist epoch of the development of primary production for export at the periphery (the phase of the internationalization of finance capital), and the second corresponding to the development in some peripheral areas of industrialized systems of production in the wake of the long capitalist crisis stretching from 1914 to 1945. This latter phase, characteristically dominated by the multinational corporation, consists of the internationalization of production.

We suggest that the first stage of the modern international system, that of the export of capital to stimulate peripheral primary production, responded to a specific contradiction in the dominant system of production of surplus value whose essence is obscured by reference to "the falling rate of profit" and "monopoly capital" (which were mere symptoms). Following closely Palloix's (1978) analysis of nineteenth century English capitalist development, we may say that the dominant system of surplus value in the nineteenth century (even in the advanced capitalist areas) was one of absolute surplus value, i.e., a system based upon the intensification of labor and the extension of the working day. Two striking aspects of the situation of the emerging proletariat were, on the one hand, the rigors factory discipline imposed upon them, and, on the other, their — even to contemporary observers — astonishing poverty (see Marcus, 1975). It is worthwhile considering briefly the nature of this poverty, for, in a certain sense, it shapes the struggle over the intensity and length of the working day as well as the particular character the global system of differentiated production was to assume under imperialism (though not through direct mechanisms such as "underconsumption").

The value of labor in this period was not in large measure determined within the capitalist industrial system. The working class did not consume large amounts of industrialized products in the process of its reproduction. For example, in 1853 approximately 60 percent by value of all British cotton goods were *exported*. This is rather paradoxical, for we associate the rise of industrial capitalism in England to the vast expansion of the industrial production of what appear to be basic wage goods, i.e., textiles. Nonetheless, a very large part of this production went not to the reproduction of the work force, but to the sumptuary requirements of the nonproductive sections of the population (upper and middle classes) and to foreign markets. The obverse side of this situation was that a significant part of the reproduction of labor took place outside of the sphere of capitalist production proper — in the domestic systems of production of both town and country.

A significant conclusion which can be drawn from this is that the revolution in the forces of production in the period (i.e., the much vaunted increase in the efficiency of human labor in the machine system) could not contribute significantly to the rate of surplus value except insofar as it provided means for the intensification of labor. The crisis character of this situation is evident: on the one hand, a rising organic composition of capital; on the other, restriction within a system of absolute surplus value — the possibility of expansion of which was clearly circumscribed by natural (human capacity) and social (worker organization, etc.) limits. Given upper limits on the extension/intensification of core labor, the sole means of transcendence of the immediate crisis of surplus value in the core was to address the nonindustrialized sector of the means of consumption, i.e., that which produced foodstuffs for consumption by the core working class (and raw materials for industrial production). It was on precisely this basis that the massive expansion of the international economic system took place in the last part of the nineteenth century. That is to say, the expansion of the primary producing role of the periphery reflected a determined crisis of surplus value in the core which could only be resolved through reorganization of production in the nonindustrial branch of the section of the means of consumption.

Here we see the export of products giving way to the export of capital, though both in varying degrees correspond to the same conditions — i.e., the reproduction of labor beyond the sphere of capitalist industry. It is imperative to grasp the fact that the export of capital necessarily involved the reorganization of peripheral production (otherwise how would surplus value be extracted?), which was necessarily oriented to the site of disequilibrium in the core (as the point of realization). That is, it was an export of capital in specific forms, shaped by a specific contradiction in the core.

That the periphery (or certain areas within it) assumed the role of major supplier of nonindustrial means of consumption in the global process of production of surplus value is, in part, explicable from the "demand" side. However, the fact that the *periphery* could meet this demand was itself contingent upon the existence or development (easier than in the core itself) of its specific relations of production. The periphery's insertion into the world market as a supplier of primary materials represented the union of a system of international capitalist commodity circulation with a system of production dominated by precapitalist social relations. Hence, the characteristic "anomaly" of the combination of "feudalism" and "capitalism" in Latin American transformations. These relations of production were not anomalous in this world-wide expansion of capitalist production. On the contrary, they were the very basis of the internationalization of production, determining the possibility of entry of products into the core as "cheap" raw materials. While in no way wishing to make light of cultural and other factors in the development of the system of precapitalist relations of production in Latin America, for example, their preservation (and extension) in the era of imperialism corresponds to a singular aspect of the production of agricultural commodities. Notwithstanding the efficiency gains to be had from capital investment in agriculture production, there is a tendency for the products of precapitalist agriculture to (be able to) circulate at prices below those which are possible for equivalent products of capitalist production proper. This phenomenon has been recognized for some time (cf. Marx, 1967b: 805-806), and corresponds to the fact that agricultural products extracted from precapitalist producers tend to be the *surplus* products of the producer (i.e., what remains *after* he has reproduced himself), with the implication that the value received by the producer from the sale of his (surplus) products does not have to cover the costs of his reproduction (as must be the case even in simple commodity production). In consequence, the price *may* be lower than the equilibrium price of the capitalist producer — the actual price typically corresponding to political conditions and the organization of land tenure (as the means of forcible extraction of surplus). The optimum condition for the maximum production of surplus value in an industrial system dominated by absolute surplus value is, then, not the subsumption of all producers directly under capitalist relations of production, but, as Rey (1973) has pointed out, the articulation of modes of production, the subjugation of a (more or less) preserved precapitalist mode of production, a subjugation taking the practical form of enforced production of surplus products.

The immanent logic of the first phase of imperialism might be represented less as a process of homogenization, which it *appears* to be from the point of view of the theory of distribution, than as a process of increasing heterogeneity, involving in the periphery the massive encouragement of primary production (in contrast to the secondary concentration in the core) and the consolidation (within transformation) of precapitalist relations of production — both aspects being determined by the problematic of the production of surplus value in the dominant capitalist social formations at a particular point of development of their own relations and forces of production. The relative concentration of exported capital in infrastructural projects in the periphery illustrates the salient characteristics of the emergent system: the importance of the export of products to the core (necessitating development of means of communication and entrepôt centers) and the salience of precapitalist relations in the productive process (hence the low level of investment directly in the productive process itself). In this respect, it is important to note that the development of seemingly free labor regimes in the place of slavery in the periphery at this period in no way refutes the proposition that production was organized within precapitalist relations of production. For example, labor relations involving imported "free" labor in the coffee plantations of Brazil were permeated with noncapitalist elements, e.g., coercive and extended labor contracts and, not least, the importance of subsistence production (sometimes in the form of intercalary crops) in self-reproduction of the plantation labor force (this entered into the *first* clause of the standard contract for colonos — cf. Netto, 1959: 132). It is worthwhile noting, against possible nationalist arguments, that this productive complex of precapitalist production of foodstuffs for the core working class was not reserved by core capital for the periphery alone. In fact, this surge of precapitalist relations was experienced in the agricultural branch of the means of consumption more or less everywhere — for example, in the generalized retreat from large-scale capitalist production of wheat to family-farm production in the last third of the nineteenth century. This was concentrated in new expanding frontier areas such as the United States, but it was also eventually to penetrate even British agriculture (see Friedman, 1976). The point is quite simple; the dynamics of the system involved, in the first instance, not the reorganization of relations between regions but between sections and branches of production involved in the process of production of surplus value. It eventually required a regional complexion not because of the imposition by nation upon nation but because of different regional economic and political possibilities of expanding production in the precapitalist sector according to the level of development of relations of production and class conflict. On the whole it seems unwise to see the path of peripheral development as corresponding *only* to core interests, except in a very restricted number of cases. On the contrary, this particular mode of insertion into the world capitalist system offered distinct advantages to the ruling classes of the periphery (particularly in Latin America), classes whose situation can be characterized as being long on political power and short on capital. The preservation of precapitalist relations in producing for the world market corresponded perfectly to the interests of the peripheral ruling classes insofar as accumulation could be based almost entirely on their political relations with producers (as mediated through the politically constructed system of private property and "rent") — just as, one might add, the international market offered opportunities for the realization of surplus value such as were unavailable in the periphery by virtue of the absence of capitalist relations of production.

The structure of the international economic system emerging at the end of the nineteenth century corresponded to contradictions in both core and periphery — the crisis of surplus value of the core (and its particular location) and the realization crisis of the dominant classes of the periphery. It is only as a result of the interaction between these two sets of factors that the particular form of peripheral production and foreign investment can be understood — it being clear that neither set of factors is reducible to the autonomous will of interested parties but corresponds to the nature of the modes of production involved and the dominant classes within them. That the path of development of production in the periphery was, indeed, ultimately shaped by the crisis of surplus value in the core is undeniable, but this subordination was not of a political kind. Rather, the most appropriate way of conceptualizing the situation is of the development of "needs" in one part of a system which allows for the expansion of production in another part — on the basis of pre-existing relations of production and in order to overcome a pre-existing local contradiction. The logic of the system is one of articulation of the structural compatibility of demands arising from the tension within both sides of the system. It is, truly, a system of submission of core to periphery — but this submission must be understood in terms of the logic of relations between modes of production rather than in subjectivist terms (a point to which we shall return below). In terms of a very different style of discourse, the point is not that the international system is ostensibly organized by those pursuing returns to capital or political power, for this is both undeniable and unilluminating. The real issue is the series of contradictions which make this or that production in specific relations of production profitable in the first instance. For that, we have to leave reluctantly the world of subjective greed to enter the realm of the logic of the system of the production of surplus value as a whole.

The fruitfulness of an approach to the first stage of imperialism in terms of a crisis in the core production of surplus value requiring a determinate solution involving a specific combination of forces and relations of production on an international level is apparent — not least in suggesting a structural solution to international differentiation. However, the analysis appears to have less to offer in the secondary (contemporary) stage of imperialism, which commonly gives the appearance of a reversal (in some areas) of the trends of the first stage — i.e., it appears as a move toward the homogenization of forces/relations of production (cf. Warren, 1973). Moreover, in the case of Brazil, for example, this second stage (particularly after 1945) appears to be one in which the representation of its international economic relations in terms of the complementarity of contradictions in social relations of production is less and less valid. The organization of the relation through the international market may have granted Brazil formal autonomy in the first stage, but this appears less true for the second period given the growing direct control (in the form of local investment) exercised by the core over the peripheral economy. Moreover, analysis in terms of the articulation of national systems of production appears increasingly anachronistic by virtue of the rise of the multinational corporation. We will argue that all these appearances are false. The current international system is, even in its tendencies, characterized and determined by the uneven and complementary development of forces and relations of production. The form of peripheral integration into the international system is still in large measure determined by contradictions in the periphery itself. And the multinational corporation, rather than transcending the prior system of the articulation of national systems is precisely the mechanism through which this is achieved in contemporary capitalism (cf. Palloix, 1975). To be sure, the second stage of imperialism is different from the first, but this difference lies less in a passage from competitive to monopoly capitalism (involving new rules of the international economy) than in the development of new forces and relations of production in the core giving rise to a new crisis of surplus value — this time centered more in the United States than in the United Kingdom.

We suggest that the second stage of imperialism (as a system of articulation of modes of production) corresponds to the maturation and stagnation of a new system of production of surplus value in the core. Specifically, it involves the rise to dominance of the system of relative surplus value — corresponding to the "industrialization" of the reproduction of the working class (Ewen, 1977). Braverman (1974) has discussed this from the point of view of the work experience of the proletariat, and little needs to be added here — except that the development of mass production involved first, the growing reproduction of labor in the realm of industrial commodities, and, second, the possible reduction in the value of labor through the application of "Fordism" (mass assembly line production) and "Taylorism" (Scientific Management/dequalification of labor) in the production of wage goods. The production of surplus value was liberated from the straitjacket of the system of absolute surplus value, with the problematic of surplus value being increasingly addressed by revolutionization of forces of production and relations of real appropriation in the section of production (the section of the means of consumption) directly determining the value of labor. This system developed for the first time in the United States at the end of the nineteenth century but was brought to maturation only after the First World War with the widespread adoption of mechanized assembly line production.

## ORGANIZATION OF LABOR IN PRODUCTIVE PROCESS

While this reorganization of productive forces and relations of production was to provide a temporary relief to the crisis of capital, it brought into play a new set of contradictions eventually necessitating a reorganization of the international system of production — the dominant contradiction being that work relations necessary for the mass production of "cheap" wage goods also provided the conditions for the "production" of mass working class economic organizations militating against "cheap" labor.

This is not the place to chart in detail the vicissitudes of fate of the core working class in the period of transition from one form of imperialism to another, i.e., in the period of global economic dislocation, fascism, and world wars. However, by the end of the period we see a relative fortification of the position of labor in the productive process (if not in the political process), a change in position in the United States which can be charted in the rise of C.I.O., i.e., precisely that organization providing labor's answer to the massification and dequalification of work in the section of the means of consumption. The development of the industrialized system of production in the section of the means of consumption completely reorganized the work process, cutting across all existing lines of skill and craft — a reorganization contingent in the earlier period upon the mobilization of an industrially inexperienced and unorganized immigrant labor force. The emergence of the C.I.O. represented the reorganization of labor organization from craft to industry, the mobilization within and against the new organization of production in the section of the means of consumption.

It is part of the folklore of the left that trade unionism represents no threat to the maintenance of capitalist domination. However, it does represent a threat to the capitalist system of production of surplus value. The character of trade union demands (wages) and the relative strength with which they have been pursued have enthroned the industrial section of the means of consumption as the critical area for the determination of global surplus value. The problem of the falling rate of profit can only be resolved through a constant increase in relative surplus value, which is itself contingent upon constant reorganization of the work process. However, and here the contradiction of core capital, precisely that labor organization which has made the industrialized section of the means of consumption the major sphere of reproduction of labor also acts as a major obstacle to the constant transformation of the work process (the seriousness of which is evidenced by resort to major recessions to intimidate labor into accepting the reorganization of work). If the system of absolute value dominant in the first stage of industrialization was blocked in part by workers' opposition (necessitating reorganization of the international system), so the system of relative surplus value has been blocked by a new form of labor organization. The response to the first crisis in the system of mass production was fascism and a resurgence of political imperialism. We suggest that the response to its maturation is a new reorganization of the global system. The first reaction to the initial development of the contradiction was consolidation of the existing international division of labor, the attempt to overcome the crisis of production through control of circulation (in a throw-back to mercantilism). The limitations of this strategy are all too evident — involving an attempt to expropriate a mass of surplus value (that of the periphery) whose volume is severely limited by the role in the production system which such control over trade consolidated. Put in other terms, in a situation in which raw materials (and especially foodstuffs) were of decreasing significance in the total system of circulation (and reproduction of core labor), core expropriation of surplus value extracted in the primary production process could hardly represent a long-term solution to the crisis of production of surplus value.

Given the fundamental crisis in the production system, we suggest that the logic of the situation was not one of consolidating the existing international division of labor, but of transforming it. Specifically, it involved a shift of elements of the industrialized section of the means of consumption (not industry in general) to the periphery — resolving the immediate crisis of surplus value not by revolutionizing the work process of the section of the means of consumption (which would lead to an increase in relative surplus value), but by introducing precapitalist elements of production into the *industrial* work process — by mobilizing a work force whose very being (and means of day to day existence) is produced outside the sphere of commodities (thus lowering the "value" of labor in the section of the means of consumption and counteracting the problem of declining rate of profit in this particular section of production — the sector where mass labor organization is perhaps most advanced). Such an introduction of labor, historically produced outside the realm of commodities, can take two forms: the injection of migrant labor into the core industrial process on a massive scale (see Piore, 1979) or the internationalization of parts of the industrial work process. As we know, both of these possibilities have been realized — the first in large internal and international population movements to the industrial areas of the core, the second in selective but intense industrialization of particular peripheral areas (in a movement which gives the lie to the original formulations of dependency theory). While this is not absolutely central to an understanding of the dynamics of peripheral industrialization (as a response to a crisis in the existing global system of production of surplus value), it is worthwhile noting that a great deal of this industrialization has taken place under the direct and indirect control of core capital. Rather than defend the core's monopoly of industrial production, core capital has, in fact, promoted the expansion of certain industrial processes at the periphery.

The case of the so-called "export platforms" provides the most obvious but, perhaps, least illuminating example of core promotion of peripheral expansion in the industrialized section of the means of consumption and, to a limited extent, in the section of intermediary means (see Frobel et al., 1980). Here we have the simplest possible scenario of the exploitation of cheap peripheral labor by core capital in manufacturing processes, with the low priced products being directly shipped to the core working class. Yet these industries, simply by virtue of being so alien to the rest of the "host" country, do little to exemplify the processes of internal contradiction in the periphery, necessarily shifting industrial structures toward compatibility with the needs of the core system of production of surplus value — contradictions which block the pursuit of alternative, more "national" paths of transformation of the local organization of production.

Thus far we have developed the rudiments of an analysis of the interests of core capital in initiating a new stage of imperialism. It is worth elucidating elements of this for the comprehension of the *politics* of imperialism. The benefits of imperialism are not limited to the profit derived from this or that foreign investment. On the contrary, they extend to broad sections of core capital insofar as the effect is the lowering of the reproduction cost of labor in the core. Thus support for imperialism is general — except to the extent that capital in the core section of the means of consumption seeks to amortize its existing investments. However, this grasps only one side of the coin, a side privileging the core contradiction as the sole motor force of internationalization. To be consistent with the terms of our argument, we must now turn to the peripheral contradictions (in relations and forces of production), generating the conditions of acceptance of the complementary role — a role which involves the uneven internal development of the productive system and a nonnational path of development. Maintaining continuity in our illustrative examples, we will turn to the vicissitudes of industrial capitalist development in Brazil.

The contradiction within the section of the means of consumption at the core involved a particular and a general crisis. On the one hand, it accelerated the decline of the rate of profit in that section; on the other, it eroded global surplus value in the system of relative surplus value. In this respect it is clear that while investment in peripheral production in the section might well serve to stave off the crisis of profitability for capitals in that section, such investment did not necessarily contribute to the solution of the global crisis. Such would be the case only if the products of the peripheral branches of the section entered into the reproduction of the core working class. This did not happen in the case of foreign-led industrialization in Brazil, and in this measure the Brazilian case is more typical of the internationalization of the section of the means of consumption than the case of export platforms. Very schematically, in the first stages in Brazil production was overwhelmingly for local markets, and it was not destined for the working class (Tavares, 1978; Jenkins, 1977: 256). Apart from profit remittances it did not contribute to the relief of the profits crisis of the core nor did it contribute decisively to the level of surplus value in Brazil — which remained entrenched in the system of absolute surplus value.

This situation is changing in Brazil and a number of other semiperipheral areas — a change involving a gradual increase in the export of manufactured products (cf. Tyler, 1976; Frobel at al., 1980; Chenery and Keesing, 1979) to the core ( and to other peripheral areas). The phase of an internally oriented (albeit foreign financed) industrialization of branches of the section of the means of consumption (and, to a lesser extent, the section of intermediary means), made possible by the first crisis of the section in the core, is being superseded by a phase of reintegration of production into the international division of labor (export of means of consumption produced in basic industrial processes). This reintegration, which certainly serves to alleviate the general crisis of surplus value at the core, is not dictated by the foreign character of much capital involved in the section at the periphery but by the organization of the production process of surplus value there. The accumulations of capital in the industrialized branches of the section of the means of consumption at the periphery presents several basic problems for capital. Policies of income concentration designed to bolster the luxury goods market limit the expansion of the market for all industrial branches. On the other hand, the possibilities of mounting a new industrial section supplying means of production to the means of consumption section must be severely limited. The relative advantages of location of mass production industries in the periphery is linked to the articulation of a precapitalist system of production into the capitalist industrial work process (Oliveira, 1972; Duarte and Queda, 1974) — to the use of labor which is cheap, to be sure, but whose cheapness reflects the fact that it is not specifically produced for insertion into the industrial work process, and thus is, so to speak, labor *sans phrase*, absolutely unencumbered by any special knowledge or skill. This labor may be integrated into the work process of the mass section of the means of consumption, which was specifically designed for the integration of industrially illiterate migrant workers (as was well appreciated by Lenin — see Linhart, 1976). On the other hand, it may *not* (in its uncorrupted state) be directly integrated into the more "technical" processes characteristic of the advanced section of intermediary means and the section of the means of production. Limited by its relations of production (of labor) to "massified" productive processes compatible to only a very limited extent with the most advanced areas of the sections of intermediary means and means of production, the peripheral section of the means of consumption must find its avenue of expansion in a direction to which the peripheral ruling class is not stranger — the international market.

## CONCLUSION

We began with a discussion of the collapse of dependency theory as an expression of the necessary destruction of the fragile class alliance (and the consequent theoretical mystification of the character of capitalist production) upon which it was based. Dependency theory built a theory of international differentiation on a vision of capitalism restricted to a permanent struggle over spoils, for the sharing out of wealth among nations. Ostensibly concerned with the international division of labor, its primary concern, in fact, was distribution rather than production — and even then with distribution among nations rather than classes. As such it could have precisely nothing to say about the real dynamics of the capitalist international system. Both sides of the developmental alliance behind the early formulations of dependency theory advanced from the primitive form of economic theorizing which it represented: the bourgeoisie to Ricardo, the anti-imperialist forces to Marx. Unfortunately, the classic Marxist comments on the international economy seemed less than promising. Mesmerized by the tendential laws of falling rate of profit and equalization rates of profit, the dominant emphasis was upon international homogenization — though there was little explicit discussion of whether this process referred to rates of profit, relations of production, distribution of branches and sections of production, or what. In contrast with these positions, Lenin seemed to offer a more useful approach in addressing the clear nonhomogenization of the international system of production — an advantage gained only by constituting forces (which are the products of the laws of value) above the laws of value (we refer to monopolies), and by defining economic relations in largely financial terms. Notwithstanding its apparent immediate applicability to the "facts" of the case, this could hardly be termed a real theoretical advance in understanding the international system of capitalism. Reviving Lenin in a semantic set studded with "monopoly capital," "multinational corporations" and the like involved practically no development beyond the original dependency vision — insofar as it kept within the cosmos of systems resulting from the interaction of analytically independent and logically prior "forces." The sole significant difference resided less in the theoretical reconstruction of the world system than in the political symbolism of the new terms used to describe it. In this case the terms and the underlying logic pointed in different directions, for the approach in terms of multinational corporations, etc., puts any coherent form of analysis upon its head by explaining the economic system in terms of the form of the firm rather than vice versa — a form of economic reductionism more associated with bourgeois economics than with Marx's theory of the social production of surplus value.

In the ultimate instance, of course, the result of this choice was no theory at all — or, at best, a minimal thesis of conflict over surplus value within a world full of particulars. The alternative we have suggested is not an attempt to suppress the particular by reference to "laws" of capitalist development, least of all it is a call to return to economism. We have simply suggested that there is a principle of coherence in the international capitalist system, that this resides in the articulation of unevenly developed forces and relations of production, and that the form of this articulation is constantly transformed by the determined development of contradictions within systems of production — it being understood that this development resides in the formation of classes and the sharpening of class struggle (as the combination of forces and relations of production). Of course, there are significant differences (and conflict!) within the core, which signify that different sorts of imperialist relations exist side by side. At this point, given the collapse of general theories of imperialism, the point is not the identification of this or that specific articulation (although one can argue for a general change expressed in the "new international division of labor"), but the identification of the *principle* of articulation and its dynamic (i.e., unequal development of relations of production). The organizing elements in relations on the world level are neither "nations" nor "monopoly capital" but complementary contradictions in the system of production and realization as a whole. The global system is differentiated, to be sure, but in the form of differentiation in unity — a unity ultimately expressing not the problematic of particular capitals, but that of capital as a whole, i.e., the reproduction of the capitalist mode of production through the integration of different systems of production in the *global, social* system of production and realization of surplus value.

## REFERENCES

Anderson, Perry
   1976 *Considerations on Western Marxism*, London: New Left Books

Arrighi, Giovanni
   1978 *The Geometry of Imperialism*, London: New Left Books

Baer, Werner
   1965 *Industrialization and Economic Development in Brazil*, Homewood, Illinois: Richard Irwin

Baran, Paul A.
   1957 *The Political Economy of Growth*, New York: Monthly Review Press

Baran, P. and Paul M. Sweezy
   1966 *Monopoly Capital*, New York: Monthly Review Press

Basbaum, Leoncio
   1962 *História sincera da república*, Volume III, Rio de Janeiro: Edalgit

Braverman, Harry
   1974 *Labor and Monopoly Capital*, New York: Monthly Review Press

Brenner, Robert
   1977 "The origins of Capitalist Development: A Critique of Neo-Smithian Marxism," *New Left Review* 104 (July-August) 25-92

Cardoso, Fernando Henrique
   1973 "Associated-Dependent Development: Theoretical and Practical Implications," pp. 142-176 in A. Stepan (ed.), *Authoritarian Brazil*, New Haven: Yale University Press

Chenery, Hollis Burnley and D. B. Keesing
  1979 *The Changing Composition of Developing Country Exports*, Washington, World Bank

Cohn, Gabriel
  1968 *Petróleo e nacionalismo*, São Paulo: DIFEL

Crisenoy, Chantal
  1979 "Capitalism and Agriculture," *Economy and Society*, VIII (1), 9-25

Dean, Warren
  1969 *The Industrialization of São Paulo*, Austin: University of Texas Press

Duarte, João Carlos and O. Queda
  1974 "Agricultura e accumulação," *Debate e Crítica* (2), 90-97

Erickson, Kenneth Paul
  1977 *The Brazilian Corporative State and Working-Class Politics*, Berkeley: University of California Press

Ewen, Stuart
  1977 *Captains of Consciousness*, New York: McGraw-Hill

Foster-Carter, Aidan
  1978 "The Modes of Production Controversy," *New Left Review*, 107 (January-February), 47-77

Frank, André Gunder
  1971 *Capitalism and Underdevelopment in Latin America*, Harmondsworth: Penguin

  1972a "The Development of Underdevelopment," pp. 317 in J. D. Cockcroft, A. G. Frank and D. L. Johnson (eds.), *Dependence and Underdevelopment in Latin America*, New York: Anchor

  1972b *Lumpenbourgeoisie — Lumpendevelopment*, New York: Monthly Review Press

Friedman, Harriet
  1976 "The Transformation of Wheat Production in the Era of the World Market, 1973-1935. A Global Analysis of Production and Exchange," unpublished Ph.D. dissertation, Harvard University

Frobel, Fricker et al.
  1980 *The New International Division of Labour*, Cambridge: Cambridge University Press

Furtado, Celso
  1963 *The Economic Growth of Brazil*, Berkeley: University of California Press

Hobson, John A.
  1938 *Imperialism, A Study*, London: Unwin

Howe, Gary N. and A. Sica
  1980 "Political Economy, Imperialism, and the Problem of World System theory," pp. 235-286 in S. G. McNall and G. N. Howe (eds.), *Current Perspectives in Social Theory*, Volume I, Greenwich, Connecticut: JAI Press

Jenkins, Rhys O.
  1977 *Dependent Industrialization in Latin America*, New York: Praeger

Kautsky, Karl
  1970 *La question agraire*, Paris: Maspero

Laclau, Ernesto
  1977 *Politics and Ideology in Marxist Theory*, London: New Left Books

Lenin, V. I.
  1975 *Imperialism — The Highest Stage of Capitalism*, Moscow: Progress

Linhart, Robert L.
  1976 *Lenine, les paysans, Taylor*, Paris: Seuil

Luxemburg, Rosa
  1972 "The Accumulation of Capital — An Anti-Critique," pp. 47-150 in R. Luxemburg and N. Bukharin, *Imperialism and the Accumulation of Capital*, London: Allen Lane

  1977 *The Industrial Development of Poland*, New York: Campaigner Publications

Mandel, Ernest
1978 *The Second Slump*, London: New Left Books
1980 *Capitalist Long Waves*, Cambridge: Cambridge University Press
Marcus, Steven
1975 *Engels, Manchester and the Working Class*, New York, Vintage
Martins, Luciano
1976 *Pouvoir et développement économique*, Paris: Anthropos
Marx, Karl
1966 *Theories of Surplus Value*, Volume II, Moscow: Progress
1967a *Capital*, Volume I, London: Lawrence and Wishart
1967b *Capital*, Volume III, New York: International Publishers
Netto, Antonio D.
1959 *O problema de café no Brasil*, São Paulo: FCEA/USP
Oliveira, Francisco de
1972 "A economia brasileira: crítica à razão dualista," *Estudos CEBRAP* (2), 3-82
Owen, Roger and Bob Sutcliffe (eds.)
1972 *Studies in the Theory of Imperialism*, London: Longman
Palloix, Christian
1975 *L'internationalisation du capital*, Paris: Maspero
1978 *Travail et production*, Paris: Maspero
Pignaton, Alvaro
1973 *Capital estrangeiro e expansão industrial no Brasil*, Brasília: Department of Economics, Universidade de Brasília
Piore, Michael J.
1979 *Birds of Passage: Migrant Labor and Industrial Societies* Cambridge: Cambridge University Press
Rey, Pierre-Philippe
*1973 Les alliances de classes*, Paris: Maspero
Roxborough, Ian
1979 *Theories of Underdevelopment*, Atlantic Highlands: Humanities Press
Tavares, Maria de Conceição
1978 "Distribuição da renda, accumulação e padrão de industrialização," pp. 36-69 in R. Tolipan and M. C. Tinelli (eds.), *A controversia sobre a distribuição de renda e desenvolvimento*, Rio de Janeiro: Zahar
Topik, Steven C.
1978 "Economic Nationalism and the State in an Underdeveloped Country: Brazil, 1889-1930," unpublished, Ph.D. dissertation, University of Texas
Tyler, William G.
1976 *Manufactured Export Expansion and Industrialization in Brazil*, Tubingen: Mohr
Warren, Bill
1973 "Imperialism and Capitalist Industrialization," *New Left Review*, 81 (September-October), 3-44
Weffort, Francisco C.
1978 *O populismo na política brasileira*, Rio de Janeiro: Paz e Terra

# 5

# DEPENDENCY: A SPECIAL THEORY WITHIN MARXIAN ANALYSIS

by

*Joel C. Edelstein**

A dependency theory which purports to explain underdevelopment in Latin America exclusively as a consequence of the transfer of surplus from backward areas to the metropolis (the "exploitation" of one nation by another) fails to comprehend the central role of the labor process in the formation of classes as well as class struggle as the motor of history. Divorced from the material reality of the working classes, it ignores the role of the masses in making history. It is static. Despite occasional calls for socialist revolution, it is based in idealism and is therefore incapable of guiding revolutionary action. Moreover, such a dependency theory presents the poverty, hunger, and oppression of peasants and workers as a consequence of a capitalism "deformed" by foreign monopoly capital. It imagines that an anti-imperialist coalition led by local capital could bring about "normal" capitalist development. Thus, this dependency theory defends the interest of local capital against Marxism-Leninism and against the struggle of the working classes for socialist revolution.

This dependency theory is implicit in the work of Raúl Prebisch and the Economic Commission for Latin America, which identified the long-term tendency in the terms of trade to be a decline in the relation of prices of primary products to prices of manufacturers. (Ironically, though this "theory" did truly speak on behalf of local capital, it set the stage for the penetration of foreign monopoly capital into the industrial sector under the recipe of import-substitution.) This formulation was replaced in the mid-1960s by more adequate, radical, and Marxist efforts. However, the bourgeois nationalist concept of dependency reappeared in the 1970s beginning with Raúl Fernández and José Ocampo's article in the first issue of *Latin American Perspectives.* They and other left sectarians have equated the work of radical and Marxist writers such as André Gunder Frank, Theotônio dos Santos, and Ruy Mauro Marini with the limited bourgeois nationalist concept of dependency. In this fashion, the left sectarian critics ignore the explicit object of their attacks, the radical and Marxist dependentistas, and use bourgeois dependency as a straw man.

*The author is an Associate Professor of Political Science at the University of Colorado, Denver.

In my opinion, this misrepresentation by the sectarians is doubly unfortunate because it obscures both the genuine and important positive contributions which they have made as well as the real contribution of the left dependentistas. The sectarians are simply wrong in ignoring the emphasis on class by radical dependentistas such as Frank. They are similarly mistaken in their portrayal of left dependency as an apology for a "normal" capitalism or the voice of local capital. Most importantly, their tendency to represent the dependency perspective as an alternative to Marxist analysis is incorrect. It is, nonetheless, worthwhile to put aside these errors of the sectarian critique in order to assimilate its accurate and important criticism of left dependency: the neglect of the role of the labor process in shaping the dependent capitalist social formation and its consequent failure to serve as a guide for revolutionary struggle and for the project of the transition to socialism.

Radical dependency theory arose as a negation of bourgeois theory which presents history as a process in which a diffusion of capital and technology from the advanced capitalist countries to the "less developed" countries leads to the destruction of feudal stagnation and the rise of universal capitalist development, prosperity, and democracy. We can see in Frank, for example, an effort to refute this notion in part by turning it on its head. Thus, Frank observed in the interaction of more advanced with less advanced countries a flow of resources from underdeveloped to more developed nations. In the face of a formulation which blamed underdevelopment on feudal isolation from the dynamic forces of capitalism, Frank focused on exchange and even defined seventeenth century Latin America as capitalist. In the heat of ideological struggle, Frank's work had the virtue of simplicity. Those who understood a different perspective could easily grasp this simple reversal (though a more fundamental contribution of Frank was his analysis of the internalization of imperialism in its impact on shaping of classes and class forces which Frank identified as a process of underdevelopment '— and this element seems to have escaped the understanding of bourgeois theorists).

The sectarian critique of dependency is correct in the sense that dependency theorists have dwelt on the question: why Latin America did not undergo a capitalist development like that of England and Northern Europe. Stating the problem in this fashion does put forth implicitly the assumption that without reinforcement of the position of an agrocommercial bourgeoisie by external forces, industrial capitalism would have developed in Latin America as it did in England. And some critical junctures have been located in which local capital has contested for power and been crushed by domestic agrocommercial ruling classes in combination with foreign interests. It answers the question essentially by looking to the integration of the area into the expanding capitalist core, thus emphasizing the reflexive aspect of Latin American development — that colonial and neocolonial economy and, consequently, class structure have been shaped by the needs of the center.

It seems to me that the analyses generated by posing the question of development in terms of participation in the world system have generated useful explanation, supported by solid historical evidence. The explanation is not merely why capitalist development characteristic of the core did not develop in Latin America. The dependency perspective has also explained, though partially, the development of dependent capitalism.

To what extent has Latin American development been determined, not reflexively in response to external forces, but as a result of internal forces and contradictions? Obviously, no European market could call forth silver mines in Cuba or sugar plantations on the Pampas of Argentina. But would local capital have responded differently had the role of foreign capital been less influential? For example, would the effort to increase surplus value have moved beyond extending the length of the work day or intensifying the labor process to altering production, itself. In its focus on the interaction with the world system, the dependency perspective tends to draw attention away from this question.

In its beginnings as a negation of bourgeois theories of development, radical dependency had strength in simplicity, but also a weakness. It is one thing to turn on its head the Hegelian dialectic. A similar effort worked upon a lesser set of concepts has an impoverished result. Although it does not substitute nation for class as the sectarians charge, it has indeed defined a mode of production by an analysis of circulation. It ignores the labor process and thus tends to understand history as a conflict among the owning classes. It fails as a guide to revolutionary action.

The labor theory of value is central in the Marxist understanding of history. The process by which surplus value is appropriated by the owning classes is critical in determining the objective antagonistic interests of the owning and the producing classes. The nature and the rate of exploitation imbedded in the labor process shape consciousness and, ultimately, the forms and level of class struggle. In the dialectical transition from feudalism to capitalism, a manufacturing bourgeoisie becomes ascendent through its efforts to increase the rate of surplus value which goes beyond lengthening the workday and intensifying the labor process. In their competitive struggle for survival and a higher rate of surplus, the capitalists transform the labor process. The triumph of the bourgeoisie is a new mode of production in which feudal classes have been reduced to the status of remnants; servile labor has been replaced by wage labor, a new concept of property and a new legal structure have been implanted which provide for investment mechanisms required by industrial capitalism; and the nature of the labor process has been changed and with it the creation of new classes, class interests, and class consciousness. Though the change is dialectical and remnants of the past remain, nonetheless there is a consistency within the new mode of production. With the new labor process of capitalist production, the producing classes are formed by a social existence which shapes a proletarian consciousness as well as proletarian class interest and proletarian forms of class struggle. The competition among capitalists forces investment, which creates a higher organic composition of capital with its tendency toward a falling rate of profit. As Marx analyzed the tendencies of capitalism, this mode of production with its unplanned anarchy of production and its fundamental contradiction between the social nature of production and the private nature of appropriation generates crises. Capitalism also creates class forces which are shaped and mobilized by its increasing crises. In its development it creates not only the agents of its own destruction but the productive forces upon which a transition to socialism can go forward.

This understanding of a historical movement is the result of analysis of real historical experience leading to a specification of the tendencies within capitalist development. It specifies how capitalism as a closed system develops. With the recognition that capitalism is not a closed system but is still in an accelerating process of internationalization toward closure, and beneath the confusing complexities of working class cooptation in periods of rapid capital accumulation and of revolutions which have arisen not from the contradictions of advanced capitalism but rather from the contradictions of imperialism, this Marxian understanding of historical development remains accurate and fundamental. An analysis can only be useful as a guide to revolutionary action if it includes an understanding of the labor process as the locus of social existence, shaping class consciousness and the forms of class struggle.

The radical dependency perspective does not deny analysis of the labor process. It does point out that production for external markets has been a basic element in the formation of underdevelopment. Production for external markets has been vitally important in establishing the interests of dominant classes in Latin America as well as in the specific correlation of class forces. Failure to recognize this element in the historical development of Latin America precludes an understanding of that history.

It is true that just as markets created by English imperialism favored the manufacturing bourgeoisie in England, the availability of markets for primary products of Latin America strengthened the position of agrocommercial and mining classes in Latin America. In this sense, the dependency perspective helps to identify the impact of relations with the world system on the correlation of class forces within all nations which have entered into such relations. However, in the English case, these market opportunities arose largely as a result of foreign policies which reflected ascendency of the manufacturing bourgeoisie which was the principal beneficiary. This history is directly consistent with the Marxist analysis of capitalism as a closed system. That is, the manufacturing bourgeoise became dominant over its feudal predecessors fundamentally because the forces of production had advanced to a point that maintenance of feudal productive relations was no longer possible. The interaction with undeveloped and underdeveloped societies only confirmed and accentuated the rise of a manufacturing bourgeoisie, which Marxixt analysis of historical development would expect.

Latin America's relation to the world system was significantly different in that it resulted in the establishment of economies and, consequently, of class systems initially as the exclusive result of the policies of the more developed countries. The ruling classes in Latin America arose on the basis of these colonial economies. Once established, the dominance of the export sector was supported by imperialism.

The development of industrial capitalism in England and Northern Europe has been characterized by the elegant dialectical movement described by Marxist analysis, driven by its own internal contradictions. The context of dependent capitalist development contains forces which influence historical development, causing it to deviate from the course which it would follow if development occurred without this influence. While dependent capitalist development is in no way "unnatural" or "distorted" in any absolute sense, since it is one locus of the process of world capitalist development, its context is different from that which was the locus of analysis upon which the Marxist understanding of capitalist development was created. In my opinion, the sectarian critics' refusal to accept the significance of the differential loci results in an inadequate, rigidified analysis.

While the radical dependency perspective only brings out elements in the context of dependent capitalist development which differ from that of the development of the now advanced capitalist countries, some sectarian critics have raised this perspective to the level of a general theory. In so doing, they attempt to make dependency into a competitor with Marxist theory and methodology. In my opinion, the concepts used by left dependentistas do not sufficiently specify a set of relationships to constitute a theory. But if these concepts were to add up to a theory, it is a special rather than a general theory. As a special theory, it seeks an understanding of social formations which have been created essentially through their integration into an expanding world capitalist system. It is not an alternative to Marxist analysis. It can be a perspective which makes a Marxist analysis of these social formations possible by exploring the totality of Latin American dependent capitalist development.

# 6

# ECONOMISM AND DETERMINISM IN DEPENDENCY THEORY

by
*Dale L. Johnson**

The wide acceptance of dependency theory throughout the Third World constitutes a conceptual revolution in a scientific understanding of large-scale questions of capitalist development. The perspective has succeeded in discrediting the system, legitimating tenents of modernization theory, and in undermining the "developmentalist" approach of reform nationalisms. Yet its intellectual and political weight as a now dominant paradigm for analyzing development and underdevelopment has caused a considerable consternation among some Marxists, especially those inclined toward orthodoxy.

Dependency theory is particularly attacked for being excessively based on analyses of exchange and spacial relations rather than production relations; it is criticized as not having an adequate approach to stages of development of the mode of production, as economistic, and as lacking in class analysis. Each of these criticisms has some merit. Yet, in my view, the problem with almost all of the critiques is that, while they specify the problems with dependency theory, they do not offer any serious theoretical development beyond it, much less an alternative to it. I do not think this is at all accidental. The critics have been unable to develop an alternative because neither the classical theory of imperialism nor contemporary strains of orthodox Marxism provide ready answers to the problems of underdevelopment that dependency theory has addressed. Dependency theory developed not just in reaction to conventional modernization theory and the 1950s nationalist and reformist formulations of the Economic Commission for Latin America (ECLA) and of the ideologues of "developmentalism" but as a so-called "neo-Marxism," because traditional Marxism was inadequate to the task, in both its theoretical manifestations and its political conceptions (e.g., the limitations of Lenin's theory of imperialism; the "feudalism" thesis of backwardness; Trotsky's law of uneven and combined development; the reformist line of the communist parties of the region; the inability of the left generally to develop a coherent alternative to developmentalist reformism).

* The author, who teaches sociology at Livingston College (Rutgers University), has adapted this article from his forthcoming book, *Social Class and Social Development: Comparative Studies of Class Relations and Middle Classes.*

Serious theoretical development "beyond dependency theory" has simply not come about: not from the "original principles" purists who believe all is explained by immanent "laws" (e.g., Weeks and Dore, 1979; Taylor, 1979); nor from the eclectics, who would reject theory for the empirics of the concrete (e.g., Palma, 1978); nor from those who subordinate intellectual endeavor to a rigid political line (e.g., Fernández and Ocampo, 1974).

Still, even in the absence of substantive contribution, theoretical criticism has its place. The most serious criticisms raised by orthodox Marxists have their origin in Laclau's classic 1972 article in the *New Left Review* (reprinted in Laclau, 1977). While I would not include Laclau among the most orthodox of Marxists, others have taken his main points, reread *Capital* as if it were gospel, and sallied forth to combat dependency heresy. Laclau argues that André Gunder Frank's thesis of the development of underdevelopment confuses the concepts of the capitalist mode of production and participation in a world capitalist economy. Capitalism is not defined by the existence of markets but by the relations of production that involve free laborers' sale of labor power; the servile relations of Third World latifundia and plantations are anything but free. Laclau suggests that capitalist development on a world scale has preserved precapitalist relations on the periphery. Primary production for export became the basis for "feudalization" or even "refeudalization" of peripheral areas.

These criticisms have been given wide circulation and credence, especially the view that dependency theory in general overemphasizes the structural relations of center and periphery that result in the appropriation of surplus through exchange mechanisms. This emphasis does not allow, it is claimed, for analyses of the articulations of precapitalist and capitalist modes of production and of the course of development of regional and national modes of production. There is some foundation for this view, but in the main the critics suffer the burden of narrow polemic. The sharp distinction drawn between production and circulation is considerably overdrawn, inasmuch as the economic process is a unitary one. Such dichotomies lead to theoretical rigidity. Production and consumption are two sides of a coin that are fused together by commodity distribution and circulation of money; the cycle of economic activity, jealously guarded over by the state, is a contradictory unity, and to emphasize production to the exclusion of surplus appropriation through exchange mechanisms is to ignore the dialectic of the economic process. It simply will not do to attack dependency theory for its exclusive emphasis on circulation, while "production relations" are formalistically stated, or even reduced to calculations of value. Still less acceptable is it to assert that dependency theory is devoid of class analysis, while generalizations about the immanent workings of the law of value and "laws" of uneven development are invoked as the method of class analysis (see especially Weeks and Dore, 1979). Nothing could be more remote from a historical dialectics of class than restatements of abstract laws.

Authors like Frank, Samir Amin, and Arghiri Emmanuel have indeed overemphasized the circulation side. At the same time this is really one of their great contributions. They have identified the mechanisms utilized by the metropolitan bourgeoisies, at different points in history, to appropriate the surplus produced in the colonial and dependent regions. In the historical relations of imperialism, the subordination of production and productive classes in the colonial and dependent regions to the metropolitan class forces (first mercantile and later industrial and financial interests) benefiting from the assymetrical terms of international commerce is a well-established pattern; the primacy of the appropriation of surplus in the sphere of circulation is simply an established, indisputable historical fact. Surplus appropriation by the bourgeoisies of the center, primarily through exchange mechanisms, is changing only in the most recent phase of transnationalism under the impact of large-scale transnational corporate investments in industrial production within Third World economies and producer cartels in primary exports.

## MODE OF PRODUCTION ANALYSIS

The critics would substitute "mode of production" formulations for dependency theory. In general there is relatively little substantive research carried out within a mode of production perspective — most is still confined to criticism or rhetorical polemic (exceptions are the colonial period research by Assadourian, et.al., 1973; and Dieterich, 1978). That which is accomplished seems to either (a) call for a reversion to a presumed "Leninist" concept of imperialism which stresses production relations or (b) to place a great deal of emphasis on the internal development of the relations of production within particular nations.

The reversion to a theory of imperialism ignores the great contribution of the dependency literature, which goes to the heart of the central question and presents a new and relatively coherent framework that facilitates understanding of the historical development of the national societies of Latin America, Asia, and Africa. As Cardoso argues, Lenin's thesis of imperialism was valid in its day (and, in fact, is a principal basis for the "development of underdevelopment" and other theses of the dependency framework) but is no longer adequate to explain what he has termed "development with dependence" (Cardoso, 1972) and "associated development" (Cardoso, 1973) of parts of the periphery in recent years. A critique of classical imperialism theory is also implicit in Dos Santos' early work (1968) and explicit in his latest (1978). Moreover, classical or modern-day theories of imperialism (such as the good synthetic work of Magdoff, 1969) are distorted in that the vision of the world proceeds from the center to the periphery. Dependency theory reverses the field of vision. True history, one which scientifically illuminates while it liberates, needs to be written from the bottom up. This history has to be grasped in its regional and national specificity. At best, a top-down perspective of imperialism only outlines the global parameters, which of course is a necessary step.

The studies that emphasize the internal development of the mode of production often conceptualize production relations formalistically rather than historically and empirically (the extreme example is Hindess and Hirst, 1975). Applied to dependent societies these studies ignore the degree to which these relations are, over time and with great regional and national variation, structured by the region's articulation with international capitalism — or differently (and better) stated, the degree to which relations of dependence become internalized so that they take the appearance of locally rooted backwardness and underdevelopment. Among these Marxist analysts there seems almost to be a reversion to the old bourgeois method of looking at particular regions and nations in relative isolation from the historical and international context.

What is necessary is a dialectical conception of the "external/internal" nexus. If *dependentistas* too often overgeneralize "external" structuring, it is an even more serious methodological error to mistake the specificity of national or regional phenomena or the great variations in the development of the capitalist mode of production in different areas of the world for localized "backward" or "precapitalist" structures or processes.

A steady carping away from the point of view of a narrow Marxist "mode of production" orthodoxy (see especially Carlos Johnson, 1977, and Cueva, 1976) or from a politically motivated or sectarian standpoint (see especially Fernández and Ocampo, 1974, and Romagnolo, 1975) will not advance a sounder theory. Nor will the vicious malignment of André Gunder Frank detract from his contribution. A noneconomistic approach that is not overdeterministic, that makes production relations, class analysis, and development of the mode of production central, that adequately poses the "external/internal" nexus, is more likely to emerge from the efforts of those who work within a theory of underdevelopment and dependency than from those outside it. The best substantive work in the field continues to be produced by pioneers like Dos Santos, Frank, Aníbal Quijano, Ruy Mauro Marini, Cardoso, Amin and by others who are creatively adapting a dependency perspective to particular questions. Dependency theory after all, as a development within Marxism and as it should be, is an approach that places determinism within a dialectic of world history; dependency theory has developed at least a rudimentary class analysis, particularly of metropolitan and local bourgeoisie relations; and it rightly began and continues primarily as a historical approach to development of world society, within which framework the course of local histories can be charted in their specificity. The bases of a sound theory are there. To be sure, what is now more a perspective than a theory needs refinement, correction of misplaced emphasis, and further conceptual development.

## CRITICISM OF DEPENDENCY

Some of the criticisms of dependency can be dealt with summarily. An obvious shortcoming of some of the 1960s formulations (including my own, 1972 and 1973a) was the polemical statement of the deformed character of capitalist underdevelopment and the stagnation thesis associated with the idea of the development of underdevelopment. In the political context of the 1960s, we were correct to denounce these deformations but wrong to see them as permanent, short of a socialist revolution. Obviously parts of the Third World have leaped out of the real stagnation of the 1950s and have experienced a considerable and rapid process of capitalist development over the last decade or two. But Dos Santos' work on the "new dependency" and Cardoso's on "development with dependency" anticipated this before it became as obvious as today. Gabriel Palma (awarded a $500 Ford Foundation prize for his critical *World Development* essay) is right to say:

I have criticized those who fail to understand the specificity of the historical process of the penetration of capitalism into Latin America, and only condemn its negative aspects, complementing their analysis with a series of stagnationist theses, in an attempt to build a formal theory of underdevelopment (Palma, 1979).

But Palma is wrong in saying that dependency theorists have rendered "both static and unhistorical" work; that they are "unable to explain the specificity of economic development and political domination in Latin America;" and that "their models lack the sensitivity to detect the social processes of Latin America . . . " Palma would still be writing about "feudalism," "dualism," "obstacles to development," "modernization," and "development strategies" if it were not for nearly two decades of theoretical endeavor and historical research by dependentistas.

Within the dependency perspective the most serious deficiency, it seems to me, has not been given serious or systematic attention. It has been its rather heavy concentration on economics and lack of emphasis on sociology. It has tended to exaggerate the determining impact of international political economy and to down play the importance, complexity, and international impact of local social struggles. The main thrust is too often a nondialectical theory of the mechanics of imperialist domination. When work on dependency moves away from "bottom up" history, it sometimes tends toward just another version of the political economy of imperialism. This can result in a structuralist "superdeterminism," which in the end is an indeterminism, since it cannot satisfactorily account for the complex interrelations of the international and national forces that propel history.

A corollary to the economism and overdeterminism too often associated with analyses within a dependency framework is explanation by conspiracy. Various studies (especially by North Americans) invoke the assumption that foreign economic penetration in national economies and the political machinations of imperialism, particularly of the CIA, contain the explanation of Third World events. Actually, the growing penetration of transnational corporate capital corresponds to a new "transnational" phase in the stage of monopoly capitalism and imperialism. The expansion of transnational capital undergirds rapidly shifting forms of dependence in the Third World, but it is by no means sufficient to explain conjunctures at regional and national levels. In the Southern Cone of South America, for example, it explains in part how "dependent development" in the "transnational phase" of international development has superseded the prior stages of "national development" (1930-1950) and the "development of underdevelopment" (1870-1930), but it does not adequately explain the "national security state" imposed by military juntas (Dale Johnson, forthcoming). Nor do critical analyses of the policies of imperialist nations (foreign policy, aid, economic sanctions, covert interventions, military adventures) in themselves explain political events; for these policies are primarily buttresses to the underlying imperial structural relationships, the grease that keeps the obsolete machinery of international economy running; they are also attempts to politically manage an unmanageable process.

In short, many have taken the structural explanations of the theorists who have made real contributions, for example Dos Santos' work on transnational corporations and the "new dependency," and used them to promote conspiratorial explanations. Those who do this ignore Dos Santos' careful conceptualization of dependence as a "structural conditioning" that permeates the structure, life, and movement of dependent societies. From this angle, dependency theory is not a strict determinism, but a basis for unraveling the dynamics of national economic, social, and political processes. These flow from the class relations attendent to national patterns of underdevelopment and dependent development that in turn dialectically interelate with international forces that are in constant movement according to the processes of capital accumulation and the unraveling of contradictions on a world scale.

Excessive deterministic zeal at the level of macro political economy has a far more serious consequence than explanation by conspiracy; and this is the implication that the impotence of internal social forces does not permit dependent societies to write their own histories. This remains characteristic of Frank's work even when — perhaps especially when — he specifically attempts a class analysis of underdevelopment.

There is no doubt as to the historical and contemporary validity of one of the central tenents of dependency theory: dependency is a centuries-long and ever-continuing process of historical structuring, as Frank and the entire "world systems" school have demonstrated, of the economic and social structures of societies impacted by international capitalist development. In my work on Chile of the early 1970s (1973b: chapter 1), dependency was viewed from a related angle: under conditions of dependence, power and decision making are removed from national societies; constraints of extra-national origin are many and severe; dependency is a severely limiting situation and nation-states and local power wielders must negotiate the conditions of their dependence, and the terms of negotiation are continually shifting. With respect to the external/internal relationship, then, we can say that the field of social struggle within dependent nations does not uniquely proceed, at any given historical conjuncture, from the free unraveling of local histories.

This is well and good, but lends itself, when taken too strictly, to a deterministic rather than dialectical stance. The problem is that much of the work by those utilizing the dependency framework has focused on external economic constraints and impulses and proceeded to view internal social struggle as a kind of dramatic production with a certain amount of improvisional theatre perhaps, but somehow not a real existence. The main actors in the Latin America theatre — military officers, local businesmen, and suffering masses — may believe their drama is real life, it is implied, but the roles they play are written abroad and transmitted to them by the latest Madison Avenue technique and by covert imperial agents, backed up by explicit pressures from international lenders and Washington and sweetened with junior partner contracts with international capital. There is of course a certain descriptive validity and ideological appeal in this characterization of local actors as puppets. But a dialectical science of society cannot assume that the life of any nation is an orchestrated production computer programmed by the powerful of another nation.

Imperialism and dependency are not a theatre of the absurd; the forms of international domination do not ordain overwhelming structures (even if, as in the Altusserian formulation, they are "relatively autonomous"); nor are events determined by the inexorable working out of immanent laws of motion of the capitalist mode of production. Ruling classes do not write history — their experience is a never-ending and largely failing struggle to achieve a workable hegemony. People make history by struggling against oppressive social realities and their oppressors; and this is nowhere more vivid today than in the dependent regions.

Marx's famous dictum is important to keep in mind when considering class struggles in dependent nations and their roots in and articulations with international forces: people make history, but only under circumstances that are objectively given. In dependent areas these circumstances are exceedingly hard and oppressive ones. Those who work within a dependency framework have emphasized mainly the "external" origin of these objective circumstances, too often ignored are people making history.

If one examines, for example, the problem of military dictatorship, the correlation between contemporary forms of capital accumulation on a world scale and the growing incidence of new forms of highly repressive states can hardly be ignored. Argentina, Brasil, Chile, Uruguay, the Philippines, Taiwan, and South Korea are the most "modernized," the most industrially developed, of the Third World nations. They are recipients of hundreds of millions of dollars in investments by transnational capital and are locked into the newest pattern of international economy, export-oriented industrialization. But to point to a correlation between the degree of integration into the most advanced forms of international accumulation and the incidence of military dictatorship is not sufficient to explain the latter.

Are these states simply consequences of the inexorable workings of international political economy? Are they, in this context, the political result of an unholy class alliance of transnational corporate interests, the North American state, and local bourgeoisies? Only at the most generalized level of explanation. The methodological problem is to identify the interrelations of the international, historical, and social roots of contemporary forms of the state in the Third World. The form of the state is not directly derived from the accumulation process. The state is an institutional expression of class relations. As such the state assumes various forms in different stages of development, depending in the main upon the outcome of class struggles. To be sure, class relations and the state as an expression of these relations are ultimately derived from the accumulation process; for what is accumulation other than a process of unfolding class relations, of changing forms of exploitation and domination. While these may be internationally "induced," they are locally rooted.

The salient features of the societies suffering the new face of militaristic barbarism is the highly antagonistic relations resulting from new forms of exploitation and oppression between the different classes and strata of increasingly complex national social structures. Dictatorship has been imposed by the necessity to contain the increasingly sharp social struggles of oppressed peoples, by the attempts of dominant classes to achieve a viable hegemony. But the largely unviable projects of hegemony, conceived and acted upon by local dominant classes and transnational centers of power, depend upon fragile alliances with local support classes, especially petty bourgeoisies and salaried middle classes, as well as the tolerance, today increasingly precarious, of social forces within the international community. The dictatorships that have emerged of late in South America and Asia are responses by local power blocs — an alliance of classes spearheaded by a fraction of the local bourgeoisie — enjoying the support of the international business community to the difficult conditions and challenges presented by the accumulated history of underdevelopment, by the uneven, warped dependent development of the current phase of transnationalism and, most of all, by the struggles of ordinary people to liberate themselves from the oppression of dependence and underdevelopment.

In a dialectical explanation of phenomena such as military dictatorships, at least two levels of explanation are required. The immediate source of these onslaughts of reaction reside in the relations of local social forces, their alliances (including with foreign centers of power), their struggles and objectives. That is, military coups are not given in external causes, neither structurally in relation to the increasingly close integration of dependent economies in the newest forms of transnational capital accumulation, nor politically in terms of policies adopted in Washington and Wall Street.

At this level of analysis the specific conditions that exist within nations are what is important. The withering away of the nation-state in the face of increasingly concentrated centers of transnational power, implied in both recent apologist and critical literature on multinational corporations, is pure mythology. The "modern world system" is constituted in terms of two organizing principles, territory and class. While capitalist development is one of polarization of classes on a world scale, it remains that classes socially coalesce within territorial states. The primary relation of class antagonism in the current transnational phase of development is undoubtedly between the bourgeoisie of the center and the working class of the periphery — and this increasingly salient antagonism is central to understanding military dictatorship in the most developed of the underdeveloped countries (that is, in locations where polarization of classes has proceeded furthest). But this relation is played out in diverse national contexts and is mediated by a range of intervening class relations (which must be studied in their specificity).

The methodological principle is therefore to look first at the concrete relations of social forces in particular locations. But these "internal" relations, their roots in the accumulation process (seen as one of unfolding relations of exploitation and domination), and the social and political circumstances that surround them, will make no sense apart from consideration of their articulation with "external" forces. This higher order of explanation is provided within a dependency framework, which specifies the direction of the accumulation process, the forms of economic subordination, the changing character of exploitation and surplus appropriation, and points toward the necessity for a class analysis under conditions of dependence.

If I could avoid the language of "internal" and "external," I surely would. It is a question of the interrelation of general determinants (the external) with specific determinants (the internal) of particular phenomena (such as militarized forms of the state) in concrete, historical circumstances. Perhaps it is better to say that the general (the process of capitalist development on a world scale) finds concrete expression in the specific (modalities of class relations, structural features of underdevelopment, forms of the states . . . in dependent societies) rather than that imperialism "conditions," "structures," or "develops" underdevelopment and all the ills associated with this condition. But even this formulation downplays the dialectic of the external/internal nexus. For, while the relation external/internal is decidedly assymetrical, it is nevertheless contradictory, often explosively so; and the conditions of underdevelopment, the events within dependent societies, have their impact on the actual course of development on a world scale. How else, apart from the accumulated effects of international class struggles, does one account for the recent incipient disintegration of U.S. hegemony?

The dynamics of the nexus is best unraveled through class analysis. Palma makes another good point in his lengthy critique:

> The system of "external domination" reappears as an "internal" phenomenon through the social practices of local groups and classes, who share its interests and values. Other internal groups and forces oppose this domination, and in the concrete development of these contradictions the specific dynamic of the society is generated (1978).

I return briefly and by way of conclusion to the class forces involved in the question of military dictatorship, of which the brutal regimes of the Southern Cone of South America are the prime example. In the stage of dependent development, fixed within the international accumulation process to which these regimes have *chosen* to firmly integrate national political economy, local capital is being restructured; the local dominant class is assuming a new dependent face; the relations between different fractions of the dominant class are transformed; important social interests tied to the old order of classic underdevelopment and national development are eclipsed or subordinated; a considerable maturity is accorded newer classes and social forces. In the context of a crisis of transition from one stage of development to another stage, an explosive quality has been added to the struggles of classes and the various social and institutional forces. And this explosive quality in the sharp struggles of the 1960s and 1970s has, in the Southern Cone, transformed transitional crises into conjunctures of *organic crises,* out of which have come the especially brutal dictatorships of Argentina, Chile, and Uruguay.

In appreciating the two orders of explanation that I have tried to draw out, the specific and general determinants which merge in a dialectic of the internal/external nexus, foremost is that history always reverts to the never-ending struggle of ordinary people, oppressed by the objective circumstances presented to them, for a better and freer existence. The heeled boot, torture, and official terrorism represent the depth of contradiction and the sharpness of struggle in Latin America and elsewhere. When viewing the dramatic events of particular nations, rulers' projects, and peoples' actions in the context of "external" structural forces, "internal" contradictions, and generalized crises in the emerging phase of international development are the starting point of a liberating and dialectical social science.

# REFERENCES

Assadourian, Carlos Sempat , et.al.
1973 *Modos de producción en América Latina*, Mexico City: Cuadernos de Pasado y Presente (40)

Cardoso, Fernando Henrique
1972 "Dependency and Development in Latin America," *New Left Review*, 74 (July-August), 83-95

1973 "Associated-Dependent Development: Theoretical and Practical Implications," in Alfred Stepan (ed.), *Authoritarian Brazil*, New Haven: Yale University Press

Cueva, Agustín
1976 "A Summary of 'Problems and Perspective of Dependency Theory'," *Latin American Perspectives*, III (Fall), 12-16

Dieterich, Heinz
1978 *Relaciones de producción en América Latina*, Mexico City: Ediciones de Cultura Popular

Dos Santos, Theotônio
1968 *El nuevo caracter de la dependencia*, Santiago, Chile: Universidad de Chile, *Cuadernos del Centro de Estudios Socio-Económicos* (10)

1978 *Imperialismo y dependencia*, Mexico City: Ediciones Era

Fernández, Raúl A. and José F. Ocampo
1974 "The Latin American Revolution: A Theory of Imperialism, Not Dependence," *Latin American Perspectives*, I (Spring, 1974), 4-29

Hindess, Barry and Paul Hirst
1975 *Pre-Capitalist Modes of Production*, Boston: Routledge and Kegan Paul

Johnson, Carlos
1977 *La teoría de la dependencia: ciéncia e ideología*, Mexico City: UNAM, Instituto de Investigaciones Sociales

Johnson, Dale L. (with James D. Cockcroft and André Gunder Frank)
1972 *Dependence and Underdevelopment: Latin America's Political Economy*, New York: Doubleday Anchor

Johnson, Dale L.
1973a *The Sociology of Change and Reaction in Latin America*, Indianapolis: Bobbs-Merrill

1973b *The Chilean Road to Socialism*, New York: Doubleday Anchor

forthcoming *Social Class and Social Development: Comparative Studies of Class Relations and the Middle Classes*

Laclau, Ernesto
1977 *Politics and Ideology in Marxist Theory*, London and New York: New Left Books and Schocken Books

Magdoff, Harry
1969 *The Age of Imperialism: The Economics of U.S. Foreign Policy*, New York: Monthly Review Press

Palma, Gabriel
1978 "Dependency: A Formal Theory of Underdevelopment or a Methodology the Analysis of Concrete Situations of Underdevelopment?," *World Development* (July and August)

Romagnolo, David
1975 "The So-called 'Law' of Uneven and Combined Development," *Latin American Perspectives*, II (Spring), 7-32

Taylor, John G.
1979 *From Modernization to Modes of Production: A Critique of the Sociologies of Development and Underdevelopment*, Atlantic Highlands, N.J.: Humanities Press

Weeks, John and Elizabeth Dore
1979 "International Exchange and the Causes of Backwardness," *Latin American Perspectives*, VI (Spring), 62-87

# 7

# THE DIFFERENCES BETWEEN MATERIALIST THEORY AND DEPENDENCY THEORY AND WHY THEY MATTER

by

*John Weeks**

In reading the debate over the relevance and theoretical basis of dependency theory, much of which one can find in the pages of *Latin American Perspectives* (Chilcote, 1974; Dore and Weeks, 1979; Fernández and Ocampo, 1974; Frank, 1974), those not versed in the debate might be forgiven for not always divining what the basic issues are. In particular, are "Marxist" theory[1] and dependency theory branches on the same intellectual and ideological tree? Is one theory a subset of the other, complementary to the other? Are they separate and competing theories? The purpose of this brief essay is to demonstrate that they are indeed separate, alternative theories, largely incompatible. To do this, we first summarize the main features of each theory and relate them to their separate intellectual origins. In a brief presentation, this must necessarily result in reducing each theory to a rather bare and stark structure and all aspects of each cannot be dealt with. The intention is not agnostically to offer two alternatives but to demonstrate that dependency theory neither can claim empirical verification nor theoretical validity.

We live in a world dominated by capitalism. As a consequence of this fact (over which there is presumably no controversy), the theory of the operation of the world economy must have a theory of capitalist reproduction as its basis. By "capitalist reproduction" is meant the process by which a specifically capitalist society evolves and reproduces its social relations on an expanding scale. Second, a theory of the operation of the world economy must locate itself *internationally*. By this we mean that one needs to derive within the theory a distinction between the "domestic" reproduction of capitalist society and its "international" reproduction. It is through this

---

*The author teaches at the American University in Washington, D.C.

[1]Since a central conclusion of the theory Marx initiated is that great people do not make history, it is inconsistent for one in the analytical tradition of Marx to refer to his or her framework as "Marxian theory." This implies that theory is the work of one (or several) people, while in fact it is the result of material conditions. Therefore, the term "materialist theory" will be used throughout this discussion.

distinction that one can analyze capitalist reproduction in the context of the division of the world along political lines. In other words, a theory of the world economy ("theory of imperialism" or "theory of dependency") need have two (obviously related, but distinct) elements: a theory of capitalist accumulation and a theory of the relevant division of the world for purposes of considering that accumulation as international. In our analysis of materialist theory and dependency theory we shall see how each deals with these two components of the analysis.

## DEPENDENCY THEORY

A theory of capitalist accumulation encompasses two related but qualitatively different processes: the initial development of capitalism and its reproduction and expansion once established as a mature social system. Most dependency writers do not deal at length with the first element of a theory of accumulation, so perhaps it is necessary to show why an explanation of the initial development of capitalism is important to the analysis of the world economy. Presumably, one of the central purposes of an analysis of the world economy (leaving aside bourgeois apologists) is to explain the pattern of uneven development in the world and to explain why that uneven development — pattern of poverty and riches — seems to have a systematic geographic character. Further, both "dependentistas" and materialists would agree that the uneven development is the result of capitalist accumulation. With these points in mind, it should be clear that any theory which restricts itself to dealing with uneven development in the era of mature capitalism (say, the last hundred years) presupposes what it seeks to prove. The purpose of theory is to explain why some areas are developed and others underdeveloped, and this purpose is avoided by taking *as given* the existence of developed and underdeveloped areas and proceeding without a backward look to how what has been presupposed is reproduced. Thus, a theory of the development of capitalism is central to the theory of the uneven development of contemporary world society.

We find the clearest analysis of the development of capitalism in the works of Paul Baran (1956) and André Gunder Frank (Baran, 1956; and Frank, 1967), and a similar position in the works of later writers (Amin, 1976).[2] We find the hypothesis that the presently developed capitalist countries reached their developed status by the transfer of resources from the presently underdeveloped world. In this view, the epoch-making transition from feudalism to capitalism in Europe is achieved by the appropriation of the surplus product from one set of countries by another set of countries (see Dore and Weeks, 1979). The set of countries which loses its surplus stagnates into underdevelopment, and the set of appropriating countries accumulates wealth at a rapid rate, based strategically upon the impetus of a larger available surplus product. This mechanism, of de-accumulation on the one hand and accumulation on the other, continues as capitalism matures, though in more sophisticated form. In the early stage of capitalist development in Eu-

---

[2]And no dependency writer to our knowledge has explicitly rejected this analysis. Indeed, the dependency analysis of contemporary underdevelopment and its reproduction is an extension of this analysis to the present.

rope, the appropriation was more violent and crude — "looting and plundering" — and gives way to "surplus extraction" through "unequal exchange" (Mandel, 1975: chapter 11; Amin, 1976; and Emmanuel, 1972) or profit remittances (Baran and Sweezy, 1966). Closely entwined with this theory of accumulation is an underconsumptionist view of the limits to that accumulation (Dore and Weeks, 1979), which is beyond the space of this essay to consider.

This theory of accumulation necessarily implies an analytical division of the world relevant to it. While dependency theorists write of the relationships between *countries* in their treatment of uneven development, in fact there is no concept of a "country" present in their theory. Rather, the "international" dimension of their theory of accumulation is achieved by dividing the world into developed and underdeveloped *areas*, and the de-accumulation and accumulation process occurs in this context. It so happens that political boundaries in many cases coincide with the developed and underdeveloped distinction. But this is in no way implied by the theory, and the theory is equally applicable *within* countries as *between* them, as Frank makes explicit (Frank, 1967). As a consequence, dependency theory comes forth with a clear and unambiguous empirical prediction. In as far as contemporary capitalism is characterized by the export of money and productive capital, this export should be from developed capitalist countries to underdeveloped countries.

In summary, dependency theory explains the rise of capitalism and the division of the world into developed and underdeveloped areas by surplus transfer; this uneven development is reproduced by the continuation of such transfers (in more "purely economic" form); the analytical space in which this occurs does not involve countries except by political accident; and predicted is the flow of capital from developed to underdeveloped areas.

## MATERIALIST THEORY

It is difficult to summarize the materialist theory of accumulation with equal brevity because of the concepts one must develop; so what follows is exceedingly schematic (in more detail, see Weeks, 1979). All class societies are characterized by exploitation[3] and the specific character of each class society is determined by the specific manner in which the surplus product of direct producers is appropriated (Marx, 1972: 783). Exploitation by definition implies a surplus product (production above the needs of direct producers), but a surplus product does not in itself imply accumulation. Accumulation on an expanding scale results from the progressive development of the productive forces rather than from the redistribution of a surplus product among societies. Thus, the explanation for uneven development on a world scale becomes the question of how and under what circumstances societies are characterized by the progressive development of the productive forces.

The process Marx called "primitive accumulation" — the separation of the peasantry from their means of labor (primarily land) — creates such circumstances. With the forcible separation of labor from rights in land, a "free" wage labor force is created. Along with this "freeing" of labor, the means of production become commodities (see Dore and Weeks, 1979). Once

[3]With the exception of socialism, in which classes persist but exploitation is eliminated.

there exists free wage labor, and the means of production are commodities, it becomes possible to bring these two together by the medium of money. Indeed, monetary exchange becomes the prior condition for the reuniting of the worker and the means of production. Such a social mechanism for organizing production is *capital* (money exchanged for the elements of production), and the expansion of this social mechanism (or social relation) results in capitalist society.

In capitalist society products circulate as commodities, which means that the surplus product of capitalist production assumes monetary form. This surplus product or surplus *value* is the material basis for accumulation and arises from the exploitation of direct producers (the proletariat). Surplus value, however, is only the *basis* of accumulation, and accumulation is forced upon individual capitalists by the conflict among capitals ("firms"). Because the products of capitalist production must be realized in money form in order for capitalists to initiate production afresh, the conflict among capitals necessarily assumes the form of an economic struggle. This struggle is fought out by the cheapening of commodities through technical change. Technical change leads to production on an expanding scale, so that the capitalist mode of production is an expanding one. This in itself is sufficient to explain why capitalism should reach out to underdeveloped areas. In materialist theory it is predicted that capital will expand into all areas, and once there is more than one capitalist area, the movement of capital *between developed capitalist areas* is as much to be expected as between developed capitalist areas and underdeveloped areas (Lenin, 1974).[4] Materialist theory converts its theory of accumulation into a theory of the world economy by locating it explicitly in the context of *countries.* What makes a political territory a "country" is that the territory is controlled by a distinct ruling class, the vehicle for such rule being the state. Materialists identify their theory of the world economy as "the theory of imperialism," which can be defined as the theory of the accumulation of capital in the context of the struggle among ruling classes. Derivative from this theory are (1) the analysis of the conflicts and cooperation between the ruling classes of advanced capitalist countries (which lead to inter-imperialist wars); (2) the conflicts and cooperation between advanced capitalist ruling classes and ruling classes of underdeveloped countries ("articulation" of modes of production); and (3) conflicts between ruling classes and oppressed peoples ("the national question").

Our presentation of materialist theory could be no more than a skeleton of that analysis, given the space available. We can summarize this summary as follows: materialist theory treats accumulation as the result of the interaction of production and changing social relations and analyzes the relationship between advanced and underdeveloped areas by this means; for a theory of the world economy, it places this accumulation process in the context of a world politically divided among ruling classes.

### CRITICAL ASSESSMENT

If the outline of the contrasting theories was brief, our critique must be briefer still. First, we deal with theoretical objections to dependency theory.

[4]Given the space limitations set for the contributions to this issue, this central point cannot be elaborated. It is, however, elaborated in Weeks (1979).

As we have seen, capitalist accumulation in dependency theory is primarily the result of the redistribution of surplus product between developed and underdeveloped areas. This presupposes both the production of the surplus product (a precondition for its distribution or redistribution) and accumulation itself. Accumulation is not related to the social relations under which a surplus product is produced or appropriated, with the implicit view that a surplus product is a sufficient condition for accumulation. In materialist theory, on the other hand, accumulation is explained as the result of particular social relations in a society (capitalist social relations). In this way, it is not only possible to explain why accumulation occurred in what dependency theorists like to call "the center" rather than "the periphery," but also to explain why it did not occur *anywhere* before the capitalist epoch. Second, on an empirical level, dependency theory makes the prediction that the flow of capital should be overwhelmingly from developed to underdeveloped areas. It is difficult to see how this theory could predict anything else, and in fact the overwhelming amount of direct investment flows are *among developed countries* (Weeks, 1979).[5] This incorrect description of reality derives from (1) an erroneous theory of accumulation, and (2) a failure to analyze the division of the world into countries (ruling class conflicts). Materialist theory, with its theory of imperialism, makes no such prediction, but rather views the export of capital from developed to underdeveloped countries as one aspect of the general movement of capital.

It is not possible in a few pages to do justice to two entire schools of thought; in the case of dependency theory this is because of its strong eclecticism, and for materialist theory because of its analytical complexity. However, a brief survey reveals the former to be unsatisfactory on both theoretical and empirical grounds.

## REFERENCES

Amin, Samir
 1976 *Unequal Development*, New York: Monthly Review

Baran, Paul A.
 1968 *The Political Economy of Growth*, New York: Modern Reader

Baran, Paul A. and Paul Sweezy
 1966 *Monopoly Capital*, New York: Modern Reader

Chilcote, Ronald H.
 1974 "A Critical Analysis of the Dependency Literature," *Latin American Perspectives*, I (Spring), 4-29

Dore, Elizabeth and John Weeks
 1979 "International Exchange and the Causes of Backwardness," *Latin American Perspectives*, VI (Spring), 62-87

Emmanuel, A.
 1972 *Unequal Exchange*, London: New Left Books

Fernández, Raúl and José Ocampo
 1974 "The Latin American Revolution: A Theory of Imperialism, Not Dependency," *Latin American Perspectives*, I (Spring), 30-61

---

[5]The manuscript referred to demonstrates, using data on U.S. foreign direct investment, that the share of such investment in underdeveloping countries has been declining continuously since the end of the Second World War and is now barely a quarter of the total.

Frank, André Gunder
    1967 *Capitalism and Underdevelopment in Latin America,* New York: Monthly Review

    1974 "Dependency is Dead, Long Live Dependency and the Class Struggle," *Latin American Perspectives,* I (Spring), 87-106

Lenin, V.I.
    1974 *Imperialism; The Highest Stage of Capitalism,* Vol. XXII of *Collected Works,* Moscow: Progress Publishers

Mandel, Ernest
    1975 *Late Capitalism,* London: New Left Books

Marx, Karl
    1972 *Capital,* Vol. III, London and Moscow: Lawrence & Wishart and Progress Publishers

Weeks, John
    1979 "Theories of Imperialism and the Pattern of U.S. Foreign Investment," Washington, D.C., manuscript available from the author

# 8

# THE POLITICAL IMPLICATIONS OF DEPENDENCY THEORY

*by*
*Thomas Angotti**

The widely diverse body of theory that has come to be known as dependency theory has had a significant impact on the anti-imperialist movement and revolutionary forces particularly in Latin America. It enjoys a fairly high degree of prestige and influence not only among professional economists and social scientists — its principal advocates — but within the revolutionary movements themselves. Whether intentionally or unconsciously, the proponents of dependency theory are actually responsible for advancing two strategic political lines for the movement.[1]

The first and most influential calls for an independent road to capitalist development (and/or gradual transition to socialism) as a means of overcoming the historical legacy of underdevelopment: i.e., independence from foreign domination. This is ultimately a reformist policy that readily appeals to the apologists for neocolonialism and only leads to the proliferation of poverty and exploitation. In effect, this line underestimates the possibility and necessity of socialist revolution as a distinct, advanced stage in the struggles for national liberation and therefore serves to conciliate bourgeois nationalism. The most sophisticated advocates of this line are Fernando Henrique Cardoso (1972) and Samir Amin (1976).[2]

The second strategic line calls for world-wide socialism as a precondition for eliminating underdevelopment. This idealist view is based on the proposition that imperialism, or foreign "domination," *directly* causes underdevelopment and serves as the main obstacle to development. In effect, this ultra-"left" line underestimates the role of the national democratic stage of

---

*The author teaches in the Columbia University Division of Urban Planning, where he directs the Planning Program in Developing Nations.

[1]This assessment would obviously exclude those dependentistas who may be located far enough to the right so as to be clearly within the pro-imperialist orbit (but then are they really dependentistas?).

[2]Throughout this analysis, the general perspective of the various theoreticians of dependency is synthesized and its major thrust summed up. This does not always coincide with the self-declarations of the dependentistas. Thus, Amin definitely identifies himself against imperialism and for socialism. By summing up the objective effect of the theories, we are consistent with Marxist materialism.

the revolutions in the developing world. Its principal advocate is André Gunder Frank (1970); of the two lines it is the least elaborated and most criticized.

The main political consequence of both of these approaches is to divert support from socialist revolutions as they actually unfold in the context of the struggles for national liberation. While dependency theory has played a progressive role by linking underdevelopment to external forces as opposed to the reactionary theories that blame the victims, it holds out the prospect that "independence" — with perhaps some gradual transition to socialism — can by itself solve the most pressing problem facing the developing nations: underdevelopment. The rightist line holds out the hope for independence without a definite break with imperialism and the capitalist mode of production, and the ultra-"left" line sees no hope for independence until the communist mode of production is somehow established on a world scale.

The Marxist critique must be aimed at challenging the influence of dependency theory within the anti-imperialist movement, where it plays a diversionary role. A major thrust of the critiques to date has been to show how dependency theory departs from the scientific theories of imperialism and underdevelopment. This is a necessary and important task, especially since dependentistas often claim Marxism as their framework or use Marxist categories and since modern revisionism has distorted revolutionary theory; but this task must be taken up within the context of exposing the negative political implications of the theory for the anti-imperialist movement. Stated very simply, the basic standpoint of dependency theory, which seeks in the first place to solve the problems of poverty and underdevelopment instead of first dealing with the question of how to defeat imperialism, is not a Marxist stand, nor does it advance the anti-imperialist movement.

The most advanced Marxist critiques to date have, in general, accurately targeted the reformist assumptions of dependency theory. They include the following: Charles Bettelheim (1972) who takes Arghiri Emmanuel to task for his neo-Ricardian analysis of the doctrine of comparative advantage and the theory of "unequal exchange"; Robert Brenner (1977), who focuses on the works of Immanuel Wallerstein and Paul Sweezy on the transition from feudalism to capitalism, pointing out their unscientific analyses of the capitalist mode of production; John Weeks and Elizabeth Dore (1979), who rectify the use of the categories of development and underdevelopment and posit the Marxist law of uneven development in place of the dependentista's concept of unequal exchange; Raúl Fernández and José Ocampo (1974), who criticize André Gunder Frank in particular for ignoring feudal and semi-feudal relations in Latin America and liquidating the central role of the national democratic struggles for independence.

In this article, I will attempt to draw out the main political implications of the Marxist critique. I will focus on the weakest aspect of the critique, which has been targeting dependency theory's distortion of the transition to socialism; given that most of the critiques have focused on the category of capitalism, this aspect has been overlooked.[3] Another shortcoming is the failure to draw out the methodological error underlying dependency theory — idealism. I will show how the theories of Bettelheim and Brenner actually distort the nature and downplay the significance of the transition from capitalism to socialism, the fundamental process that defines the current historical epoch, and fall into a different form of idealism. Given space limitations, it will not be possible to fully elaborate this analysis and critique; instead, what follows is the broad outline of a more thorough critique.

## THE MARXIST CRITIQUE OF DEPENDENCY THEORY

### The Main Propositions of Dependency Theory[4]

Dependency theory is actually a very broad, eclectic school of thought whose only common ground is the assumption that underdevelopment has causes external to the underdeveloped nations. The fact that dependency theorists span the entire range from the right to far left in the political spectrum helps explain their reluctance to be associated with one another or with a "school." Nevertheless, there are perhaps four main theoretical perspectives shared to some extent by most dependentistas: (1) the critique of dualism, (2) the core/periphery theory, (3) unequal exchange, and (4) the dependent bourgeoisie.

*The critique of dualism.* The entire thrust of the dependency school is to refute the idea propounded by bourgeois social science that the main obstacle to development is to be found in the inherent sociocultural qualities of the "traditional," backward sectors of underdeveloped countries, which supposedly lack the characteristics of the "modern" Western capitalist economies. All social history is therefore explained as a gradual transition from one ideal type (the traditional underdeveloped society) to another (the modern developed society). This critique is the most progressive feature of dependency theory; it has helped direct attention to imperialism's role in national oppression and underdevelopment.

*Core/periphery theory.* The second major construct is the notion that the world is divided up into "core" and "periphery" and that this is the most generalized division. While the terminology may not be shared by all, the basic approach is the same: the core is made up of the affluent advanced countries and the periphery is made up of the underdeveloped poor countries. This distinction is also used to describe the internal structure of nations; thus, we have the "internal colony" thesis (González Casanova, 1970).

*Unequal exchange.* The idea that underdevelopment is related to the disadvantage of "peripheral" nations on the world market is given its most mature expression in Emmanuel's (1972) theory of unequal exchange, ostensibly a critique of the Ricardian doctrine of comparative advantage. The main

---

[3]There is also a tendency among the critiques to rely on quotations from Marx, Engels, and Lenin to rectify the dependency definition of capitalism. This dogmatic tendency overlooks the necessity to demonstrate how dependency theory cannot explain imperialism in the twentieth century, or socialism in the twentieth century — phenomena that Lenin only began to analyze concretely before his death.

[4]More elaborate syntheses of dependency theory have been done (e.g., Chilcote, 1974). This brief synthesis is presented only to lay the foundation for the following critique.

implication is that the terms of trade and wages need to be revised so that labor (and capital) in the periphery are compensated in accordance with the value produced.

*Dependent bourgeoisie.* Most dependency theorists, especially those who use Marxist categories of class, tend to regard the bourgeoisie in the "periphery" as entirely dependent on external forces and therefore unable to play a progressive, anti-imperialist role. A corollary is that the working class in the "core" is both objectively and subjectively united with its own bourgeoisie rather than with the masses in the "periphery" and thus not part of the anti-imperialist front.

## The Main Political Effect

The most significant political impact of dependency theory has been to divert and dampen support for socialist revolution. The main theoretical omission underlying this is the failure to take into account the historical significance of the appearance of socialism in the world as a distinct mode of production ever since the victory of the Bolshevik Revolution in 1917.[5] Few of the existing critiques have specifically examined this question.[6]

Despite the revolutions in Russia, China, Cuba, Vietnam, Korea, and elsewhere, which have resulted in one-third of the world's population living in societies that do not function according to the laws of profit and private property and have none of the characteristics of extreme poverty, underdevelopment, and dependency found in the capitalist world, dependentistas continue to see dependency as the constant phenomenon. Although many socialist countries are still "underdeveloped" by North American standards, underdevelopment under socialism has a qualitatively different dynamic than under capitalism. The main obstacles to development are technical and environmental, since imperialism as a system has been removed from within the national borders of socialist countries (though its continued dominance on a world scale tends to distort socialist development).

Dependency theory assumes that the principal contradiction in the current epoch is between dominant and dependent forces, not a class struggle between imperialism and socialism. This "domination" is attributed alternatively to multinational corporations, financial institutions, or a "technostructure," operating on an international level; when attributed to imperialism, it is viewed principally as a foreign policy that can be reversed, and not as an organic system which requires the repression of independent nations in order to guarantee the export of capital. "Domination" is therefore a superstructural element whereby the powerful subdue the weak, the rich exploit the poor, and the "superpowers" devour the small nations. This category bears little resemblance to the Leninist theory of imperialism as a system which has a material basis in the real economic relations of society.

## Idealism: The Principal Methodological Error

The common methodological error of dependency theory is idealism,

---

[5]By socialism is meant the lower stage of the communist mode of production, which nevertheless is characterized by its own distinct laws of motion.

[6]This is the focus of critiques relating to particular socialist countries; for example, Gilbert (1974) examines relations between Cuba and the Soviet Union.

particularly as manifest in the tendency to blur the distinction between quantitative and qualitative change. The idealist world is made up of substances or things that are simply "transformed" gradually in time but do not significantly alter their inner essence. Thus, major social revolutions cannot and do not result in qualitative changes. The consequence is either reformist politics (aid the process of *gradual* change towards greater development and independence, or even towards socialism) or pessimism (nothing really changes qualitatively and there will always be domination and dependence).

The idealist method obscures the following world historical processes: (1) stages in the revolutionary process; (2) changes in the mode of production; (3) stages in the development of the dominant modes of production; and (4) the class struggle.

*Stages in the Revolutionary Process.* Every socialist revolution in the last three decades has occurred within the context of a national democratic struggle for independence from imperialism. The two stages of these revolutions may be very closely interrelated and difficult to distinguish (as in the Cuban revolution), but the failure of many revolutions to move beyond the national democratic stage (e.g., the "African socialist experiments") has had the obvious effect of perpetuating dependence on imperialism. The victory of a national democratic revolution represents only a quantitative break with imperialism; only a socialist revolution which expropriates private property and stakes its future on solidarity with the socialist camp actually signifies a qualitative change in the political economy and serves as the basis for unleashing the productive forces that imperialism has maintained in their backward state.

The reformist line among the dependentistas overemphasizes the importance of the democratic stage in the revolutionary process. The ultra-"left" line, on the other hand, practically liquidates the necessity of a national democratic revolution. If the whole world is capitalist, as André Gunder Frank claims, and there are no contradictions between national bourgeoisie and imperialism, then the only relevant struggle is between the international bourgeoisie and the international proletariat (Fernández and Ocampo, 1974).

*Changes in the Mode of Production.* The transition from capitalism to socialism is obscured by the notion that dependency continues after socialist revolution (one "superpower" is simply exchanged for another). Socialism is pictured as simply a transitional form of exploitative society differing only slightly from capitalism. The complete muddle made of the transition between capitalism and socialism corresponds to the muddled analysis of the transition from feudalism to capitalism that Brenner (1977) and others have criticized. Thus, dependentistas make no basic distinction between precapitalist commodity exchange and capitalist commodity production based on the accumulation and reproduction of surplus value (Weeks and Dore, 1979).

*Stages in the Development of the Dominant Modes of Production.* Dependency theory blurs the distinctions between the incipient mercantile stage of capitalist development based on small-scale commodity production and coinciding with the expansion of long-distance trade and colonialism; the industrial stage of capitalism, where the direct producers have been separated from the means of production and the production of surplus value is generalized; and the highest stage — imperialism — where the export and re-production of capital on a world scale becomes the main organizing principle.

Dependentistas also tend to mechanically separate capitalism (seen as internal to the nation) and imperialism (seen as external). This creates the il-lusion that capitalism can be eliminated (or shall we say "transformed" into a nondependent form?) without waging a struggle against and defeating imperialism. Indeed, the very category "dependent capitalism" implies that there could be such a thing as nondependent capitalism in the Third World, a capitalism that would benefit the masses of working people.

Just as the historical stages of development in the capitalist mode of production are obscured, so also are the stages in the communist mode of pro-duction. Thus, even among those who identify themselves with socialism, there is a tendency to assess post-revolutionary society according to the criteria of communism at its highest stage. If these ideal criteria do not match reality, these societies are considered to be some new form of exploitative en-tity (Sweezy, 1980) or transitional formations that exhibit all the major economic characteristics of capitalism. The political effect of this is pessi-mism and defeatism: why bother with the struggle for socialism if it only leads to a new form of exploitation?

*The Class Struggle.* Dependency theory tends to substitute a schematic stratification of society for an objective, particularized analysis of the class struggle. According to the ultra-"left" version, all classes in the "periphery" are somehow "dependent" and all classes in the "core" are "dominant." This blurs the distinction between the working class and the peasantry, obviates the need for any vanguard force in society, and again leads to pessimism. It removes any independent role for the national bourgeoisie in the anti-imperialist front. And it reduces the class struggle in the advanced capitalist nations to sibling rivalry.

While the ultra-"left" line fails to consider the contradictions between nations as part of the international class struggle, the rightist line reduces the class struggle to nothing more than a struggle between nations (or "social formations"). In effect, it abandons the theory of class struggle.

The theory of unequal exchange appeals to the class base of the commercial bourgeoisie and petty bourgeoisie, whose interests lie in securing better prices on the world market for national products. It also offers an appealing argument to trade unionists who are convinced the way forward is simply achieving higher wages (so workers would presumably be remunerat-ed at the value of their labor power).

In sum, the idealist method cannot provide a correct strategy for changing the world because it does not allow for a scientific understanding of the historical process of the transition from capitalism to socialism. Because it fails to place the whole question of economic development and underdevelop-ment within the context of the struggle against imperialism and for socialism, it cannot even pose useful solutions to that problem.

The methodology of dependency theory is also noted for its lack of rigor. Thus, both Marxist and non-Marxist categories are used interchangeably with very little explanation. For example, Sweezy substitutes "surplus product" for "surplus value" so that imperialist expansion is explained as simply a means of disposing of surplus commodities. This turns around completely the Leninist view that the driving force behind imperialism is the export of capital and not the export of commodities (Brenner, 1977). Similarly, the category "labor" and "labor power" are used interchangeably, "value" and "exchange value" and so forth. And in the end such unscientific notions as "primitive accumulation" are introduced, all in the interest of updating Marx. Our concern here is not in "preserving" a "pure" Marxism, but in demanding that dialectical and historical materialism, like every science, has a certain integrity upon whose maintenance depends the future course of the revolutionary process.

## CRITIQUE OF THE CRITIQUES

### Charles Bettelheim's Anarcho-syndicalist Critique

Charles Bettelheim's critique (1972) of the theory of unequal exchange accurately targets Emmanuel's distortion of the law of value and the role of commodity exchange. Emmanuel (1972) sees the source of capitalist exploitation in trade relations, where the prices offered to producers in Third World nations are supposed to be below their value, and in the wage structure, where labor power is supposedly remunerated below its value. Bettelheim correctly shows how this is at odds with the fundamental principles of Marxist political economy in which prices and wages are merely outward forms of value and generally tend to fluctuate around value. For Marxists, the source of capitalist exploitation is the extraction of surplus value from the production process, its exchange and reproduction.

Bettelheim, however, offers us another one-sided view of capitalism when he claims that "relations of exploitation cannot be constituted at the 'level of exchange'; they necessarily have to be rooted at the level of *production*, or otherwise exchange could not be renewed" (1972: 300). Also, "One of the serious weaknesses of the terms 'commercial exploitation' and 'unequal exchange' is that they obscure the fact that what is described by them is necessarily rooted in production relations."

This perspective fails to see capitalism as a system involving the production, circulation, and reproduction of capital and *every facet* of economic relations in society. Particularly in its highest stage — imperialism — capitalist relations not only consume and subordinate the precapitalist modes of production but permeate every sphere of social interaction and every region of the world. In short, the fetishism of commodities increasingly becomes universalized and is not simply limited to the sphere of exchange.[7]

Capitalist relations of exploitation are not simply "rooted at the level of

[7]In Volume I of *Capital*, for example, Marx shows how money and other outward forms of capital take on a mystical appearance that only obscures their being a social relation and not simply a *thing* that is exchanged. Marx explains commodity fetishism: "There is a physical relation between physical things. But it is different with commodities. There, the existence of the things *qua* commodities, and the value relations between the products of labor which stamps them as commodities, have absolutely no connexion with their physical properties and with the material relations arising therefrom . . . This I call the Fetishism which attaches itself to the products of labour, so soon as they are produced as commodities, and which is therefore inseparable from the production of commodities" (1867, I: 72).

*production."* Without competition between capitalists and commodity exchange, there could be no reproduction of capital; capitalism is the production of commodities specifically *for exchange*. Thus, Marx notes:

> . . . *competition* is nothing other than the inner *nature of capital*, its essential character . . . (1973: 414).

> Production of surplus-value is the absolute law of this mode of production. Labour-power is only saleable so far as it preserves the means of production in their capacity of capital, reproduces its own value as capital, and yields in unpaid labor a source of additional capital. The conditions of its sale, whether more or less favourable to the labourer, include therefore the necessity of its constant re-selling, and the constantly extended reproduction of all wealth in the shape of capital (1967, I: 618-619).

In other words, while the starting point of all capitalist production is the creation of surplus value, that very creation depends on the constant exchange and reproduction of capital; in the imperialist age in particular, the extended reproduction of capital requires a far more complex and all-encompassing system of exchange and reproduction than the nineteenth century industrial entrepreneurs could ever have imagined.[8]

Bettelheim's overemphasis on the sphere of production is no less one-sided than Emmanuel's overemphasis on the sphere of exchange. It represents a more profound tendency within Bettelheim's work towards syndicalism. In his *Economic Calculations and Forms of Property* (1975), Bettelheim emphasizes the necessity of increasing the "direct control" of the "immediate producers" over the production process as a key element in building socialism. In his analyses of China (1974, 1978a) and the Soviet Union (1976, 1978b), Bettelheim focuses on the process of production at the point of production — at the factory level and on the farms — and criticizes any attempts to implement central economic planning that do not strengthen the "direct control" of the producers but instead enhance the role of managers, the party, and the state (Goldfield and Rothenberg, 1980).

In his critique of Emmanuel, Bettelheim incorrectly attributes "the appearance of large-scale industry" in the world to "the transformation of the relations of production" in some countries. This analysis drops out entirely the role of the development of the productive forces and introduction of new technology as the principal *condition* that sets the historical stage for the transformation of production relations. These conditions make it possible for revolutionary changes in production relations to occur.

Bettelheim also tries to explain underdevelopment in anarchosyndicalist terms. For him, underdevelopment entails an:

> . . . international division of labor that renders inevitable *a polarized development of the world's productive forces* . . . (and thus) . . . *the expanded reproduction of economic inequalities* . . . (resulting from) . . . the domination of the world by capitalist production relations (1972: 289, emphasis in original).

Thus, the international division of labor is said to "block" development in

---

[8]For example, the third volume *Capital*, entitled "The Process of Capitalist Production as a Whole," deals almost entirely with the circulation, reproduction, and realization of capital.

some countries while it apparently promotes development in the more advanced countries.

This "blockage," however, is not due to the division of labor, as Bettelheim implies. It is an organic function of capitalism at its highest stage, whereby the oppression of entire nations — including the peasants, working class, petty bourgeoisie and national bourgeoisie — is a necessary condition for the proliferation and protection of capital on a world scale. The result of this oppression is the reinforcement of backwardness because national development can only occur within the context of and according to the needs of imperialism. When the technical and environmental conditions in the Third World meet the needs of imperialist expansion, then industry and other economic activities are located there. This determination is always made relative to the conditions available in the advanced capitalist countries, of course.

The division of labor between the primary-producing "periphery" and the industrial "core", for example, is more a function of the unevenness of capitalist production and — as dependentistas have documented — is becoming less and less significant to the extent that manufacturing spreads to many areas of the Third World.[9] In itself, it is not a determining factor nor is it the source of capitalism's evils. Those who see the world mainly from the factory floor harp about the division of labor; from the point of view of the international proletariat, the main effect of imperialism in the underdeveloped nations is that it holds back national development that is in the interests of the masses of people.

Underdevelopment is a historical condition related to the *uneven development* of capitalism which, like all social processes, does not evolve uniformly. It is bound up with the relatively low level of development of the productive forces in the colonial and neocolonial world — relative to the capitalist countries that developed first and most rapidly. Bettelheim sees the resulting inequalities as being *reproduced* as a result of the division of labor which "polarizes" development. But this completely distorts the increasingly important changes going on *within* the neocolonial world. Inequalities are not simply reproduced, but the relationships among the underdeveloped nations and between the various nations and the imperialist countries are constantly changing. Although inequalities are "reproduced," they always take a new form as imperialism constantly expands and transforms the preexisting modes of production and integrates parts of the "periphery" more and more into the "core." Thus, inequalities *within* the neocolonial world are growing as a portion of it develops on capitalist terms. To overlook this factor can lead to the liberal politics that pose a false unity among the "poor" countries.

Bettelheim's syndicalist outlook leads him to make a negative concession to the dependency school by posing the determining role of the "world relationships of domination and exploitation." Throughout the major works of Bettelheim, this "domination" is defined as essentially a political and ideological phenomenon, while the ultimately determinant role of the material and economic base is dropped out altogether. For example, his analyses of the

[9]Thus, in 1977, 31.4 percent of all exports from underdeveloped countries were manufactures, compared to 19.3 percent in 1972 (Vuskovic, 1980).

USSR and China are filled with admonitions that the key to building socialism is in revolutionizing the relations between the masses and the party and the masses and the state, in order to keep the institutions of authority on a revolutionary course. This idealist approach completely ignores the main political task of socialist revolutions, particularly in underdeveloped nations: the development of the productive forces in order to meet the constantly expanding needs of the masses. This provides a concrete material basis for raising the level of class consciousness of the masses — not at some distant future stage, but in conjunction with the elimination of backwardness and poverty. To pose the key task of the revolution as "improving relations" between the masses and "authority" (the main source of "domination") — which is what Bettelheim means by "production relations" — is a thoroughly idealist theory of socialist construction. Its consequences are the glorification of backwardness, small-scale production, and the unsocialized rural life they engender.

The root of the problem with Bettelheim is his idealist view of the world as made up of independent structures — relatively autonomous institutions within the international division of labor. These structures tend to "reproduce" themselves just as "inequality" is reproduced. This is a structuralist and not a dialectical materialist method because it does not understand history as motion generated by contradiction and not structures.

Bettelheim therefore looks at the structure of "social formations" and "the world structure": basically an imbalanced division of labor that is reproduced by imperialism. It is "the structure of underdevelopment" — a "left" version of dualism. Underdeveloped countries are trapped in these structures of capitalist development and cannot extricate themselves, or so Bettelheim's analysis would have us believe. From his studies of the Soviet and Chinese revolutions, it is obvious he does not think even a major socialist revolution can break down the divisions in the structure. Only a constantly recurring cultural revolution can *begin* to make a dent in them (for a somewhat half-hearted critique of Bettelheim's structuralism, see Clawson and Keenan, 1979).

The political implications of Bettelheim's theory for the anti-imperialist and socialist movements are significant. As with structuralism in general, it leads ultimately to pessimism and inertia. Despite Bettelheim's formal adherence to the theory of the two-stage revolution, the essential thrust of this theory is to downplay and even oppose advancement to the proletarian stage; for example, he clearly opposes the consolidation of the Bolshevik Revolution in 1929, as it entailed the initiation of central planning, priority development of the means of production, and consolidation of the proletarian dictatorship. Thus, Bettelheim adopts the petty-bourgeois line of Nikolai Bukharin that would have held back consolidation of the second stage by continuing the New Economic Policy (NEP). This line favored the perpetuation of rural backwardness in the interests of achieving some ideal "equilibrium" in economic development; it would give priority to consumption instead of production and promote the "relatively autonomous" structures like the trade unions and local peasant organizations in place of the organs of national proletarian power. This line, while it may formally unite with the goal of proletarian revolution, in the end thwarts its consolidation and advancement and may even create the conditions in which capitalist restoration is possible (as in the current situation in Poland). The most influential version of this line in the Third World today is the official policy of Tanzania. (For a more detailed analysis of Bettelheim's and Bukharin's theories of socialist construction, see Angotti, 1981).

## Brenner's Idealism

Robert Brenner's analysis (1977) very rigorously demonstrates how dependency theory distorts the basic Marxist category of capital, in particular the emergence of capital as a social relation in the world through the historical process of transition from feudalism. Brenner shows how dependency theory identifies the source of exploitation and accumulation of capital as trade relations and exchange; in the process, he does not fall into the blatant one-sidedness of Bettelheim and notes the crucial role played by the changes in technology and productivity in advancing the level of the productive forces. Brenner shows how "primitive accumulation" is really only a descriptive category and how imperialism mainly relies on the production of relative surplus value and extended reproduction in order to expand.

Brenner, however, completely misjudges the main methodological error in the theories of Wallerstein, Sweezy, Frank, and the other dependentistas. It is not mechanical materialism but idealism. This appears to conceal a certain idealism on Brenner's part.

Wallerstein's "world system," for example, is basically idealist because in it the superstructure — the state — inevitably determines the base and not the other way around. Sweezy fails to ground his theory in the real economic relations of production, and therefore the transitions from feudalism to capitalism and capitalism to socialism are depicted as quantitative, gradual processes without any qualitative change; and Frank's schematic model also idealizes social relations by fitting reality into a priori categories (core/periphery; development/underdevelopment) rather than developing categories from observation and scientific analysis of history.

As Brenner demonstrates, the dependentistas fail to grasp the historical significance of the appearance of capitalism in the world, and fail to see it as qualitatively distinct from precapitalist trade and exchange on the market. But this is an idealist error, not mechanical materialism.

Why should the identification of the methodological error be so important? Because it also underlies the dependentista's view of the transition from capitalism to socialism — and Brenner's. Brenner sees "socialism in one country" as a "utopia." In other words, after the capitalist mode of production is eliminated, the change is still only quantitative, and no nation — particularly underdeveloped ones, according to Brenner's method — can enter the lower stage of communism alone. The implications for the anti-imperialist movement are apparent. On the one hand, it liquidates the necessity of two-stage revolution: what would its purpose be? On the other hand, it downplays the significance of the proletarian revolutions that have actually been consolidated. Objectively, the nations established on the basis of scientific socialism in which capitalism is no longer the dominant mode of production are the natural allies of the anti-imperialist movement because their very stability and growth depend upon the ultimate demise of imperialism on a world scale. This is so despite revisionist distortions and even outright class collaboration on behalf of the parties in power.

Brenner's view ultimately fails to grasp the importance of the united front against imperialism. In this front, the establishment, defense, and construction of socialism are inextricably bound up with the defeat of imperialism. And socialism appears on the world scene in the same way capitalism did — unevenly, in separate nations. Brenner's critique of the dependentistas faults them for failing to understand this process when it involves the transition from feudalism to capitalism; but he himself fails to apply the dialectical method to the transition to socialism.

## CONCLUDING REMARKS

In this paper, only the main aspects of the critique of Bettelheim and Brenner have been outlined; a more in-depth analysis as yet remains to be done. It is important to reiterate, however, the positive contributions of their work to the repudiation of dependency theory.

The task before Marxists at this point is not simply to demonstrate the incompatability of dependency theory with the principles laid down by Marx, Engels, and Lenin, but to sum up the critique and further develop the scientific theory of underdevelopment and dependency as part and parcel of revolutionary theory and the theory of socialist construction. After all, it was the failure of the Marxist movement in the first place to establish a leading revolutionary line that opened the way for every sort of academic and bourgeois theory to enter the anti-imperialist movement under the guise of Marxism.

In the current epoch of the transition from capitalism to socialism, no development theory that fails to deal with socialist construction can be relevant. This is also why the theory cannot rely on quotations from Marx, Engels, and Lenin, who could not observe the actual experiences of socialist economic development and draw the universal lessons from the experiences. Similarly, the critique of dependency theory has to ultimately rest on the demonstration that it cannot solve the real problems of the less developed nations: the defeat of imperialism and the development of production to meet the expanding needs of the masses.

The reformist line that flows from dependency theory holds out the hope that underdevelopment can be overcome through autarky, while the ultra-"left" line awaits the ultimate defeat of imperialism. Neither of these perspectives can actually chart a correct course for the anti-imperialist movement. They instead lead to the justification of neocolonial exploitation, "nonalignment," and the perpetuation of backwardness.

The debate over dependency remains by and large within the anti-imperialist movement. It is therefore critical that Marxists play a leading role in both the critique and a positive affirmation of the role of imperialism in underdevelopment, as a basis for raising the level of unity within the movement. Unfortunately, the one-sided critiques of Bettelheim and Brenner, and such unscientific muddles as "the noncapitalist" road to development (Solodovnikov and Bogoslovsky, 1975) only hold back this development.

# REFERENCES

Angotti, Thomas
  1981 *Charles Bettelheim's Version of Soviet History: Historical Idealism*, San Francisco: The Soviet Union Study Project

Amin, Samir
  1976 *Unequal Development: An Essay on the Social Formations of Peripheral Capitalism*, New York: Monthly Review

Bettelheim, Charles
  1972 "Theoretical Comments," pp. 271-322 in Arghiri Emmanuel, *Unequal Exchange: A Study of the Imperialism of Trade*, New York; Monthly Review

  1974 *Cultural Revolution and Industrial Organization in China*, New York: Monthly Review

  1975 *Economic Calculations and Forms of Property*, New York: Monthly Review

  1976 *Class Struggles in the USSR*, (First Period: 1917-1923), New York: Monthly Review

  1978a *China Since Mao*, New York: Monthly Review

  1978b *Class Struggles in the USSR*, (Second Period: 1923-30)

Brenner, Robert
  1977 "The Origins of Capitalist Development: A Critique of Neo-Smithian Marxism," *New Left Review*, 104 (July-August), 25-93

Cardoso, Fernando Henrique
  1972 "Dependency and Development in Latin America," *New Left Review*, 74 (July-August), 83-95

Chilcote, Ronald H.
  1974 "A Critical Synthesis of the Dependency Literature," *Latin American Perspectives*, I (Spring) 4-29

Clawson, Pat and James Keenan
  1979 "Economism Exposed: Bettelheim on the Bolshevik Revolution," *The Insurgent Sociologist*, VIII (Summer), 80-87

Emmanuel, Arghiri
  1972 *Unequal Exchange: A Study of the Imperialism of Trade*, New York: Monthly Review

Fernández, Raúl A. and José F. Ocampo
  1974 "The Latin American Revolution: A Theory of Imperialism, Not Dependence," *Latin American Perspectives*, I (Spring) 30-61

Frank, André Gunder
  1970 *Latin America: Underdevelopment or Revolution*, New York: Monthly Review

Gilbert, Guy J.
  1974 "Socialism and Dependency," *Latin American Perspectives*, I (Spring) 107-123

Goldfield, Michael and Melvin Rothenberg
  1980 *The Myth of Capitalism Reborn: A Marxist Critique of Theories of Capitalist Restoration in the USSR*, San Fransisco: The Soviet Union Study Project

González Casanova, Pablo
  1970 *Sociologia de la Explotación*, 2nd ed., Mexico City: Siglo, XXI Editores

Marx, Karl
  1967 *Capital*, 3 Vols., New York: International Publishers

  1973 *Grundrisse*, New York: Vintage

Solodovnikov, V. and V. Bogoslovsky
  1975 *Non-Capitalist Development: An Historical Outline*, Moscow: Progress Publishers

Sweezy, Paul
  1980 "Post-Revolutionary Society," *Monthly Review*, XXXII (November), 1-13

Vuskovic, Pedro
  1980 "Latin America and the Changing World Economy," *NACLA Report on the Americas*, XIV(January-February) 2-15.

Weeks, John and Elizabeth Dore
  1979 "International Exchange and the Causes of Backwardness," *Latin American Perspectives*, VI (Spring), 62-87

# 9

# TOWARD
# A NEW UNDERSTANDING OF DEVELOPMENT
# AND UNDERDEVELOPMENT

*by*

*Norma Stoltz Chinchilla and James Lowell Dietz* *

Dependency theory has contributed to contemporary Marxist analysis by questioning outmoded interpretations of imperialism, pointing out weaknesses in many theoretical explanations of development and underdevelopment, and advocating a study of the dynamics and effects of imperialism from the point of view of "imperialized" ("satellite") societies rather than imperialist ("metropolis") ones. It directly confronted Marxists with the need to reexamine the conventional wisdom on the causes of underdevelopment. The widely read and popularized formulations of André Gunder Frank (1967, 1969) as well as the works of Paul Baran (1957), Fernando Henrique Cardoso (1969, 1972, 1973) Theotônio Dos Santos (1970), and the father of dependency, Sergio Bagú (1949), forced Marxists to confront the issue of development and imperialism once again and replace often unquestioned formulas with more profound and complex theoretical formulations. The flurry of intense inquiry and debate stimulated by the emergence of the dependency perspective has been perhaps its most enduring contribution to Marxist scholarship.

For many scholars and activists, the dependency perspective has been not only the radical but the Marxist interpretation of imperialism. Many Marxists, or persons sympathetic to and influenced by Marxist theory, are found in the ranks of its advocates, but the relationship between the dependency paradigm and Marxist theory has been anything but unproblematic. Dependency advocates have posed important questions, their Marxist critics acknowledge, but they have failed to answer them within a Marxist framework, choosing instead to insert new theoretical categories (like dependent capitalism) and elaborate ad hoc explanations. Not only were dependency theory's categories and methodological assumptions inadequate to the task of understanding development, but its political implications were often unacceptable or overly ambiguous. While dependency analyses had put the questions on the agenda, it has not been able to provide adequate alternative theoretical answers to the

---

*The authors teach respectively in the School of Social Sciences at the University of California, Irvine, and in the Department of Economics at California State University, Fullerton.

causes of underdevelopment and the specificity of capitalism in Latin America.

Extensive Marxist critiques of dependency theory are increasingly well-known (see Cueva, 1976; Laclau, 1977; Foster-Carter, 1978; Brenner, 1977; Dietrich, 1978). But most of these critiques suffer from the same weakness as dependency theory itself — the lack of an alternative theory. In fact, the failure of most critiques to outline an alternative has reinforced the view that the differences in the debate are insignificant semantic differences and that dependency critiques are dogmatic or ill-founded. The greatest weakness of most critiques of dependency theory has been this failure to go beyond mere criticism to an alternative theoretical perspective with demonstrated theoretical, empirical (i.e., historical), and political differences of consequence. The discussion which follows is based on the belief that the beginnings of an alternative conception now exist; we offer a sketch of this approach and briefly indicate the possibilities for encouraging the kind of complex and detailed studies that are needed to push forward our understanding of capitalist development and underdevelopment.

## OVERCOMING THEORETICAL WEAKNESSES

Neither the concept of "development" nor "underdevelopment" was elaborated adequately in dependency theory. Often, developed countries were defined as those that were wealthy and underdeveloped nations those that were poor; the definitions seemed to be imbedded in the terms themselves. Frank borrowed his definitions directly from orthodox, neoclassical economics. Development meant growth and underdevelopment stagnation. Thus, Frank's famous "development of underdevelopment" implied increasing stagnation for "underdeveloped" countries. This equation of underdevelopment and stagnation, however, could not be maintained once many underdeveloped (poor) nations began to show sustained signs of development (growth) in the 1960s and early 1970s. Frank introduced the concept of "lumpendevelopment" (1972) to describe this new situation, and Cardoso, in many ways the most sophisticated of dependency writers, wrote of "associated dependent development" (1973) and the possibility of development within dependent countries (1972). None of this terminology, however, went beyond describing the changes taking place in Latin America. The descriptive categories lacked a theoretical foundation to explain the changes that Frank, Cardoso, and other dependency theorists were attempting to account for. What was missing was a theoretical understanding of capitalist development, i.e., of the movement of capitalism in national economies and at the world level. In the absence of this framework, it was difficult to explain the coexistence of growth and "underdevelopment" without resorting to ad hoc argument.

Virtually all of the theoretical weaknesses of dependency analysis have revolved around its understanding of the history and nature of capitalist development. In reaction to both orthodox dualist theories of development and the official communist parties' view that feudalism was the cause of underdevelopment, dependency theories argued the opposite: Latin America and the Caribbean were capitalist and had been integrated into the capitalist world system for a long time (for some, like Frank, since the conquest). The dependent capitalism of these areas, however, resulted in their underdevelopment rather than the development which took place in Western Europe as a result of its *nondependent* capitalism. Dependency theorists seemed to argue that dependent capitalism was a new, historical mode of production, a deformed capitalism which did not result in development (growth). What defined dependent capitalism was the impossibility of autonomous capitalist development and the export of the surplus from peripheral countries to the nondependent capitalist (core, center) countries resulting in a tendency toward stagnation in the periphery and growth in the center. It was the outward flow of surplus (via unequal exchange, profit remittances, technological transfers, etc.) that accounted for the dual but united process of underdevelopment at one pole and development at the other. The flow of surplus certainly meshed with the facts, but as an edifice upon which to hang the poverty of the Third World, it turned out to be weak.

This theoretical weakness can be examined at two levels. First, in their attempt to force underdeveloped nations into the mold of a capitalist mode of production, dependency theorists were required to do violence to much of observable reality. They argued, for example, that what might appear to be feudal or precapitalist relations of production in agriculture were not and are not precapitalist. Instead, apparent precapitalist labor relations are simply the *forms* of labor domination used by the capitalist mode of production in the periphery. Wage labor was only the historically specific means by which capitalism extracted surplus value in the center countries where the land/labor ratio was low, while forced labor and other servile labor forms have been the necessary means of surplus extraction adopted by capitalist enterprises in the periphery where the land/labor ratio is large. From the dependency perspective, in Latin America (and the world), there is only capitalism and the capitalist mode of production. This view fails, however, to distinguish between "mode of production" and "social formation" (as Lenin [1967] implicitly did in his study of the multiplicity of relations of production in Russia) and fails to perceive the political implications of different relations of production and the corresponding class structures during different historical periods. With the exception of Marini's (unsuccessful) attempt to link dependence and stagnation, this has left a significant theoretical gap. In what ways does dependent capitalism operate according to different "laws" or tendencies than nondependent capitalism, and what are these new laws? Is dependent capitalism actually a new mode of production distinct from the capitalist mode? How does the internal class structure of dependent capitalist societies differ from that of nondependent capitalist societies? Dependent capitalism is given the theoretical status of a mode of production, but its structure and meaning have not been defined and its grounding in a Marxist context is left unclear.

## GROWTH AS A RESULT OF CAPITALIST PENETRATION

Confronted with these questions, some scholars have returned to classical writings in an attempt to develop an explicitly Marxist analysis of dependency and underdevelopment (Kay, 1975; Palloix, 1975; Warren, 1973). They argue that economic growth in Latin America is the result of increased capitalist (imperialist) penetration into areas which, though long integrated into the world capitalist market via exchange, have not been transformed internally to any significant degree. In their view, imperialist penetration of the Third World economies is creating conditions for the full emergence of industrial capitalism and capitalist relations of production. It is this internal transformation that explains the growth which is increasingly the norm in Latin America. This change is not the result of autonomous and internally generated national control in underdeveloped countries but is due instead to the expansion of monopoly capitalism, its productive apparatus, its culture, etc., into the "periphery."

In this view, expansion of international commodity production via transnational corporations spreads the capitalist mode of production and capitalist industrialization throughout the Third World by destroying precapitalist forms and creating the conditions necessary for its own reproduction. This theoretical position seems to be more compatible than dependency theory with Marx's thinking in *Capital:* "The country that is more developed industrially only shows, to the less developed, the image of its own future" (Marx, 1967: 8-9). As well, it seems to be Lenin's meaning when he wrote that,

> The export of capital greatly affects and accelerates the development of capitalism in those countries to which it is exported. While therefore, the export of capital may tend to a certain extent to arrest development in the countries exporting capital, it can only do so by expanding and deepening the further development of capitalism throughout the world (Lenin, 1939: 65).

Kay, Palloix, Warren and others, however, reproduce an error that permeates dependency theory by assuming that capitalism is basically an unchanging system subject to the same "laws" in the late twentieth century as it was in the nineteenth. Like dependency analysis, these theories of increasing homogenization of production and social relations in the world have no concept of *stages* of capitalist development or of the maturing and decaying of the capitalist mode of production (as occurred for earlier modes of production). There is simply capitalism. When imperialism is mentioned, it has no theoretical meaning beyond signifying capitalist expansion. In the view of these writers, there is no difference between imperialist-induced growth and a hypothetical nationally controlled capitalist growth process in terms of the development/industrialization dialectic; they are simply different forms of capitalist class rule subject to invariable capitalist laws of motion, i.e., to the inexorable weight of "capitalogic." In other words, in this perspective, capitalism is capitalism — even when it is imperialism. It is Volume I Marx without Lenin.

The existence of underdevelopment cannot be explained by these authors except by the absence of capitalism. Usually implicitly, but at times explicitly (Kay, 1975), underdevelopment persists because of the lack of capitalist development so that a higher level of capitalist (imperialist) penetration — even if such development is foreign dominated — would mean less underdevelopment for the Third World.

We believe this perspective remains partially flawed and politically dangerous since it implies that imperialism is progressive. But the efforts by these authors to develop a Marxist analysis to account for the reality which dependency theorists had described was valuable. It forced a further interface of Marxist theory with the concrete conditions of Latin America. Out of this came another spurt of Marxist analysis, mostly from France and Latin America itself, that has attempted to explain the place of Latin America and the Caribbean in the world economy and account for both the current growth process and continued poverty and "underdevelopment."

This alternative analysis is known as the "modes of production" or "articulation" perspective. It is this explanation that we believe improves upon the theory described above while providing a consistent theoretical framework within which to understand the reality dependency analysis described.

## THE MEANING OF DEVELOPMENT

Before developing the alternative approach, it is important to realize that there is more than one meaning that can be given to development (or underdevelopment). First, development can be understood in orthodox economic terms, i.e., as a certain threshhold level of GNP (gross national product) per capita and underdevelopment as its opposite, a low level of GNP per capita. A country experiencing development would exhibit an increasing GNP. Development thus can be viewed as both a condition and a process. It is this meaning of development (and underdevelopment as its opposite) with which both dependency analysis and the theories of Warren, Kay, and others have worked.

Second, development and underdevelopment are often used to refer to (typically undefined) ideal states. Development has a positive connotation as a condition of economic well-being and autonomy while underdevelopment has the opposite meaning. Thus it is possible to have "development within underdevelopment," i.e., growth taking place in a country which exhibits the negative characteristics of underdevelopment. For both Frank and Cardoso, "development within underdevelopment" could [or can] continue without development leading to development, i.e., without growth (the first meaning of development) leading to the ideal state of development (its second meaning). Why this might be expected to be a permanent feature in underdeveloped countries is, however, not clear.

There is also a third possible meaning of development that considers its specificity, that is, which attempts to understand the process of *capitalist* development. From this perspective, there is no predisposition to imbue "development" with either a positive moral connotation or to give it the orthodox economic definition. Instead, capitalist development is understood to be the extension of capitalist social relations (wage labor, proletarianization, alienation of peasants and independent commodity producers from their means of production, etc.) to an ever greater part of the population and of capitalist dominance over an ever larger part of society's production. The question of whether or not this process results in an improvement in the conditions of life for the majority depends not upon whether growth occurs or not, but on the class divisions of society and their strengths in reaping the benefits of production. This is a question separate from whether growth is taking place or whether capitalist relations are spreading. Denis Goulet once phrased this dichotomy, "Development . . . or Liberation?" (1973). It is first necessary to understand the nature of capitalist development as capitalism before it is possible to talk about development as liberation (i.e., an ideal state).

## THE MODES OF PRODUCTION APPROACH

The modes of production approach begins with four premises (Rey, 1976; Godelier, 1974, 1977). Analyses of these perspectives can be found in Chinchilla (1980), Dietz (1979a, 1979b, forthcoming), and Dietrich (1978).

(1) Though it is essential to analyze the functioning of capitalism at the world level, the fundamental unit of analysis remains the national economy. Each national economy is a concrete, historically created *social formation* which is formed by the "articulation" (interaction, linking, relationship) of two or more *modes* of production. The particular way in which these modes of production and their classes interface, in complementary as well as contradictory patterns, influences the structure, class nature, and direction of development of that society. Different social formations (national economies) having the same modes of production will not be the same due to historical variations in the articulation of their particular modes of production and classes within each social formation. Except during periods of rapid transition, one mode of production (and hence one class) will tend to be dominant within a social formation and may rise to dominance through internal or external means (capitalism, for example, arose from *within* most Western European social formations but was introduced from *without* into many Third World societies). The other modes of production retain their basic relations of exploitation (and thus class conflict) within the social formation, but these are mediated and affected by their relation to and with the classes of the dominant mode. The emergence of a new dominant mode of production does not result necessarily in the dissolution and decline of pre-existing modes; rather former modes of production and their classes may be able to preserve themselves, and may even be reinforced by the dominant mode of production, for long periods of time.

For example, when the capitalist mode of production is dominant, the nature of the articulation within the social formation is affected primarily by the needs of the capitalist mode and secondarily, but significantly, by the internal structure and class strength of the precapitalist modes. The speed and success with which capitalism dominates, penetrates, and destroys precapitalist modes has to do with the internal structure of these modes as well as external factors. As a result, since these factors vary widely in each concrete case, the process is neither mechanistically predictable nor uniform among social formations (Rey, 1976; Bradby, 1975). It is not only that Third World social formations differ in significant ways from the proto-typical (English) capitalist model described by Marx, but even the Western European capitalist formations differ from one another (for example, in the degree to which the peasantry has been preserved in France and Germany) due to different articulations with and degrees of preservation or destruction of previous modes and classes.

The view of social change embodied in the mode of production approach thus explicitly rejects both the universal evolutionary view of the orthodox economic paradigm and the simple Marxist perspective (which Marx himself warned against) of a fixed, linear sequence of modes of production. It also avoids the forced simplicity of the dependency approach which theorizes that there is one and only one mode of production — (dependent) capitalism.

(2) The mode of production approach takes into consideration the stages of development of the different modes of production which articulate within any social formation. Modes of production have periods of ascendancy and decline that affect not only their own tendencies and internal processes of re-production but also the nature of their relationship to the other modes within the social formation. It is necessary to determine the stages of development of the different modes, to study the process of their reproduction (especially the class relationships and conflicts), and to discover the nature of the articulation between the modes and the classes within the entire social formation. For example, this view recognizes that the capitalist mode of production has different tendencies and functions differently depending on its level (stage) of development, e.g., competitive vs. monopoly capitalism, and that the nature of capitalism dominating the international system as a whole can influence the kind of capitalism dominant in concrete social formations in specific historical periods.

(3) Development is not understood in some abstract, ideal sense, but rather as the "development of capitalist development," that is, as the process by which the capitalist mode and its classes come into contact with other modes of production and their classes and replace or dominate the precapitalist modes. It recognizes that capitalism is always "underdeveloped" in the ideal sense of development; that in rich and poor countries alike it brings progress only for the few at the cost of appropriating the labor, the control, the power, the creativity, and at times the lives, of the many.

(4) External control and influence, in this view, are modified and shaped by the internal structure — the structure of classes, the level and forms of the class struggle, and the nature of the state. Neither external relations nor internal ones, however, are "determining" a priori; rather, they exert different forces at different points in time and in different ways which must be studied in their concrete specific forms; the changes of a social formation are not based on general "laws of development" that are always moving forward unambiguously.

Mode of production is a general theoretical category that indicates general tendencies (not laws) of societal change; the exact forms of change and the process of their development are mediated in class struggle and, therefore, are not wholly predictable. Any real understanding of social change must be accompanied by detailed investigation of concrete societies. The general method for such investigation includes: (a) identifying the types, stages, and nature of the modes of production within the national economy; (b) determining the forms and nature of the articulations of the various modes, including the determination of the dominant mode of production and the impact of this dominant relation on the other modes, especially in terms of their class structure, ideology, etc., and the reciprocal influence of the subordinant modes of production on the dominant mode and its class relations, ideology, etc.; (c) identifying the different aspects and functions of the social, political, and ideological superstructure of the social formation in terms of their origin and functions vis à vis the different modes of production and determining the ways in which the reproduction of the social formation and the separate modes of production is secured (and to what extent they are reproduced individually). This would include analysis of the state as a site of both class struggle and class dominance by the ruling class of the dominant mode of production.

What theoretical advances does the mode of production alternative contribute? The realization that there are *parallel processes of development* in advanced capitalist and Third World countries makes it possible to begin to explain similarities and differences within the same theoretical framework without resort to ad hoc explanations. The similarities of capitalist development can be seen to derive from the consistent, underlying logic and internal dynamic of the capitalist mode wherever it appears. The differences derive from the ways in which capitalism satisfies its need to reproduce itself through its articulation with the other modes within a specific social formation. Class alliances and the forms of class struggle which emerge (as well as the nature of the classes) in the Third World can be understood as resulting from and affecting these articulations. Different stages in the dominant mode of production and different stages of the articulation relations among the modes within the social formation will have different consequences for growth possibilities. Contact with and penetration by foreign capital in the social formation of a Third World country do not inevitably result in underdevelopment (in its first sense); rather, capitalist social formations (i.e., those where the capitalist mode of production is dominant) can experience either growth or stagnation. The stagnation which dependency theorists observed was not caused by external dependency but by the internal dynamic between production and reproduction of different modes of production at different stages within the social formation. In the same way, the current situation of economic growth in these social formations is the result of changes in the nature of the articulation of the various modes and the power of the classes in the social formation; it reflects the increasing strength of the capitalist mode and classes vis à vis the precapitalist.

This is not to say that the fact that capitalism in Latin America and the Caribbean has been transplanted to the region is unimportant. The fact that it is monopoly capitalism now operating in Third World social formation is significant and has clearly affected the development of these social formations. But it is also significant to recognize the internal process and interaction of articulations that result when foreign monopoly capital confronts existing modes of production in Third World social formations.

What the articulation approach promises are analyses which look at modes of production as more than just structures which "act" (e.g., "capitalism expands") and which are able to see both structures *and* actors (classes) within those structures. For example, in studying Latin America it is clear that the tendencies of capitalist development result in expansion both across national borders and within them; but the specific structure of classes which are part of the capitalist mode of production (workers in general, national capitalists vis à vis international capitalists, etc.) affect the "tendencies" of capitalism. Furthermore, since noncapitalist modes of production exist simultaneously with capitalist ones in the world economy and within specific social formations, their class structures affect the dominant mode and its reproduction possibilities and shape the character of and possibilities for the dominant class. In a related fashion, the articulation perspective offers, to a greater degree than any other, a beginning understanding of the complex but fundamental questions of ideology and class position for individuals who are not easily categorized as peasant or proletarian in a classical sense but who embody characteristics of both.

## REFERENCES

Bagú, Sergio
　　1949 *Economía de la sociedad colonial*, Buenos Aires: El Ateneo

Baran, Paul
　　1957 *The Political Economy of Growth*, New York: Monthly Review Press

Bradby, Barbara
　　1975 "The Destruction of Natural Economy," *Economy and Society*, IV (May), 127-161

Brenner, Robert
　　1977 "The Origins of Capitalist Development: A critique of Neo-Smithian Marxism," *New Left Review*, 104 (July-August), 25-92

Cardoso, Fernando Henrique
　　1969 *Dependencia y desarrollo en América Latina*, Mexico City: Siglo XXI

　　1972 "Dependency and Development in Latin America," *New Left Review*, 74 (June-August), 83-95

　　1973 "Associated Dependent Development: Theoretical and Practical Implications," pp. 142-176 in Alfred Stepan (ed.) *Authoritarian Brazil*, New Haven: Yale University Press

Chinchilla, Norma Stoltz
　　1980 "Articulation of Modes of Production and the Latin American Debate," unpublished manuscript

Cueva, Agustín
　　1976 "A Summary of 'Problems and Perspectives of Dependency Theory,' " *Latin American Perspectives*, III (Fall), 12-16

Dieterich, Heinz
　　1978 *Relaciones de producción en América Latina*, Mexico City: Ediciones Cultura Popular

Dietz, James
　　1979a "Capitalist Development in Latin America," *Latin American Perspectives*, VI (Winter), 88-92

　　1979b "Imperialism and Underdevelopment: A Theoretical Perspective and a Case Study of Puerto Rico," *Review of Radical Political Economics*, 11 (Winter), 16-32

　　Forthcoming *Capitalism, Class and Industrialization: A Political Economic History of Puerto Rico Since the Nineteenth Century*

Dos Santos, Theotônio
　　1970 "The Structure of Dependency," *American Economic Review*, LX (May), 231-236

Foster-Carter, A.
　　1978 "The Modes of Production Controversy," *New Left Review*, 107 (January-February), 47-77

Frank, André Gunder
　　1967 *Capitalism and Underdevelopment in Latin America*, New York: Monthly Review Press

1969 *Latin America: Underdevelopment or Revolution*, New York: Monthly Review Press

1972 *Lumpenbourgeoisie — Lumpendevelopment*, New York: Monthly Review Press

Godelier, Maurice
    1974 "On the Definition of a Social Formation," *Critique of Anthropology* (I), 63-73

    1977 *Perspectives in Marxist Anthropology*, London: Cambridge University Press

Goulet, Denis
    1973 "Development . . . of Liberation?," in Charles K. Wilber (ed.) *The Political Economy of Development and Underdevelopment*, New York: Random House

Kay, Geoffrey.
    1975 *Development and Underdevelopment: A Marxist Analysis*, New York: Macmillan

Laclau, Ernesto
    1977 *Politics and Ideology in Marxist Theory*, London: New Left Books

Lenin, V.I.
    1939 *Imperialism*, New York: International Publishers

    1967 *The Development of Capitalism in Russia*, Moscow: Progress Publishers

Marx, Karl
    1967 *Capital*, Vol. I, New York: International Publishers

Palloix, C.
    1975 "The Internationalization of Capital and the Circuits of Social Capital," pp. 63-88 in Hugo Radice (ed.), *International Firms and Modern Imperialism*, Baltimore: Penguin Books

Rey, Pierre-Phillipe
    1976 *Las alianzas de clases*, Mexico City: Siglo XXI

Warren, Bill
    1973 "Imperialism and Capitalist Industrialization," *New Left Review*, 81 (September-October), 3-44

# 10

# DEPENDENCY AND WORLD SYSTEM THEORY: A CRITIQUE AND NEW DIRECTIONS

*by*
*James Petras\**

World system theory (so designated by one of its major practitioners, Immanuel Wallerstein, 1975) is derived from the intellectual heritage found in the critique of the developmentalist perspective of liberal political economy. This critique was articulated in the work of Paul Baran (1957), A. G. Frank (1967, 1969), Theotônio Dos Santos (1971), and other dependency theorists (for a recent review and effort to defend the dependency perspective, see Cardoso, 1977). Recently, dependency has achieved a new status in the attention given to the "unequal exchange" theses of Arghiri Emmanuel (1972), Samir Amin's discussion (1974) of the "accumulation of world capital," and Immanuel Wallerstein's historical interpretation (1974, 1976) of the rise of a "single capitalist world economy."

The basic framework of a world systems theorist is strikingly elementary. The problematic to be explained is the fact that there exist different stages or levels of national development within what appears to be a unified global economy. The key to explaining this phenomenon, it is argued, is to specify the different political and economic roles which a state or geographic area plays within the overall system. This notion gives rise to the basic categories of analysis: core, semiperiphery and periphery; core and periphery; metropole and satellite.

The real innovation of the world systems approach lies in the choice of the primary unit of analysis — the capitalist world economy. All phenomena are to be explained in terms of their consequence for both the whole of the system and its parts. It is asserted that the internal class contradictions and political struggles of a particular state, like Rhodesia for example, can be explained as "efforts to alter or preserve a position within the world economy which is to the advantage or disadvantage of particular groups located within a particular state" (Wallerstein, 1975: 16).

What is important to notice is the direction of generalization in world systems theory, for that is the key to understanding the approach. Specific events within the world system are to be explained in terms of the demands of the system as a whole. Actors are acting, not for their immediate concrete interests, but because the system dictates that they act. As Wallerstein (1975:

*The author is a Professor of Sociology at the State University of New York, Binghamton.

26) has put it: "Where then in this picture do the forces of change, the movements of liberation, come in? They come in precisely as not totally coherent pressures of groups which arise out of the structural contradictions of the capitalist world economy" (Wallerstein, 1975: 16).

The central theme of the world systems approach is the proposition that core regions exploit peripheral regions through various mechanisms of unequal exchange. Superficially, this idea of unequal exchange seems similar to the focus by structuralists on unequal economic transactions. In fact, the world systems conceptualization is distinguished by an effort to ground unequal exchange in a labor theory of value. This labor theory of value forms the basis of an attempt to explain how surplus value extracted from the working class of the periphery is transferred to core regions. It is further hypothesized that the transfer of value from one region of the world capitalist economy to another is a form of primary accumulation that is necessary to the maintenance of monopoly forms of capitalism in the core. As a means of extracting surplus, unequal exchange is not only different from the extended reproduction of capital that is characteristic of the core, but it is the principal contradiction of the modern capitalist world.

The economic arguments purporting to demonstrate the functioning of unequal exchange are most fully developed by Emmanuel. He begins by critiquing Ricardo's theory of international trade for being based on unrealistic assumptions. According to Emmanuel, it is statistically more accurate to assume that capital is mobile and labor is immobile on the international market. With this revised set of assumptions, it is possible to demonstrate a tendency for profits to become equalized internationally while wages remain different. Emmanuel then claims that it is these two tendencies which explain the deterioration in the terms of trade of peripheral regions which are emphasized by structuralists. In this analysis, the wage differential between core and periphery is the independent variable that accounts for the phenomenon of unequal exchange. Amin and Wallerstein agree with Emmanuel regarding the centrality of wages, but they also draw attention to other differences between core capitalism and peripheral capitalism.

Given this analysis of world capitalism, the salient question for radical praxis becomes, "What can regions of peripheral capitalism do in order to mitigate or eliminate the effects of unequal exchange?" Assuming that a sudden raising of the level of wages in the periphery to that prevailing in the core is impossible, the logical tactic is to develop means for preventing the movement abroad of the surplus value extracted from workers in the periphery. Emmanuel argues that since somebody has to benefit from these low wages, and since it is desired that foreign consumers not be the beneficiaries, it is best that the benefits accrue to national capitalists. He proposes taxes on exports and diversification of production as two mechanism for accomplishing this goal. It is assumed that this excess surplus will be used for development purposes.

## AN EVALUATION OF WORLD SYSTEMS APPROACHES

To conceptualize the issues of the Third World in terms of dependency or as part of a world system is to lose sight of the most decisive processes of class formation and social relations which beget change and the particular configurations of social forces which emerge on a world scale.

It is not the world system that begets change in social relations, but rather social forces that emerge and extend their activities that produce the world market. The transformations wrought within societies by their insertion in the world market must be seen as an ongoing reciprocal relationship: between the forces and relations of production within a social formation and those that operate through the world market. From the perspective of international political economy, a comprehensive analytical framework must focus on the structural variations and transformations within the capitalist mode of production and the state capacities for exercising hegemony, both within a social formation and on a global basis.

The principal features which characterize capitalist development have varied considerably over time: the process of primitive accumulation, the growth of commercial capital, the expansion and growth of industrial and later financial capital each have their own laws of development, generating their own class structures and appropriate state organization. The class and state variations within core countries are determinants of their relative position in the world capitalist system. Among the capitalist countries (core), the variations in imperial state organization, development of the productive forces, and homogenization of the social formation (absence of precapitalist social formation), affect the relative competitive position of each in terms of establishing areas of hegemony. The differential in class formation contained within each core society is, in turn, essential to understanding the types of class alliances within a social formation and between capitalist countries. Finally, the crystallization of class forces — the degree of polarization within a social formation, outcome of the combined developments of productive forces, external expansion, and internal polarization — determines the level and scope of class conflict, which itself feeds into and influences the worldwide position of a given capitalist class.

The metaphor of a metropole/satellite relation eliminates the most essential factors that account for the specific relations and processes that shape historical development. The focus on the external relationships between social systems leads to an incapacity to differentiate the different moments of capital development, the specific configuration of types of capitals, the particular class relationships and conflicts engendered between capital and labor. This, in turn, leads to overly abstract sets of assertions: core exploits the periphery through unequal exchange or the metropole appropriates surplus. Vague enough to be sure. But not only is the core constantly changing in its internal organization of capital — shifts from merchant to industrial to financial — but the relationships of capitals within the core are in unstable competition; moreover, the social relations of production themselves are changing, creating new sets of demands and crises.

The long-term cycles of capital expansion and contraction on a world scale, the particular forms they take — wars, colonialism, imperialism, etc. — are reflections of the unstable relationships between competing and expanding capitals within the core and the crises (depression or stagnation) which are engendered. The notion of core and periphery, especially in the work of

Amin, sets up a set of fixed exploitative relations that leaves unexamined the internal crises that disrupt the operations of expansion and what he describes as surplus appropriation.

Moreover, the general crises of core capital have engendered, in specific but recurring instances, class conflicts and shifts in the axis of state power. Changes of class forces alter the boundaries for the continued reproduction of capital — decisively affecting the global position of the ruling class, i.e., its capacity to appropriate surplus. The indefiniteness of systems analysis before the historic confrontation of classes and the absence of any notion of how the class struggle interacts with the actions of the ruling class — specifically related with its movement in the international arena — substantially weakens the theory's capacity to explain societal change. The conception of the world system remains a static description of national features abstracted from the class realities which produce it.

From the other side of the metaphor, the imposition of satellite status is not a uniform or completed process: the persistence of precapitalist classes and institutions within the restructured peripheral society inserted in the world system suggest a whole complex of social forces that conflict or collaborate in the subordination of peripheral society.

The heterogenity of precapitalist social formations and the particular ways in which imperialist forces interlock makes notions of dependency and periphery rather vacuous. The internal variations in class development are largely a product of the interface of the original organization of production and the particular moment of imperialist domination. The social relations of production that emerge from and shape the further development of the subordinated peripheral society cannot be encapsulated in any vague and amorphous notion of "underdevelopment."

The pivotal unit which facilitates core subordination of peripheral society is the existence within the latter of collaborator classes whose function is to organize the state and economy in accordance with the core definitions of the international division of labor. The creation of an international political economic order based on the inequalities of nations is rooted in the existence of an expanding center of capitalism and a set of classes within the periphery whose own expansion and position is enhanced in the process. The insertion of particular social formations within the world capitalist market and division of labor is largely the product of classes which combine a double role — exploit within the society and exchange outside the society. This dual process leads to the expansion of production relations and antagonistic class relations within peripheral society, growing exchange relations and competition with the core.

The political economy of world systems analysis emphasizes the aggregate economic and technological levels of societal development as the decisive features in defining roles and conflict in the world order. This approach understates the centrality of conflicts between social systems — Zaire and Angola, Mozambique and South Africa, Eritrea and Ethiopia — and the fundamental contradictions within social systems, i.e., conflict between classes; the conflicts between capital and labor in Italy and France, for instance.

Obviously all societies participate in the world capitalist system at different levels and, depending on the development of their productive forces, with differing degrees of influence within it. Nevertheless, what is more important is the organization of production, the class relationship, and the class character of the state which differentiates societies and ultimately provides meaning to their insertion within the world system. In understanding the processes of world historic change, it is not as important to know that Zaire and Mozambique are peripheral societies as it is to recognize the profound class transformations that affect one and not another. The same could be said for Cuba and China in comparison to the Dominican Republic and India: both are peripheral countries (or perhaps one or the other is semiperipheral), but their participation in the world capitalist market is informed by a different set of class interests which act decisively to affect the character and shape of the development of the productive forces within society and to contribute to undermining the organizing principles of the world capitalist system in the larger historical perspective. Thus the decisive factors differentiating societies are found in their internal class relationships and struggles; the external articulation (between the class structure/world market) of these internal changes influences and shapes, but in no decisive sense develops and initiates the basic changes that mark the scope of the transformation to new forms of capitalist domination or socialism and the direction of the transition. Insofar as imperialist forces act, they operate within the class formation and cannot be conceptualized as the impersonal forces of the market; but rather they must be marked as part of the internal class alignments.

Having stated the above, however, it is important to recognize that the capitalist world market does have a profound effect in shaping the developments within a social formation: obviously the lower the level of productive forces within a transitional society, the greater its vulnerability to forces operating through the market. In the case of revolutionary societies this increases the chances of distortions and aberrations from the original class project. This contest between internal class developments and the operation and demands of antagonistic class forces acting through the world market is one of the central issues to be confronted by socialist theorists; but it is not dealt with adequately by simply looking at the fact of insertion in the world market in isolation from the decisive shifts and changes in class formation. Without a clear notion of the antagonistic class interests located in the interior of a social formation, there is a tendency among world system theorists to dissolve the issue into a series of abstract developmental imperatives deduced from a static global stratification system which increasingly resembles the functional requisites and equilibrium models of Parsonian sociology. The purpose of social revolution is not development; nor is the development of the productive forces an instrument of mobility toward higher levels in the world stratification pyramid (shifts from periphery toward core). The problematics of social revolution are focused on transforming social relations of production in order to create the bonds of class solidarity (internationalism in the world sphere) to transform the world social order. The analysis of world system through its use of formal stratification criteria of differentiation *subsumes* specific class differences into general developmental categories, *subordinates* notions of class conflict to mechanisms of (international) social mobility, and *amalgamates* social transformations with their opposite, by abstracting power relations from their historic class context. Here the notions of system-convergence are buttressed by an analysis in which structural position in a system of (world) stratification leads to internal homogenization: all peripheral countries as they ascend the ladder become more and more like the core states which, in turn, are increasingly alike because of their common position within the world capitalist system, etc. The great revolutionary conflicts then are reduced to becoming merely one of several instruments to a common outcome: Russia becomes like the United States, China like the Russians, Cuba follows China, Vietnam, etc.; the functional imperatives of the world system demand conformity to its operating principles as the price of ascent.

The general weakness of this theory, of course, is that it explains everything and explains nothing: Why the particular collectivist, revolutionary forms of struggle? Why the egalitarian aspirations, and why the profound efforts to transform capitalist society? This is a roundabout way of becoming part of the world capitalist system — to say the least.

While one can analytically conceive of a world capitalist system, in historical experience it is made up of specific imperial and revolutionary societies which enter into conflict precisely over its existence. Herein lies the contradictory phenomenon: of anticapitalist societies which both participate in and struggle against the forces within the capitalist market. The form and outcome of that struggle depend on the organization and consciousness of the classes within the anticapitalist society. The manner in which the fundamental contradiction (between anticapitalist social formations and capitalist world market) will be resolved depends on the evolution of class forces within the country and the proliferation of revolutionary forces in other societies. The capitalist world market thus must be demystified from a set of static institutions and described essentially for what it is: a series of class relationships that have their anchorage and instrumentation in the imperialist states. The world market operates through the class directed institutions that impose the exploitative class relationship throughout the world. The world capitalist system can best be analyzed by examining the hegemonic class relationship and imperialist state and the conflicting class relationships that emerge in each social formation.

## NEW DIRECTIONS

The political economy of the periphery is moving in a new direction which involves redefining the problematic, reformulating the key concepts, and developing a more dynamic and inclusive analytical framework. In the preceding section, we outlined what some of these issues and problems encompassed. We will restate our position in summary form:

(1) The previous problematic, which focused on development, abstracted from the social relations of production and emphasized to a great degree the extension and increase in productive forces. The result has been to downgrade the degree to which labor is the creator of value and the source of wealth. The focus on social relations of production allows us to focus on the

issue of exploitation and to focus on the forms and techniques by which labor is degraded, as well as to understand the forms by which exploitative relations of production can be transformed.

(2) By redefining the problematic of political economy away from development to exploitation, we thus are required to reformulate the key concepts with which we analyze the new problematics. Notions such as dependence and modernization which operate to explain or discuss development are inappropriate. Rather, our focus should be on the class relationships, both at the internal as well as the international level, and the types of class relationships which are engendered in the process of accumulation.

(3) These class relationships, however, are evolving phenomena, products of changes in the level and forms of capitalist development in the core; the impact of these changes in the core on the productive systems and class forces in the periphery in turn produce impacts back on the core from the class forces in periphery, modifying or transforming the relationship. The notion is one of reciprocating interplay between conflicting and collaborative classes which reproduce or refashion the economy and state structures through which they operate.

(4) This approach rejects aggregate notions of national interest in defining the critical actions between or within productive and state systems and focuses instead on the idea of class differentiation. In the periphery this means that the problem is one of identifying the location of core capital within the class structure of peripheral societies and its relationship to the peripheral state and dominant classes. The implication here is that class cleavages are less confined to national boundaries and more involve class units which cut across national boundaries.

(5) Thus, this approach locates the process of capital accumulation within the framework of class/state relationships and it is within this schema, based on the determination of class coalitions and hegemonic influence, that studies of income distribution and types of regimes could be fruitfully analyzed.

(6) The problem of accumulation is not, however, local or national, but global; moreover, the source of accumulation has become dissociated from the locus of accumulation, thus creating the problems associated with movements of capital and the activities of the multinational corporations. We emphasize, however, that these movements and activities can best be understood through the notion of the imperial state, the worldwide political network which facilitates the growth and expansion of capital. Moreover, the overly economistic arguments put forth (mainly by economists) concerning the multinational corporations fail to account for the significant role of the imperial state in establishing the prior and essential conditions for the flows of capital. Imperial state activity is essential to determining the scope, direction, growth, and survival of the multinational corporations. The concerns of U.S. political scientists with a foreign policy advisory orientation toward political order, stability, and institution-building in this context are piecemeal intimations of the centrality of the imperial state in creating the conditions for long-term, large-scale expansion. Unfortunately, these policy notions are not anchored in the economic process; nor are the policy prescriptions linked to a central organizing principle that can account for the

multiplicity of contexts in which the same problematic is posed; nor is there any effort to account for the coincidence between the forms of economic development (large-scale, long-term movements of core capital) and the need for authoritarian government. The facile acceptance of authoritarian state-development strategies syndrome is rooted in a recognition of the inequalities and exploitation which result from foreign based capital accumulation and the concomitant social tensions. Lacking an anchorage in the social relations of productive systems, developmental social scientists have obscured the centrality of exploitative social relations through general references to "systemic strains," "development imperatives" or derive the authoritarian attributes from vague cultural and historical determinations within peripheral society.

## REFERENCES

Amin, Samir
    1974 *Accumulation on a World Scale,* 2 vols. New York: Monthly Review
Baran, Paul
    1957 *The Political Economy of Growth,* New York: Monthly Review
Cardoso, Fernando Henrique
    1977 "The Consumption of Dependency: Theory in the United States," *Latin American Review,* XII (3), 7-24
Dos Santos, Theotônio
    1971 "The Structure of Dependence," in K. T. Fann and Donald C. Hodges, *Readings in U.S. Imperialism,* Boston: Porter Sargent
Emmanuel, Arghiri
    1972 *Unequal Exchange: A Study of the Imperialism of Trade,* New York: Monthly Review
Frank, A. G.
    1967 *Capitalism and Underdevelopment in Latin America,* New York: Monthly Review
    1969 "The Development of Underdevelopment," in his (ed.) *Latin America: Underdevelopment or Revolution,* New York: Monthly Review
Wallerstein, Immanuel
    1974 "Dependence in an Interdependent World," *African Studies Review* (17), 1-26
    1975 "The Present State of the Debate on World Inequality," in his *World Inequality: Origins and Perspectives on the World System,* Montreal: Black Rose Books
    1976 *The Modern World-System,* New York: Academic Press

# 11

## INTERNATIONALIZATION OF CAPITAL: AN ALTERNATIVE APPROACH

*by*
*David Barkin**

In this short essay I shall argue that the "internationalization of capital" is a much more fruitful approach for studying the world economy than "dependency theory." Quite specifically, I suggest that political economy today should not try to explain the backwardness of one part of the world vis à vis other parts but rather should explain the dynamics of the emergence of the international capitalist economy. In this context, it is crucial to understand the unequal patterns of development which are characteristic of capitalist development and which leave certain areas and certain classes more impoverished than most. As a framework of analysis, the internationalization of capital obliges us to return to the basic laws of capitalist accumulation which imply a particular organization of production and the social relations specific to this mode of production.

The internationalization of capital represents a sharp departure from previous and most current work by political economists on the international economy. Rather than starting from the nation-state as the unit of analysis, this analytical approach presupposes a qualitative change in the nature of the international economy. This transformation is related to the changes in the scale of production and the locus of decision making by those empowered to direct capitalist enterprise. With the emergence of the transnational corporation as the principal organizer of production on a global basis, decisions cease to be made with reference to a single nation. It becomes increasingly clear that the nation, or the nation-state, cannot limit capitalist expansion to its own borders. In the best of circumstances, individual political units might attempt to influence the allocation of investment resources through national policies aimed at increasing the rate of profit or improving the investment climate. But increasingly the dynamics of the world capitalist economy cannot be understood with reference to a single nation or group of nations. Productive decisions are now made on a global scale.

There is another powerful reason for preferring the internationalization of capital as an explanatory theory to understand the world economy and, particularly, the plight of the nations of the "Third World." This new

*David Barkin teaches at the Universidad Autónoma Metropolitana, Xochimilco, Mexico City.

approach emphasizes production as its point of departure. Unlike conventional theory and many versions of dependency theory which pinpoint circulation
(or international trade) as the key element to be analyzed, the internationalization of capital insists on examining the determinants of production on a
global scale. As such, it seems to me, it raises crucial questions about the nature of the new international division of labor which are still not completely
resolved. Analytically, we cannot be satisfied with simple positivistic discov-
eries that there is growing industrial production in former primary producing
nations, or that there is a new group of intermediate countries producing
export products to satisfy basic consumption needs in the wealthiest
countries. By starting from production and concentrating on the process of
capitalist accumulation, the theory of the internationalization of capital
obliges us to look for new categories to use to analyze the dynamics of the reproduction of the world capitalist system. Thus, the descriptive stratification
of production into primary, secondary, and tertiary sectors seems less
revealing than a breakdown which differentiates those lines of production
which contribute to the reproduction of the labor force (means of subsistence
or wage goods) and those which are directed towards capital accumulation.

With the focus on production, the internationalization of capital also
explains the changing relationships between different parts of the world
economy. As capitalism became the dominant mode of production, theoretical
debates have arisen over the articulation of "noncapitalist" modes of
production to the rest of the system. In Latin America, the discussion of
feudal systems seemed of great concern to some dependency theorists. With
the framework advocated here, the problem is more neatly addressed by
examining the process of moving from the formal to the real subsumption of
labor to capital throughout the system (as discussed by Marx in the now famous, but originally unpublished, part seven of volume one of *Capital* (now
available as an appendix to the new Vintage edition with an excellent
introduction by Ernest Mandel). We can examine the problems of the
relationship between peasant and capitalist production by determining if and
how surplus value is generated and the ways in which it is appropriated by
different segments of the capitalist class. In this way, the complex productive
structures within individual countries can be analyzed in terms of their
particular contributions to the global process of articulation.

The internationalization of capital does not, however, dismiss the nation-
state from the analysis. Many political economists have typically identified
the state with the national economy and develop their analyses on the basis
of national economies. This focus is specifically adopted by dependency
analysts who often view their objective as explaining the subordination of
one country or grouping of countries to another. In this view, a great deal of
attention is devoted to the examination of national economic policies with a
consequent de-emphasis of trends on a transnational scale. The focus of the
internationalization of the capital changes the analysis, placing greater
importance on the problem of the relationship between global tendencies and
transnational decision makers on the one hand and the individual nation-state
on the other. It involves a still incomplete reconstruction of the role and
concept of the state. It is incomplete in several senses: (1) clearly at an
international level, no real state authority exists, and in spite of well-

intentioned efforts to forge such an authority, the efforts have not been successful to date; (2) at the national level, there is a continuing and often ill understood conflict between national and transnational bourgeoises, which translates into conflicting policies; (3) the theory itself has not been adequately developed to handle the contradictions created by the changing international economy. In spite of these problems, however, it seems clear that the questions posed about the problems of the role of the state in the accumulation of capital on a global scale now transcend the traditional notion of the nation-state, and new frameworks of analysis must be found. This is an integral part of the approach advocated here and therefore a great advantage of the theory.

The internationalization of capital, in sum, is a relatively new approach to the study of the world economy, to the problem of dynamics of global capitalism and international economic relations. Obviously production still has a geographic specificity, but this approach argues that the logic of allocative decisions is now global even when transnational capital is not involved in a particular activity. That is, even when investment and production decisions are made by national governments or local capitalists, it seems increasingly clear that global economic and political structures strongly influence the individual decision maker. It is possible to state this even more strongly: international markets and economic power structures are increasingly determining the individual decisions made in ever more isolated parts of national economies, even when "noncapitalist" productive groups are involved, such as peasant producers in many Third World economies.

Unfortunately, the body of literature referring to the internationalization of capital is relatively unknown in the United States. Before his untimely death in 1973, Stephen Hymer had begun to do research within the Marxist paradigm on the expansion and integration of the world economy. But recent developments have occurred in France, following preliminary work by people like Christian Palloix. The theory takes as a point of departure the relatively simple proposition that the analysis of the intertwining of the three circuits of capital — money-capital, productive-capital, and commodity-capital — discussed by Marx in the second volume of capital, might be usefully extended to the international economy. A historical examination of the integration of the world market economy reveals the early importance of commercial-capital (in the form of foreign trade), dating back to the very emergence of the capitalist system. The subsequent importance of money-capital was noted most persuasively by Lenin in his influential essay on imperialism. But perhaps the most significant change in recent years has been the expansion of productive-capital on a global scale and the powerful impact of the integration of the various facets of capitalist economic life into an increasingly unified global market.

The theory of the internationalization of capital explains the impact of the growth of the world economy on the productive structure of each of the participating nation-states. Although it also is fundamental for comprehending the dynamics of the global system as a whole and in analyzing tendencies in international trade and investment, in what follows, I wish to focus specifically on the impact of the internationalization of capital in altering the particular productive structures of each country. This approach is useful because it also provides a critique of the deterministic analysis of some who focus exclusively on the transnational corporation (TNC) as the motive force behind recent changes in the international economy. In its most simplistic form, these companies are identified as the objective enemy of the people. Their size and international character have conferred upon them a mystique which makes them appear to be uncontrollable. The theory of the internationalization of capital, in contrast, focuses on the laws of expansion of capitalism, the laws which Marx analyzed more than a century ago and which are still useful in understandng the dynamics of the societies in which we live. From this perspective, we can understand the behavior of the TNC in the context of the process of the accumulation of capital on a global scale which permits and, at the same time, requires the concentration and centralization of individual capitals. In this context, the TNC is understood as an actor, an important actor, in a process that transcends each actor.

Just as important, however, is the insight that this approach provides into the behavior of individual economies. No longer is it possible to explain the enthusiasm of some "developing" countries for increasing their structural dependency in terms of foreign intervention. National policy decisions are certainly influenced by international events and pressures, but the eagerness of a country like Mexico to court admission to the General Agreement on Tariffs and Trade (GATT) is the product of a sincere conviction by policy makers, supported by a domestic bourgeoise, that the country's best interests are identified with the more complete integration of the domestic economy with those of its principal trading partners. Furthermore, the recent tendency for large Mexican capitals to not only associate themselves with transnational capital but also to buy out international investments is better explained by the Marxist analysis of the competition of capitals than it is by the tools of industrial organization approaches to the expansion of the TNC or the dependency theorists' models.

It might be instructive to use the theory of the internationalization of capital in a concrete situation. My work in Mexico has documented the structural changes in agriculture which have made the country incapable of supplying itself with the basic food products which it needs for its own reproduction. This is even more striking in Mexico than in other countries where food dependency has been growing, in view of the success of agricultural development efforts to achieve self-sufficiency in the recent past and the patent underutilization of human and natural resources which could, if mobilized, guarantee the domestic production of virtually all of the agricultural products currently imported. To understand this process, it is necessary to explain that the very process of the modernization of part of the agricultural sector exposed a small group of Mexican farmers to the international market. With the expansion of irrigation and the extension of modern cultivation techniques, reinforced by heavy expenditures in research, Mexico was able to achieve self-sufficiency in basic food production by the early sixties. The farmers in that part of the country favored by these programs enjoyed a new level of prosperity that the capitalist organization of private agriculture permitted. They soon discovered, however, that wheat and corn were not as profitable as export crops (vegetables and fruits) or others destined to be industrial raw materials, like sorghum which is the principal ingredient in animal feeds. As a result, the country became even more dependent on imported foods than ever before in its history.

Clearly the availability of export opportunities and a growing market for animal feeds did not arise spontaneously. Both were the result of the active intervention of foreign capital and especially the TNC within Mexico. Fruit and vegetable brokers and merchants began stimulating the production of export production in the late fifties and by the end of the sixties these activities had expanded substantially in the most productive parts of the Mexican agriculture sector. The northwestern part of the country and the Bajio, both important grain-producing areas, witnessed a rapid transformation of their productive structures. In some cases, the foreign capitalists engaged in contract agriculture, agreeing to purchase the production under specified conditions in return for financing the production from the beginning; in other cases, the expansion of fruit and vegetable production was undertaken with the farmers assuming all of the risk. In either case, the farmers were able to take advantage of the opportunities afforded them by the international economy as a result of the successful efforts of the Mexican government to modernize these regions and expose them to the opportunities offered by the markets.

Foreign capital also played an important role in expanding the production of poultry and pork for the domestic market. Both these lines of production were designed with North American technology, which is intensive in use of energy and requires massive quantities of sorghum. This grain is of the maize family but is easier to cultivate and its harvest is more readily mechanized. As a result in the most advanced parts of the country, sorghum rapidly displaced corn as the preferred crop, offering lower costs and greater profits to the farmers who were able to afford the hybrid seeds and machinery used for its production.

As part of the same process, official resources were channeled into improving irrigation systems, assuring adequate supplies of fertilizers and other agricultural inputs, stimulating machinery production and importation and providing subsidized agricultural credits. This financial and technical assistance further broadened the prosperity of a small part of the agricultural economy and played an important role in assuring Mexico's position as an agricultural exporting nation. This strategy also sealed the fate of the traditional peasant economy, condemned to work marginal lands without adequate credit or technical support based on agricultural research. An ever growing part of peasant land lay fallow as it was unprofitable to plant the basic food products which the people needed and the country was obliged to import. By the early seventies the importation of basic grains and oil-seeds became the symbol of the new economic strategy: promoting exports without consideration for the socioeconomic consequences of changing production patterns.

The present example is designed to illustrate a process in which national decision making and international capital join together to "internationalize" the domestic economy. That is, to accelerate the impact that allocative decisions in the international economy have on a country's socioeconomic structure by changing its productive structure. In Mexico this process of official determination to insert the country into the international economy is evident on many levels. The country adopted a value-added tax at the beginning of 1980 to promote exports, stimulate modern agriculture, and simplify the tax structure; its inflationary impact and bias against consumption together with the complicated administrative structure the tax requires threw the country into chaos and heightened the bias against production for domestic mass consumption by further reducing real incomes and stimulating private investment in heavy industry. The program to liberalize trade, likewise, is making life more comfortable for the upper-income groups, while the majority is suffering from rising prices and shortages of basic food commodities.

The official commitment to continue with the internationalization of the Mexican economy augers badly for the masses. While the government urges people to be patient and argues that the long-term impact of these changes will be salutary, the people are becoming increasingly impoverished. The official explanations are based on conventional analyses of the benefits from trade, the wonders of competition, and the benefits of investment. The government is explicitly adopting the tenets of a free enterprise economy, and the catechism of the Chicago School of Economics is gaining an increasing hearing. The sectoral shortages, the bottlenecks, the disorder that these changes sow are not seriously impinging on the prosperity of private investors. National holding companies are in a good position to buy out foreign capital. Heinz, General Foods, and Pepsico are among the recent instances of "renationalization." But national capital does not operate very differently than the TNC. Mexican Bimbo bread or cupcakes are the same as ITT's Wonder bread and Twinkies. Modern Mexican hotels are indistinguishable from their international competitors. What is determinate is not the nationality of the capitalist but the social relation of exploitation and the systematic disregard for the majority within each society. The analysis of the expansion and implantation of the international economy inside each nation-state is a very promising way of analyzing the prospects for the future. This is the approach of the theory of the internationalization of capital.

The growing influence of the international economy, however, is not the only determinant of change in capitalist societies. This process creates its own contradictions: growing unemployment, the progressive immiserization of masses of people in the face of material "progress," denationalization, cultural destruction, and the other ills defined in an ample literature of denunciation; these are the phenomena usually focused upon by the "dependentistas." As an alternative, the analysis provided by the theory of the internationalization of capital also offers alternatives for concrete action. In place of proposals for a code of ethics for corporate behavior or new rules for negotiating with the TNC, the theory suggests that what is necessary is a new strategy for producing the goods which the masses of people need for their own basic survival. This is an approach which can be usefully integrated into popular struggles on a national level. Focusing on changes in the productive apparatus as part of a longer-term political struggle for structural transformations is proving to be a promising result of this new way of analyzing international economic relations.

# 12

## IMPERIALISM AND DEPENDENCY: RECENT DEBATES AND OLD DEAD-ENDS

by

*Ronaldo Munck\**

"dependency theory has not died. It still permeates the analysis and theory of the left . . . That is why the ideological struggle against this theory is not something of the past; it is an urgent task for today" *(Debate,* 1981: 5).

Thus concludes Thesis 15 of the recent Nineteenth Congress of the Mexican Communist Party. Whether this is representative of the current relation between Marxism and dependency theory and whether an adequate theory of imperialism has superseded the now soundly criticized tenets of the dependency theorists are questions I will try to answer in a review of recent (and not so recent) contributions to the "dependency debate."

Latin American Perspectives opened its pages with a thorough balance sheet of dependency studies by Ronald Chilcote (Chilcote, 1974). This was in reality a synthesis of the dependency literature as the title announced. After careful reconstruction of the main lines of debate, Chilcote pointed to a number of common assumptions "in the hope that they might guide the reader to further understanding, constructive critique, and refinement of dependency theory" (Chilcote, 1974: 21). However, the element of understanding and *constructive* critique was to be notably absent from some subsequent contributions. Perhaps such guidelines only lead to anodyne uncontroversial reviews of the literature. Not so, as shown by Kyle Steenland in a later issue when he tackled the thorny question of feudalism and capitalism in Latin America (Steenland, 1975: 49-58) and likewise, Timothy Harding in his introduction on dependency, nationalsim and the state, placed the origins of dependency studies in "the meeting of a sterile and mechanical Marxism and a plainly inadequate bourgeois theory of nationalist development" (Harding, 1976: 4). More recently, in a hard-hitting article, Weeks and Dore (1979) took up the issue of international exchange and the causes of backwardness. At one stage the authors say that "while the discussion to this point has been critical, its result has not been negative; we have not merely sought to point out errors, but to point them out in a way which can carry the analysis forward" (Weeks and Dore, 1979: 78). They then set out an alternative

---

*The author teaches in the Department of Sociology at Ulster Polytechnic in Northern Ireland.

explanation for the "causes of backwardness." The point is that whether we agree or disagree with the content of their analysis the form in which they conduct their critique/supersession is admirable.

## MARXISM AND DEPENDENCY

If the Communist Party of Mexico (PCM) can be said to uphold orthodox Marxism, then their recent "official" critique of dependency theory can be taken as representative. Thesis 15 of the recent PCM congress maintains that dependency had a positive role in "breaking with some of the old schemas of the Communist International," but that it now constitutes "an obstacle to the advance of Marxism." Among its negative theoretical effects the following are listed: denying the development of capitalism as a system of social relations of production; denying the existence of a real class enemy, that is a real, strong bourgeoisie with its own class personality; making imperialism (understood always as the economic, political and cultural presence of the United States in the continent, and not as a phase in the development of capitalism) into the main enemy of the revolution without locating the anti-imperialist struggle in its correct context; seeing the struggle for socialism purely as the development of the forces of production (i.e., economism); exaggerating the specificity of local capitalism to the point of ignoring the operation of the laws which dictate the development of capitalism (*Debate*, 1981: 5). These "deviations" allegedly lead to an anti-imperialism which becomes class-collaboration; underestimation of the class enemy—the bourgeoisie—which is seen as completely subordinated to imperialism; and an inability to analyze the transformations of the working class.

These points are all debatable, and certainly many apply to the crude oversimplified dependency polemics. A communist party is not perhaps the best placed to criticize "anti-imperialism which becomes class-collaboration," but some of the other points are quite sound, notably the neglect of the real power of the local bourgeoisie which comes from so many years of denying the very existence of a national bourgeoisie. A similar line of critique is developed by the Mexican writer Carlos Johnson in a more academic context (see Johnson 1979 or his article, this issue).

For Johnson, "dependency theory is taken to be a product of the struggle between monopoly capital and competitive capital," and more specifically it "represents an ideological substantiation of capitalism in countries where capital/labor relations are not yet dominant and reflects the class needs of competitive capital in the face of monopoly capital" (Johnson, this issue or 1979: 1). It has often been noted how dependency theory can be used to legitimate bourgeois nationalism, neglecting the class conflict, etc. Johnson carries this further and says it actually *represents* national competitive capitalism, and consequently "the dependency theorist (knowingly or unknowingly) becomes the ideologue of the local capitalist's struggle against monopoly capital" (Johnson, this issue or 1979: 8-9). This, however, ignores the complex mediations between class forces and ideological expressions, and it is sheer metaphysics to say dependency theory expresses the "needs" of competitive capital. Unaware of the contradiction, Johnson then goes on to say that "much like the Narodniks, dependency theorists elaborate the idea that in the face of monopoly capital (imperialism), national capitalism is in fact an impossibility in Latin America" (this issue or 1979: 6.) How can a theory at one and the same time incarnate the interests of a force (national competitive capital) and yet deny its existence or possibility of development? At a more basic level, Johnson is apparently unaware of Fernando Henrique Cardoso's longstanding criticism of the Latin American "Narodniks"—those who deny that dependent *development* takes place.

The real target of Johnson's polemic against dependency theorists becomes clear in a passing reference to one of their "political conclusions," namely their "incendiary revolutionarism" (Johnson, this issue or 1979: 15). What is *really* being attacked then is Guevara's position of "Socialist revolution or caricature of revolution," and not the "ideologues" of national capital. It is done, however, in the name of Marxist orthodoxy because the aim of dependency theories "is to deomonstrate the universality of the phenomenon of dependency, and ideally, to erase any differences between capitalism and socialism" (Johnson, this issue or 1979: 10). This is quite simply not true, *even* for many of those (socialists) who discuss the question of Cuba's "dependency" on the Soviet Union. As with the other points mentioned above, this is a purely *formalist* deduction. Finally, what *alternative* does Johnson provide us? Simply, it is "the theoretical conception of analysis, based on dialectical-historical materialism, which was established long ago in Marx's work on capital/labor relations—a specific form of class production and appropriation/accumulation—and on his insights into the socialist process of transformation" (Johnson, this issue or 1979: 16). What is this, if not a form of "idealism" which is Johnson's favorite term of abuse for the dependency theorists . . . Has Johnson not heard of "the crisis of Marxism," or does he believe that all is well in the old house? This is the type of Marxism rightly criticized by Cardoso which merely repeats that "the class struggle is the motor of history" instead of carrying out a concrete historical analysis.

The failure of ossified orthodox Marxists to advance a coherent and fruitful alternative to dependency theory should not blind us to well sustained Marxist criticisms. Philip O'Brien long ago pointed out how dependency could easily become a pseudo-concept which explained everything in general and hence nothing in particular (O'Brien, 1975). In the pages of this journal, Augustín Cueva argued persuasively that "dependency theory exponents possess a nostalgic longing for a frustrated autonomous capitalist development, which is precisely what makes dependency theory so nationalist in its ideology" (Cueva, 1976: 13). These points are now widely accepted, although one should not ignore the recent lucid defense of dependency theory presented by Vania Bambirra (1978) which restates the positive critical role it has played and its still fruitful research agenda. This more positive evaluation is confirmed, I believe, by the recent reopening of an important debate within the dependency problematic.

Cardoso, jointly with José Serra, takes up Ruy Mauro Marini's influential analysis of the underlying mechanisms of dependency (Serra and Cardoso, 1979). Marini is associated with the Narodniks (so thoroughly criticized by Lenin) for whom the narrowness of the internal market sets definite limits on the development of Third World capitalism. Serra and Cardoso question the "underconsumptionism" implicit in this line of analysis. They are particularly concerned with Marini's emphasis on superexploitation in the periphery as a source of international unequal exchange (the substantial literature around this concept being ignored in this article because the debate is complex and relatively self-contained). There is no "iron law" of dependent capitalism that leads to absolute impoverishment of the masses; the extraction of *relative* surplus value (through technological advance) is the essence of Brazilian capitalism, not just *absolute* surplus value (based on lengthening the working day, etc). For Marini, the basically stagnationist tendency of Brazilian capitalism would lead to its subimperialist expansionism and pose bluntly the question of "socialism or fascism." According to Serra and Cardoso, Marini's analysis in terms of an implacable logic (dialectic) of dependency is a form of economism which leads inevitably to the type of political voluntarism so evident in the Brazilian proponents of armed struggle in the early 1970s.

Marini (1980) for his part came back with a spirited reply which shows, I think, Cardoso's incomplete break with the Economic Commission for Latin America (ECLA) tradition (cf. Cardoso, 1977b). Apart from accusing Cardoso of "sociologism," this article tended to reassert his thesis that "dependent capitalism, based on the super-exploitation of labour, divorces the productive appartus from the needs of consumption of the masses, aggravating thus a *general tendency* of the capitalist mode of production . . . (Marini, 1980: 74). A telling criticism is that Serra and Cardoso tend to erase the differences between capitalism in the advanced countries and the quite specific dependent capitalism. My point, however, is not to enter this detailed debate, but rather to note the wealth of empirical material that the two sides draw on to argue their cases.

One such source in English is John Wells' (1977) discussion of the diffusion of durable consumer goods in Brazil and its implications for recent controversies concerning Brazilian development. We can also point to the ongoing debate in Brazilian economic history regarding the relative weight of the "internal axis" of capital accumulation in relation to the "external" (foreign capital, imperialism) in determining the dynamic of Brazilian capitalism (see Mantega and Moraes, 1980). The discussion on dependency in Africa is no less controversial, as witnessed by the recent reopening of debate around Colin Leys' pathbreaking analysis of Kenyan dependent capitalism (see *Review of African Political Economy,* 1980).

Another aspect of certain interest is the growing attempt by traditional historians to counter the hegemony of the dependency approach. Thus the doyen of British Latin Americanists D.C.M. Platt takes Stanley and Barbara Stein's *Colonial Heritage of Latin America* to task for its alleged historical inaccuracies (Platt, 1980). A comment by the Steins allows for a refinement and furthern development of a dependency focus on the colonial period (Stein and Stein, 1980). If a theory is assessed in terms of its openness to debate, reformulation, and progress, dependency theory must be judged positively.

In attacking what he called "the consumption of dependency theory" in the United States, Cardoso pertinently asked: "Have dependency studies been able to whet the imagination so that discussion is opened on themes and forms of comprehending reality which are compatible with the contemporary historical process?" (Cardoso, 1977a: 17). I think the record must lead us to concur with Cardoso's verdict that "on balance, the effect of dependency theories on the sociological imagination seems to me to have been positive" (Cardoso, 1977a: 19). We have the ongoing endeavors of *Latin American Perspectives* to present a critical understanding of the economic, political, and social relations in the area. There is the sustained theoretical and concrete analysis of Brazilian capitalism presented by Peter Evans (1979). For all its debatable points, there is the whole range of work on the "bureaucratic-authoritarian" state, which has spawned amongst others the collection edited by David Collier (1979). And what about the alleged inability to analyze the development of the working class, when faced by Hobart Spalding's brilliant historical synthesis of the Latin American labor movement (Spalding, 1977)? One could even add the recent positive contributions associated with the work of Osvaldo Sunkel, who was perhaps on the "conservative" side of the early dependency debate. A whole range of topics—technological dependence, mass communications and dependence, militarism and dependence, etc.—are broached creatively in the volume edited by José Villamil which centers around Sunkel's version of dependency theory (Villamil, 1979) and work at the Institute of Development Studies, University of Sussex.

In the confrontation between dependency theory and the sterile dogmatic Marxists (the "ideological cops"), we see many willful distortions and an inability to learn from one's opponent. The theoretical closure which the PCM would have us operate on the notion of dependency would see us denying its very real contribution to Marxism as a guide to action. Sound concrete analysis of the economy, the state, and the labor movement is of far more use in this respect than ritual incantations of the dusty old catechism of Marxism-Leninism. I find myself in this respect fully in agreement with Florestán Fernandes' foreword to Peter Evan's book: "I do not think that there is such a thing as the *theory of dependency;* what exists is a theory of imperialism of which the body of hypothesis and explanations relating to the effects of imperialist domination on the periphery of the capitalist world form one part. But this does not prevent me from being enthusiastic about his approach, which locates imperialism at the center of the theory and focuses on relations of dependency as seen in the light of the dynamics of expansion of large corporations, the modern capitalist state, and the model for control of the periphery formed by the two of them in an era when the 'division of the world' has been redefined by internationalization and worldwide counter-revolution" (Fernandes, 1979).

## IMPERIALISM AND DEPENDENCY

It was once widely accepted that dependency studied "the other side" of imperialism as it were. The dogmatic Marxists however who have rejected dependency theory tell us that "it's all in the classics." Thus Raúl Fernández in an analysis of Colombia informs us simply that "the theoretical framework of the essay is the theory of *imperialism* developed by Lenin—imperialism is capitalism in capitalism's advanced or highest stage" (Fernández, 1979: 38). This type of uncritical repetition of eternal truths—à la Little Red Book—may well breed loyal cadres, but it is hardly a substitute for critical (i.e., Marxist) analysis. In fact, the debate around imperialism has resurfaced with intensified vigor in recent years. If Marxists can apply their polemical ardor against dependency theory they should also critically reexamine the fundamental tenets of the theory of imperialism.

Giovanni Arrighi, well known for his work on Africa, has recently set out to *reconstruct* the theory of imperialism (Arrighi, 1978). He worked on the assumption that "by the end of the sixties, what had once been 'the pride' of Marxism—the theory of imperialism—has become a 'Tower of Babel,' in which not even Marxists knew any longer how to find their way. The truly surprising thing is that even those scholars who were most alert to the changing pattern of international capitalist relations felt obliged to pay a tribute to Lenin where none was due, compounding the confusion" (Arrighi, 1978: 17). The study Arrighi presents is more of a formal and structural reading of the concept of imperialism, rather than a full historical study. Nevertheless, its conclusions are seriously and rigorously derived and merit careful attention. He finds that Hobson's ideo-typical structure of imperialism (a prime source for Lenin) is, in fact,

> rigidly circumscribed in time [in its] capacity . . . to order expansionist phenomena synchronically and diachronically. This capacity is zero prior to the second half of the 17th century - that is, before the nation-state began to exercise a decisive influence over the international system; it is maximal for phenomena of the late 19th century, when the nation-state had finally become the basic structure of the international system, while its very application is dubious to times of crisis of the nation-state, such as those in which we seem to live (Arrighi, 1977. 151).

In conclusion it is anachronistic for us to attempt to ground a theory of contemporary imperialism in *historically determinate* definitions relating to processes and ideologies of the early 1900s.

A different type of venture is undertaken by Anthony Brewer (1980). This is nothing less than an ambitious reappraisal of imperialism from Marx, through Luxembourg, Hilferding, Bukharin, and Lenin, to Frank, Wallerstein, Rey, Emmanuel, and Amin. Basically, Marx expected the spread of capitalism to lead to full capitalist development everywhere, while Lenin and his contemporaries focused on the rise of monopoly and interimperialist rivalry. More recently, emphasis has shifted to the understanding of *underdevelopment*, where Brewer guides us carefully through the whole range of theories in terms of their logical coherence and their relevance to real problems. The problem with André Gunder Frank, for example, is located in the distance between his grandiose general statements—such as development and underdevelopment being opposite sides of the same coin—and his discussion of particular historical situations. There is a lack of real theory, and Brewer suggests that the Marxist analysis of relations of production can fill that gap. In conclusion, I think this book is an invaluable guide to the literature—its vast scope and explanatory emphasis cannot, however, lead us to the synthesis required today to guide future work. The main problems, however, are identified and that is a magnificent starting point for renewed theoretical clarification.

A more disparate series of contributions are brought together in a recent issue of *The Review of Radical Political Economics* (1979) dedicated to the new directions of the theory of imperialism in the 1980s. The editors note in their introduction that "the dependency theorists attempted to formulate a theoretical understanding of the observable, empirical facts of foreign domination (i.e., dependence) in Latin America and this effort was instrumental in initiating a reconsideration of the dynamics of capitalism and its penetration into, and impact upon, underdeveloped countries" (*The Review of Radical Political Economics*, 1979: 1). This seems a more nuanced Marxist appreciation of the dependency approach than usual. I believe that our understanding of contemporary imperialism is advanced by this volume although, as the editors admit, no unified political perspective emerges.

Without any doubt the most global and challenging critique to the theory of imperialism is Bill Warren's recent posthumous volume (Warren, 1980). Warren's starting point is Karl Marx's view on the historically progressive nature of capitalism and its unprecedented development of the forces of production. Colonialism did not then retard or distort indigenous capitalist development but rather acted as a powerful engine of progressive social change. For Warren, "although introduced into the Third World externally, capitalism has struck deep roots there and developed its own increasingly internal dynamic" (1980: 9). Lenin supported these views on the progressive and dynamic international role of capitalism until his famous pamphlet on "Imperialism: The Highest Stage of Capitalism" which "initiated the ideological process through which the view that capitalism could be an instrument of social advance in precapitalist societies was erased from Marxism" (Warren, 1980: 8). This shift was consolidated at the Sixth Comintern Congress (1928) where "the Marxist analysis of imperialism was sacrificed to the requirements of bourgeois anti-imperialist propaganda and, indirectly, to what were thought to be the security requirements of the encircled Soviet state" (Warren, 1980: 8). On this basis Warren then goes on to criticize the whole conception underlying the post-war analysis of imperialism, particularly the focus from Paul Baran onwards, on what he calls "the fiction of underdevelopment."

Bill Warren's critical engagement with the dependency school takes up a whole chapter trying to show it is just nationalist mythology. After setting out what he sees as its main tenet, Warren concludes that "the dependency approach, while not formally excluding alternative answers, has effectively narrowed the intellectual focus of analysis of the dynamics of Latin American society and has foreclosed the posing of critical questions in the name of an irrelevant antithesis between diffusionist (or structural-functionalist) and dependency approaches" (Warren, 1980: 162-163). Dependency theory is seen as static because only the *form* of dependency changes and because it simply *assumes* the continuing validity of the center-periphery paradigm. Dependency theorists usually equate imperialism with the world market and also incorrectly assume that there is a latent suppressed autonomous historical development alternative available. The criticisms are familiar and in some cases and in some ways quite correct. But, as often happens, the critics of dependency theory assume a theoretical/political unity which just does not exist. Warren's reference to the Latin American debate is quite limited and based on second-hand sources; for example, Osvaldo Sunkel and Dos Santos are quoted only via Philip O'Brien's critique of dependency (O'Brien, 1975).

Sometimes Warren makes points that are remarkably simple yet are at total variance with the whole "Gunder Frank" conception of underdevelopment. For example, the massive literature on surplus extraction from the Third World, the machinations of the multinational corporations, and so on, basically misses the point according to Warren. In fact, foreign investment in a Third World country implants capitalist relations of production and leads to the expanded reproduction of capitalism. The fact that for every dollar invested five are repatriated is thus irrelevant. Warren's work is, in fact, an elaboration of Kay's earlier witticism that "capital created underdevelopment not because it exploited the underdeveloped world but because it did not exploit it enough" (Kay, 1975). Warren's empirical evidence on the extent of capitalist development in Latin America had already been taken up (McMichaels, et al., 1977) in relation to an earlier article (Warren, 1973). Recent evidence for Southeast Asia shows that the South Korean and Taiwanese "economic miracles" resulted from a *particular* set of historical ingredients: hypermilitarization, ultra-dependency, and massive U.S. aid combined with popular anticommunism (Halliday, 1980). However, Warren's fundamental thesis, that imperialism leads to the development of capitalism in the Third World, can still stand though we must recognize the uneven and partial nature of this process. His book is stimulating, essentially demystifying, and must be taken seriously.

Warren is sometimes, however, carried away in his critique of the post-Marx theories of imperialism. Thus we are told that "imperialism was the means through which the techniques, culture, and institutions that had evolved in Western Europe over several centuries . . . sowed their revolutionary seeds in the rest of the world" (Warren, 1980: 136). If it is reactionary to say that imperialism was "a titanic step towards human unity," Warren's view of capitalist politics is even more so: "Capitalism and democracy are, I would argue, linked virtually as Siamese twins" (1980: 28). It is on the basis of this type of ludicrous statement (not his underlying method) that Warren has been taken up enthusiastically by Dudley Seers, father figure of the "development industry" in Britain. Seers (1979) argues that Marxism when true to Marx is basically in agreement with Milton Friedman and the whole "Chicago Boys" line that egalitarian social and economic policies are counterproductive, nationalism is an outmoded ideology, capitalism is synonomous with parliamentary democracy, etc., etc., *ad nauseum*.

Bill Warren deserves more serious political consideration than this. In the early 1970s he was a prime mover of the British and Irish communist organization which became notorious for its support of the most reactionary social groups in Ireland. It supported the proimperialist settlers of the Northeast whose historic mission was to build capitalism (in association with British imperialism) against the reactionary pretensions and outdated myths emerging from the "green fog" of Irish nationalism. I believe, however, that Warren's politics implicit in the book (they are not drawn out explicitly) are quite within the classical Marxist tradition. That is, that capitalism leads to the creation of an industrial proletariat which will be the "gravedigger" of the bourgeois system. To this end his emphasis on the development of a working class in the Third World and its socialist tasks (not to be confused with bourgeois anti-imperialism) is to my mind highly welcome.

As with many Marxist polemics the *dialectical* aspect of the Marxist method tends to be lost. Thus, Warren quotes at length Marx's views on the "progressive" aspects of British imperialism in India, perhaps best summarized in the following passage:

> The political unity of India . . . was the first condition of its regeneration. That unity, imposed by the British sword, will now be strengthened and perpetuated by the electric telegraph. The native army, organized and trained by the British drill-sergeant, was the sine qua non of Indian self-emancipation. The free press, introduced for the first time into Asiatic society . . . is a new and powerful agent of reconstruction . . . Steam has brought India into regular and rapid communication with Europe, has connected its chief ports with those of the whole southeastern ocean, and has revindicated it from the isolated position which was the prime law of its stagnation (Avineri, 1969: 13).

However, in the same article on "The Future Results of British Rule in India," Marx went on to say that "The Indians will not reap the fruits of the new elements of society . . . till in Great Britain itself the now ruling class shall have been supplanted by the industrial proletariat, or till the Hindoos themselves shall have grown strong enough to throw off the English yoke altogether" (Aniveri, 1969: 137). There is absolutely no contradiction at all between Marx's view that British rule in India created the preconditions for a massive advance (even while it was destroying preexisting industry) *and* that it must be overthrown before the benefits could be enjoyed. Bill Warren should have matched his quotes from Marx praising the historical advances of the bourgeoisie (which he did quite openly) with the following: "The profound hypocrisy and inherent barbarism of bourgeois civilization lies unveiled before our eyes, turning from its home, where it assumes respectable forms, to the colonies, where it goes naked . . . " (Avineri, 1969: 137).

## TOWARDS A SYNTHESIS

In the study of the Third World today, two major approaches can be distinguished: the world-system perspective focusing on circulation, and the modes of production approach, focusing obviously enough on production. I shall examine recent expressions of both in turn moving towards a possible systhesis and introducing the concept of *dependent reproduction*.

According to Ernesto Laclau, "a good example of the theoretical errors to which an ingenous empiricism leads in social sciences can be found in the now well-know work of Immanuel Wallerstein" (Laclau, 1977: 43-44). This author's wide-ranging articles have recently been collected together (Wallerstein, 1979) and provide us with a useful summary of this perspective. In his introduction Wallerstein restates the classical debate on the rise of capitalism between Paul Sweezy (and Frank) and Maurice Dobb (and Laclau)—again based on the circulation and production emphasis respectively. His conclusion is that "though Dobb and Laclau can both point to texts of Marx that seem clearly to indicate that they are more faithfully following Marx's argument, I believe both Sweezy and Frank better follow the spirit of Marx if not his letter . . . " (Wallerstein, 1979: 9). In support of this, a series of essays trace the historical evolution and structural characteristics of the capitalist world-economy from the sixteenth century to the present.

I think it is important to note that Marx is not unambiguously a "productionist" as the following passage makes clear: "Whether the commodities are the product of production based on slavery, the product of peasants (Chinese, Indian ryots), of a community (Dutch East Indies), of state production (such as existed in earlier epochs of Russian history, based on serfdom) or of half-savage hunting people, etc.—as commodities and money they confront the money and commodities in which industrial capital presents itself . . . The character of the production process from which they derive is immaterial . . . the circulation process of industrial capital is characterized by the many-sided character of its origins, and the existence of the market as a world market (Marx, 1978: 189-190). So, Marx was also a "circulationist" or rather he did not separate the realm of production and circulation counterposing one to the other.

The problems with Wallerstein remain, even more so with the spate of world-system studies generated by his followers. There is an all-encompassing breadth of focus (over space and over time) which tends to dissolve the historical specificity of historical social formations. As a "guide to action"— on, for example, South Africa—they are virtually useless. The basic problem is that the world capitalist economy is the starting point of analysis without any prior *theoretical* construction of the concept (this is where his "empiricism" comes in). The result according to Laclau then is "a merely factual and erudite survey" (Laclau, 1977: 46).

André Gunder Frank's more recent work shows the difficulty of criticizing this author on the basis of classical texts—his work is flexible, progresses, and is eclectic (not in a derogatory sense). His *Dependent Accumulation and Underdevelopment* (1978a) is a brilliant historical sweep through the phases of imperialism from 1500 to 1930. In a companion volume he answers the earlier criticism of his "circulationism " by Laclau and others "by undertaking an analysis of the *mutual* dialectical relations between the changing 'external' (but with respect to the capitalist system still internal) relations of exchange and the transformations of the relations of production 'internal' to each of the major regions of the world at each of the three historical stages of capitalist development on a world scale" (Frank 1978b: 14). Whether this starting point is sustained in his concrete analysis is, of course, another question. His questionable focus on what he calls "a single worldwide process of capital accumulation" leads him to conclude that the question of internal/external determination is "irrelevant and unanswerable." Nevertheless, he provides a useful analysis of primitive accumulation and we must be thankful that Frank seems to have outgrown his penchant for the catchy phrase—of which the "development of underdevelopment" was the most notorious—which made him so popular (especially among students) but also made him an easy target for critics. The reservations expressed about Wallerstein's work may, however, apply in part to the new direction taken by Frank.

At the other end of the scale we have the "modes of production" analysis. Here we have the recent collection of essays from *The Journal of Economy and Society* entitled *The articulation of modes of production* (Wolpe, 1980). Though attempting to demonstrate the analytical power of the concept, the essays also reveal a number of as yet unresolved conceptual problems. Most of the articles analyze particular social formations, constituted as they are by a combination of more than one mode of production. The process of *articulation* between these is one of the major focuses. Why it is that precapitalist modes of production tend to be preserved still seems to be explained only in terms of their being "functional" for the continued reproduction of capitalism. This may be so, but one gets an uneasy feeling that these cannot really be independent *modes* of production if their conditions of existence are so inextricably linked up with the expansion of capitalism. That there are noncapitalist *relations* of production, even Frank would not dispute today, but to see the Third World in terms of "combinations" of modes of production is another question. One of the contributors to the Wolpe volume, the French Marxist anthropologist Claude Meillassoux now has one of his recent books *Maidens, Meal and Money* (Meillassoux, 1981) available in English. This contains a quite brilliant analysis of "imperialism as a mode of reproduction of cheap labor power" which centers on the exploitation of the domestic community in the Third World. Here we find a fruitful meeting point between the studies of imperialism and that growing research field known as the new international labor studies.

The major theoretical text in this area is undoubtedly that of John Taylor (1979), which is an ambitious attempt to go beyond the neo-Marxist paradigm by laying the foundations of a comprehensive mode of production approach to the study of the Third World. Taylor's critique of the "sociology of development" treads well-known ground, and he encapsulates this in its "teleological" nature i.e., that it posits an ideal condition of development which, though non-existent, is potentially realizable. More controversial is his extension of this label to the "sociology of underdevelopment," where he picks up Paul Baran's familiar distinction between actual and potential surplus—i.e., with or without the restrictive and exploitative structures of imperialism. In Taylor's words: "The major point to be directed at this analysis is that—despite the total divergence of its conclusions from those of the Sociology of Development—it still constitutes a form of explanation in which the contemporary phenomena of an underdeveloped society are defined by being juxtaposed against a potential state, to the achievement of which they do or do not contribute . . . (Taylor, 1979: 93). Now, Bill Warren has reminded us that not all anticapitalist ideologies are socialist—they can be utopian or reactionary. Taylor is trying to say that socialism should not have an ethical component at all, which is something different. His Althusserian Marxism, based on the primacy of "theoretical practice," ignores that Marx had a *moral* critique of capitalism too—what else is Baran referring to with his "potential" surplus?

Taylor's construction of a systematic modes of production approach is even more questionable. Long pages of Althusserian theoretical practice are matched by far fewer concrete applications of the theory. He accepts Lenin's views on imperialism but tries to translate them into modes of production terms. Imperialism restricts the development of capitalism in the Third World where it might restrict its marketing requirements (or more broadly its reproductive requirements) and this restricted and uneven development is "reinforced by the continuing existence of elements of the non-capitalist mode" (Taylor, 1979: 363). These two elements jointly determine the particular pattern of capital accumulation in Third World social formations: urban unemployment, combination of different types of labor, etc. In the end, however, Taylor's elaborate theoretical construction has yet to generate the type of concrete analysis comparable in its depth and scope to that of Cardoso for example. More specifically, we find in Taylor a real retrogression to the old position of the Latin American communist parties when he refers to "the resistance put up against imperialist penetration by the non-capitalist mode (of production)" (Taylor, 1979: 221). He analyses the Latin American countryside as a semifeudal bastion bravely resisting the encroachments of capitalism. There are two criticisms: (1) modes of production are raised to the level of real "actors" with a life of their own above and independent from social classes, and (2) it misrepresents the symbiotic relation between industrial and agrarian capital in Latin America, albeit with their internal conflicts but never fundamental antagonism.

As I have already intimated, my approach to the world-system and modes of production perspectives would be to move towards a systhesis. This was already pointed to in *Latin American Perspectives* (Sternberg, 1974), and a whole volume (Oxaal et al., 1975) was dedicated to pursuing this "marriage." The first remained at the level of pointing out its need, and the second failed to bridge the gap in its various contributions, which tended to adopt just one or the other perspective. Laclau in a postscript to his classical 1971 critique of Frank points also in this direction (Laclau, 1977). The market-focused empiricism of Wallerstein is matched by the theoretical inflation of the concept of mode of production by others, resulting in such confusing categories as "colonial mode of production," which conflates two distinct levels of analysis (mode of production and economic system). Following Laclau, "Marxist thought in Latin America has found considerable difficulty in moving *simultaneously* at the level of *modes of production* and that of *economic systems,* and that its most frequent mistakes derive from a unilateral use of one or other of the two levels . . . to perpetuate confusion of the two cannot but lead to the multiplication of pseudo-problems and paradoxes" (Laclau, 1977: 42-50). This still leaves us, however, at the level of a prescriptive statement.

The missing link, I believe, is the basic Marxist concept of *reproduction.* At the same time as it produces, every social formation must reproduce the *conditions* of its production, namely the productive forces and the existing relations of production. Marx's reproduction schemes in Volume 2 of *Capital* had a more restricted purpose, but the method is still valid. There Marx showed how "Capital, as self-valorizing value . . . is a movement, a circulatory process through different stages . . . hence it can only be grasped as a movement, and not as a static thing" (Marx, 1978: 185). The function of Marx's reproduction schemes is to show how it is possible for the capitalist mode of production to survive. Bill Warren is quite correct then in noting that our analysis should not confuse a moral critique of capitalism with its possibility of existence and reproduction (which Marini and others tend to do). Does the expanded reproduction of capitalism in general, however, mean that dependent capitalism can function in the same way, and according to the same laws of motion?

There have, in fact, been a number of attempts to elaborate the concept of *dependent reproduction,* which break decisively with some of the rather static elements in the dependency approach. One of these is the essay by Bernardo Sorj and Leo Zamosc (1977) which examines the reproduction of peripheral capitalism, its structures and contradictions, in terms of the export-based économy of El Salvador. They analyze theoretically and empirically how the production and commerical circuits are integrated into the international economic system. As opposed to Wallerstein, they do not believe there is a common essence across the periphery, stressing rather the concrete determinations of each situation. The international division of labor is a basic determinant of peripheral capitalism, but only if understood in its various forms and phases. Another important conclusion is that "given the subsumptin of the non-capitalist relations of production to the dynamic of capitalist expansion, the discussion over modes of production loses sense, not that this eliminates the question of the specific reality of these forms of production, their effects on capitalist development and on the political process" (Sorj and Zamosc, 1977: 9).

A more systematic theoretical attempt is made by the Colombian economist Salomon Kalmanovitz (1980) to elaborate a theory of dependent reproduction. Marx's reproduction schemes are modified to take into account the opening of the dependent economy to international capital and commerce, insofar as this is basic to the dynamic of dependent capitalism. In part this author is following the path indicated by Warren—examine simply the expansion of capitalism in the Third World—but his conclusion is different, namely that the world capitalist system cannot guarantee the accelerated accumulation of capital in all the semicolonial and dependent countries. As against the reproduction schema of a mature capitalist economy as studied by Marx, dependent reproduction is marked by a division of labor between sectors with different relations of production. Second, outside of Mexico, Brazil, and to a certain extent Argentina, we cannot speak of an internal production goods sector. This, and the dependence on the foreign market for the realization of most commodities means that the peripheral economy does not have a self-centered circuit of capital accumulation. Kalmanovitz is aware of the limited purpose of Marx's reproduction schemes and employs them only to examine the conditions of existence of dependent capitalism, which lead to the development of accumulation or to its "blocking." To examine *all* the elements of a dependent capitalist social formation, the concept of reproduction would have to be elaborated further. So far, dependent reproduction is a rather economic notion, its full political, ideological, and social determinants remain to be incorporated. A key element in this reconstruction must be the reproduction of social classes through the class struggle of dependent capitalism, and in the first instance, the formation and reproduction of the working class which is the essence of the capital relation and the basis of its undoing.

## APPENDIX: DEBATES AND DEAD-ENDS

In recent years a fierce polemic has raged among British Marxists which might just clarify the procedures of creative debate. It concerns the reception of Louis Althusser's systematic re-reading of Marx as exemplified by his text with Etienne Balibar (Althusser and Balibar, 1970). For many, the "Althusserian revolution" represented the most original and productive development in modern Marxist theory and research. Althusser's own major statements on the status of Marxism as a science and its delimitation from humanism and historicism, were followed by the indispensible work of Poulantzas on the state; Baudelot and Establet on the school; Terray on precapitalist societies and so on. The critique of Althusser's theoreticism and structuralism has also been developed in a sometimes vigorous but always serious debate.

The reception of Althusserianism in Britain was something quiet different, being at least in part somewhat of an intellectual fashion among intellectuals who had grown weary of bourgeois sociology and wanted an aseptic "scientific" Marxism to take its place. Sometimes it took a rather bizarre turn as, for example, in the work of Barry Hindness and Paul Hirst who in their "anti-historicist" frenzy told us that "the study of history is not only scientifically, but also politically valueless" (Hindness and Hirst, 1975: 312). This was bound to rile the substantial school of British Marxist historians. It was in this context that E.P. Thompson (author of the classic *The Making of the English Working Class*) launched his (1978) onslaught against the Althusserian menace.

Thompson's was no ordinary polemic—he referred to Althusserianism as "this particular freak which has now lodged itself firmly in a particular social *couche*, the bourgeois *lumpen-intelligentsia*" (1978: 195). There are dark hints that Althusser was "responsible" for the excesses of the Khmer Rouge in Kampuchea, and more openly: "Althusserianism is Stalinism reduced to the paradigm of theory. It is Stalinism at last, theorized as ideology" (Thompson, 1978: 374). In fact, throughout the text there is a crescendo of violence in the epithets that are thrown at Althusser, ending "with the declaration of a general jihad against Althusserianism—a call to a new War of Religion on the Left" (Anderson, 1980: 128). Thompson sees himself engaged in "the defence of reason itself" and the effect of his intervention is to operate a radical act of closure on future debate. In other words, a dead-end. Some of Thompson's points—such as the role of human agency in history—are sound, others have been made before, but the end result is a terrible impoverishment of theoretical debate.

Meanwhile, some younger Marxists were engaging in a fruitful debate over the significance of history in the Marxist enterprise. Even some "Althusserians" were critically engaging with the tradition of Thompson in Marxist historiography (see R. Johnson, 1978). This led to a lively debate in the pages of *History Workshop* on the Althusserian contribution, or lack of it, to Marxist historical research. Perry Anderson was able to refer to "a common socialist culture that had grown beyond mutual anathemas . . . seeking a critical balance or synthesis between these two diverse traditions" (Anderson, 1980: 127). It was Anderson (1980), in fact, who drew out the lessons of this whole affair — basically a global consideration of Thompson's prolific historical contribution; this text is also concerned to break out of the dead-end into which Thompson (1978) had led the debate. On the one hand, he could speak of Thompson as "our finest socialist writer today," yet he also called on him to make a more balanced assessment of "the *kind* of systematic conceptual clarification attempted by Althusser and Balibar which was an original and fruitful enterprise, and which yielded an account far more specific and precise than any prior Marxist discussion . . . " (Anderson, 1980: 65).

The analogies with the debate which concern us here should be obvious. There is a body of work—Althusserianism and dependency theory—which was both legitimate and productive. It was often *mis*appropriated by others; dependency theory in the United States, for example, "has been vulgarized, sanitized and sterilized" (Fernandes, 1979). Self-appointed dragon slayers in both cases took it upon themselves to "smash" their opponents. As Thompson against Althusser, so C. Johnson, Fernández, and others entered the battle against dependency theory, in both cases using carefully constructed straw men and ridiculous accusations. Violent polemic may seem to some to follow in Lenin's footsteps when he upbraided the "renegade" Kautsky, but we would do well to remember that Stalin went easily from liquidating erroneous views to liquidating people. Meanwhile, in both cases ongoing critical discussion was actually taking the debate forward instead of into a cul-de-sac and generating a productive research program. The analogy is, of course, only a formal one and breaks down when we consider the *content* of the debate and not just its *form*. Thus, C. Johnson et al. are much closer to Althusser's "scientific" Marxism, and F.H. Cardoso would certainly feel much more at home with E.P. Thompson's socialist-humanism. The procedural lessons are I think still relevant, and in this we can conclude with Antonio Gramsci's note on "Scientific Discussion":

> In the formulation of historico-critical problems it is wrong to conceive of scientific discussion as a process at law in which there is an accused and a public prosecutor whose professional duty is to demonstrate that the accused is guilty and has to be put out of circulation.
>
> In scientific discussion, since it is assumed that the purpose of discussion is the pursuit of truth and the progress of science, the person who shows himself most "advanced" is the one who takes up the point of view that his adversary may well be expressing a need that should be incorporated, if only as a subordinate aspect, in his own construction" (Gramsci, 1971: 343-344).

## REFERENCES

Althusser, Louis and Etienne Balibar
  1970 *Reading Capital*, New York: Pantheon Books

Anderson, Perry
  1980 *Arguments Within English Marxism*, London: New Left Books

Arrighi, Giovanni
  1978 *The Geometry of Imperialism: The Limits of Hobson's Paradigm*, London: New Left Books

Avineri, Shlomo (ed.)
  1969 *Karl Marx on Colonialism and Modernization*, New York: Anchor Books

Bambirra, Vania
  1978 *Teoría de la dependencia: Una anticrítica*, Mexico City: Ediciones Era

Brewer, Anthony
1980 *Marxist Theories of Imperialism: A Critical Survey*, London: Routledge & Kegan Paul

Cardoso, Ferando Henrique
1977a "The Consumption of Dependency Theory in the United States," *Latin American Research Review*, XII (3), 7-24

1977b "The Originality of a Copy: CEPAL and the idea of Development," *CEPAL Review* (second half of 1977)

Chilcote, Ronald H.
1974 "A Critical Synthesis of the Dependency Literature," *Latin American Perspectives*, I (Spring), 4-29

Collier, David (ed.)
1979 *The New Authoritarianism in Latin America*, Princeton: Princeton University Press

Cueva, Agustín
1976 "A Summary of 'Problems and Perspectives of Dependency Theory'," *Latin American Perspectives*, III (Fall), 12-16

*Debate*
1981 "Comunismo Mexicano," issue 16 (February-March)

Evans, Peter
1979 *Dependent Development: The Alliance of Multinational, State and Local Capital in Brazil*, Princeton: Princeton University Press

Fernandes, Florestán
1979 Foreword to Peter Evans, *Dependent Development: The Alliance of Multinational, State and Local Capital in Brazil*, Princeton: Princeton University Press

Fernández, Raúl A.
1979 "Imperialist Capitalism in the Third World: Theory and Evidence from Colombia," *Latin American Perspectives*, VI (Winter), 38-64

Frank, André Gunder
1978a *Dependent Accumulation and Underdevelopment*, London: Macmillan

1978b *World Accumulation 1492-1789*, London: Macmillan

Gramsci, Antonio
1971 *Selections from the Prison Notebooks*, London: Lawrence and Wishart

Halliday, J.
1980 "Capitalism and Socialism in East Asia," *New Left Review*, 124 (November-December)

Harding, Timothy F.
1976 "Dependency, Nationalism and the State in Latin America," *Latin American Perspectives*, III (Fall), 3-11

Hindress, Barry and Paul Hirst
1975 *Pre-Capitalist Modes of Production*, London: Routledge & Kegan Paul

Johnson, Carlos
1979 "Dependency Theory and the Capitalist/Socialist Process," Montreal: Centre for Developing-Area Studies, Working Paper (25)

Johnson, R.
1978 "Thompson, Genovese and Socialist-Humanist History," *History Workshop*, 6 (Autumn)

Kalmanovitz, Salomon
1980 "Teoría de la reproducción dependiente," *Críticas de la Economía Política* (Edición Latinamericana), (11)

Kay, Geoffrey
1975 *Development and Underdevelopment: A Marxist Analysis*, London: Macmillan

Laclau, Ernesto
1977 *Politics and Ideology in Marxist Theory*, London: New Left Books

Mantega, G. and M. Moraes
    1980 "A Critique of Brazilian Political Economy," *Capital and Cass,* 10 (Spring)

Marini, Ruy Mauro
    1980 "Las razones del neo-desarrollismo (respuesta a F.H. Cardoso y J. Serra)," Revista *Mexicana de Sociología* (XL), 57-106

Marx, Karl
    1978 *Capital,* Vol. 2, London: Penguin Books

McMichael, P., James Petras, and R. Rhodes
    1974 "Imperialism and the Contraditions of Development," *New Left Review,* 85 (May-June)

Meillassoux, Claude
    1981 *Maidens, Meal and Money: Capitalism and the Domestic Community,* London: Cambridge University Press

O'Brien, Philip
    1975 "A Critique of Latin American Theories of Dependence," in Oxaal et al., *Beyond the Sociology of Development,* London: Routledge & Kegan Paul

Oxaal, Ivar, Tony Barnett and David Booth (eds.)
    1975 *Beyond the Sociology of Development,* London: Routledge & Kegan Paul

Platt, D.C.M.
    1980 "Dependency in Nineteenth-Century Latin America," *Latin American Research Review,* XV (1), 113-180

*Review of African Political Economy*
    1980 "Debate on 'Dependency' in Kenya (Kaplinsky, Henley, Leys)," 17 (January-April)

*The Review of Radical Political Economics*
    1979 "Facing the 1980s: New Directions in the Theory of Imperialism." XI (Winter)

Seers, Dudley
    1979 "The Congruence of Marxism and Other Neoclassical Theories," in K.Q. Hill (ed.), *Towards a New Strategy for Development,* New York: Pergamon Press

Serra, José and Fernando Henrique Cardoso
    1979 "As desventuras da dialêctica da dependência," in *Estudos CEBRAP,* 23 (January-February)

Sorj, Bernardo and Leo Zamosc
    1977 "La reprodución del capitalismo periférico: estructura y contradicciones," *Caderno do Departmento de Ciencia Política* (Universidad Federal de Minas Gerais), 4 (August)

Spalding, Hobart A., Jr.
    1977 *Organized Labor in Latin America: Historical Case Studies of Urban Workers in Dependent Societies,* New York: Harper & Row

Steenland, Kyle
    1975 "Notes on Feudalism and Capitalism in Chile and Latin America," *Latin American Perspectives,* II (Spring) 49-58

Stein, Stanley and Barbara
    1980 "Comment," *Latin American Research Review,* XV (1)

Sternberg, Marvin
    1974 "Dependency, Imperialism and the Relations of Production," *Latin American Perspectives,* I (Spring), 75-86

Taylor, John
    1979 *From Modernization to Modes of Production: A Critique of the Sociologies of Development and Underdevelopment,* London: Macmillan

Thompson, E.P.
    1978 *The Poverty of Theory,* London: Merlin Press

Villamil, José (ed.)
    1979 *Transnational Capitalism and National Development: New Perspectives on Dependence,* Sussex: The Harvester Press

Wallerstein, Immanuel
    1979 *The Capitalist World-Economy*, London: Cambridge University Press

Warren, Bill
    1973 "Imperialism and Capitalist Industrialization," *New Left Review*, 81 (September-October), 3-44

    1980 *Imperialism: Pioneer of Capitalism*, London: New Left Books

Weeks, John and Elizabeth Dore
    1979 "International Exchange and the Causes of Backwardness," *Latin American Perspectives*, VI (Spring), 62-87

Wells, John
    1977 "The Diffusion of Durables in Brazil and its Implications for Recent Controversies Concerning Brazil and Development," *Cambridge Journal of Economics*, I (September)

Wolpe, H. (ed.)
    1980 *The Articulation of Modes of Production*, London: Routledge & Kegan Paul